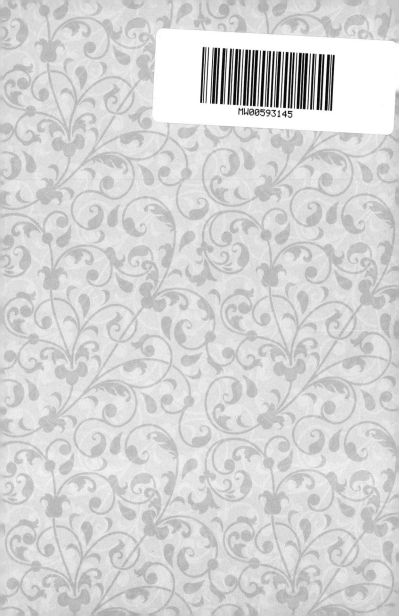

MW00593145

Mornings with Nana

with

Nana

365
Days of Love and
Encouragement

MARIETTA
TERRY

BroadStreet
P U B L I S H I N G

BroadStreet Publishing® Group, LLC
Savage, Minnesota, USA
BroadStreetPublishing.com

Mornings with Nana: 365 Days of Love and Encouragement
Copyright © 2024 Marietta Terry

9781424567874 (faux leather)
9781424567881 (ebook)

Scripture quotations marked TPT are from The Passion Translation®. Copyright © 2017, 2018, 2020 by Passion and Fire Ministries, Inc. Used by permission. All rights reserved. ThePassionTranslation.com. Scripture quotations marked NKJV are taken from the New King James Version®. Copyright © 1982 by Thomas Nelson. Used by permission. All rights reserved. Scripture quotations marked NLT are taken from the Holy Bible, New Living Translation. Copyright © 1996, 2004, 2015 by Tyndale House Foundation. Used by permission of Tyndale House Publishers, a Division of Tyndale House Ministries, Carol Stream, Illinois 60188. All rights reserved. Scripture quotations marked NIV are taken from The Holy Bible, New International Version® NIV®. Copyright © 1973, 1978, 1984, 2011 by Biblica, Inc.™ Used by permission. All rights reserved worldwide. Scripture quotations marked ESV are taken from the ESV® Bible (The Holy Bible, English Standard Version®). Copyright © 2001 by Crossway, a publishing ministry of Good News Publishers. Used by permission. All rights reserved. Scripture quotations marked NASB are taken from the New American Standard Bible® (NASB). Copyright © 1960, 1962, 1963, 1968, 1971, 1972, 1973, 1975, 1977, 1995, 2020 by The Lockman Foundation. Used by permission. www.Lockman.org. Scripture quotations marked KJV are taken from the King James Version of the Bible, public domain. Scripture quotations marked NET are taken from the NET Bible®. Copyright © 1996–2016 by Biblical Studies Press, LLC. http://netbible.com. Quoted by permission. All rights reserved. Scripture quotations marked AMP are taken from the Amplified® Bible (AMP). Copyright © 2015 by The Lockman Foundation. Used by permission. www.Lockman.org. Scripture quotations marked ASV are taken from the American Standard Version, public domain. Scripture quotations marked RSV are taken from the Revised Standard Version of the Bible. Copyright © 1946, 1952, and 1971 by the National Council of the Churches of Christ in the United States of America. Used by permission. All rights reserved worldwide. Scripture quotations marked PHILLIPS are taken from The New Testament in Modern English by J. B. Phillips. Copyright © 1960, 1972 by J. B. Phillips. Administered by The Archbishops' Council of the Church of England. Used by permission.

Cover and interior by Garborg Design Works | garborgdesign.com

Printed in China

24 25 26 27 28 5 4 3 2 1

With love, to my cherished grandchildren
and great grandchildren.

January

Choosing to Deny Ourselves

If any man would come after me, let him deny himself,
and take up his cross daily, and follow me.
LUKE 9:23 ASV

When we come to the end of ourselves, realizing our own helplessness, relinquishing control, and surrendering our authority to God, he will begin a new work within us. He readies us for service, filling us with holy expectations. What joy it brings our Savior when we come to this position out of love for him. A childlike heart that solely walks with and glorifies Jesus will bring our Lord great pleasure.

Whether it is due to seeing ourselves in the true light of our sin or readily offering God our lives due to his great affection for us, let us choose self-denial. We should see it as an honor to share in the sufferings of Christ. None of us have ever suffered to the point of sweating blood, but he endured that level of agony for us. What joy is ours when we offer up our lives out of adoration for Jesus!

Lord, how desperately I need you! Help me choose to surrender myself, deny myself, and follow you. Amen.

Afforded a Royal Position

Fear not, little flock; for it is your Father's good pleasure
to give you the kingdom.

LUKE 12:32 KJV

Christ is the perfect Shepherd. He is our provider, caregiver,
guide, restorer, comforter, and protector. He is everything!
Christ the Lamb left the glory and total adoration of heaven,
humbly offering himself as our sacrificial Lamb so that we may
be made righteous by his blood. How can we help but proclaim,
"Hallelujah! What a Savior!" Shouts of worship continue to
erupt when we consider that it is the Father's joy to give us the
kingdom. Sinners are redeemed as the children of God and
positioned to freely join in the inheritance that is in Jesus Christ.

What we had to offer and what Jesus sacrificed are in
complete opposition. We were poor, without hope, wretched,
and destitute but afforded a royal position because Jesus gave up
his holy life for us. We share in the riches of salvation in Christ.
Undeserving, yet we are gifted all that his glory has to offer. Let
our praises ring out and continue throughout eternity in honor
of our Savior and King.

Lord, may I not waste your precious promises but through the
power of your promised Holy Spirit, my Helper, may I live them
out in my life. Help me remember all that you have richly given to
me in Jesus. Amen.

Boldly Magnify His Holy Name

The four living creatures, each of them with six wings, are full of eyes all around and within, and day and night they never cease to say, "Holy, holy, holy, is the Lord God Almighty, who was and is and is to come!"

REVELATION 4:8 ESV

May we humbly ask God for a glimpse of his perfect, holy righteousness to permeate and transform our whole being and the way we live. May his gift of faith and belief propel us to finish the race and hear the words, "Well done." May we bow before his throne and proclaim, "Holy, holy, holy, Lord God Almighty." As we gaze on his righteousness, we may be tempted to shrink back as we consider our depravity in the light of his divinity. If we feel shame, he will surely lift our head, for we stand in his presence because of his own Son's sacrifice.

God sees Jesus when he looks at us. Christ made certain that God would accept our offering of praise through the power of his cross. We can proclaim his glory now and throughout eternity in assurance that our praises will honor him. Let us boldly magnify his holy name.

Holy God, thank you for your redeeming grace that blots out my sin by the power of your blood. Amen.

Stepping into Authority

Submit yourselves therefore to God.
Resist the devil, and he will flee from you.
JAMES 4:7 KJV

The Lord is our strength, for he tells us that he has given us the spirit "of power and of love and of a sound mind" (2 Timothy 1:7 NKJV). The darkness may toy with the thoughts in our head, but they cannot remain when we resist. We have the same power that God exerted when he raised Christ from the dead to shut down principalities, destroying any evil perpetrated against our redeemed soul. Our God has given us in Jesus the right to step into our authority to tear down any thought that does not come into agreement with our secured position in Christ.

As we lift our voices in gratitude to God, Satan will turn his vile tail and slither away, for he cannot stand for a single second in the presence of worship to our holy King. Remember that "greater is He who is in you than he who is in the world" (1 John 4:4 NASB).

Divine Holy Spirit, thank you for this assurance. Amen.

Faith to Move Mountains

I heard the voice of the Lord saying, "Whom shall I send, and who will go for us?" Then I said, "Here I am! Send me."
ISAIAH 6:8 ESV

Isaiah saw the Lord and heard the host of heaven cry, "Holy, holy, holy is the LORD of hosts" (v. 3 ESV). He stammered and said, "Woe is me" (v. 5 ESV). Then an angel of fire flew to him and touched his lips with a burning coal from the altar, saying, "Behold, this has touched your lips; your guilt is taken away, and your sin atoned for" (v. 7 ESV). Then the Lord said, "Whom shall I send, and who will go for us?" And Isaiah responded, "Here I am! Send me" (v. 8 ESV).

For a moment, I retreat as I count the cost. Will you, Lord, ask me to leave my loved ones or sacrifice my safety by going to a foreign land? Will I move forward or faint under the weight of uncertainty? Will I fail to obey or to have the faith to move mountains? Grant me your power and unwavering belief in your purpose for my path. May I continually build my life on you, the Word, and allow you to use me as a living stone. May I honestly and earnestly trust as I continually say, "Lord, send me!"

Dear Lord, put feet and hands to my response, "Here am I. Use me. Send me." Amen.

God's Glorious Grace toward Us

May God be gracious to us and bless us and make his face shine on us—so that your ways may be known on earth, your salvation among all nations.

PSALM 67:1-2 NIV

God, in his kindness and love, gives us what we don't deserve and saves us, through Christ, from what we do deserve. For us to think that this benevolence is our entitled benefit is a mistake of massive proportions. Due to his goodness alone, we are royal heirs with Jesus. Consider how he showers us with his affection. He counts the hairs on our head and raises his voice in song over us. May we never think for a moment that this is due to anything we have done, but purely a result of his glorious grace.

The purpose of this display of grace is to bring attention to who God is. He is love, he is trustworthy, he is our salvation, and without redemption in Christ, we would be damned to hell. Doesn't he merit the fame, the acknowledgement from every knee that one day will bow? We are the recipients of the care and adoration of a righteous God who is worthy of our greatest praise.

Father, thank you for your gift of grace. I'm unworthy yet so grateful for the blood of Christ. I worship your name. Amen.

God's Loving Provision and Plan

Humble yourselves, therefore, under God's mighty hand,
that he may lift you up in due time. Cast all your anxiety
on him because he cares for you.

1 PETER 5:6–7 NIV

I wondered why humility toward God and others and giving God all my cares and anxieties are connected in this verse. Is it because I have pride in thinking I can work it out, I have the answer, or I can remedy the situation without God's help? How often I have made a total mess because I held tight to my own control rather than relinquishing my cares and concerns to God's loving provision and plan? How haughty of me to think I can handle anything outside of his power and grace!

May God sweep away the pride and ego that keep me from submitting my battles, burdens, fears, and frustrations to him. May I strike from my consciousness the sinful thoughts that I am enough on my own and that I alone command the solution. I want to receive the confident peace of knowing that my God is orchestrating every divine moment for his perfect will. I want the strict boundaries that his eternal love creates to pen me in and only open the gate when he calls me out to follow him.

Lord, thank you for your forgiveness of my sins as I humbly surrender them to you. Amen and hallelujah.

Do Not Fear Delays

This is the confidence we have in approaching God:
that if we ask anything according to his will, he hears us.
And if we know that he hears us—whatever we ask—
we know that we have what we asked of him.

1 JOHN 5:14–15 NIV

As a little girl, I had a beautiful doll whose head I accidentally smashed as I was showing off that it was unbreakable. I sobbed in my mother's arms for what seemed like hours. That night, I placed Betsy, my doll, on my dresser and asked God to heal her head. I totally believed that the next day she would be all put together. She wasn't. It crushed my heart. Unbeknownst to me, Mom took her back to the store, and a few weeks later, Betsy was back, perfect as before. Years later, as an adult, God's Spirit reminded me of Betsy. She had been put back together, just not in the way or time I thought it should happen.

Satan often creeps in during times of delay and uses them to discourage and introduce doubt. However, God always hears and answers in his timing and according to his good will. His answer is always perfect and perfectly timed.

Lord, my request today is that my heart will trust that your ways and answers to my petitions and prayers are always perfect. Thank you and amen.

God's Guiding Light

Jesus answered, "Are there not twelve hours of daylight? Anyone who walks in the daytime will not stumble, for they see by this world's light. It is when a person walks at night that they stumble, for they have no light."

JOHN 11:9–10 NIV

The disciples questioned Jesus about the wisdom of going to Bethany. The people there had tried to kill him. Jesus answered that it is at night, without a light, when people will stumble.

I once heard a story that in the early 1900s, two young female evangelists wanted to minister in a remote town in the hills of the Ozarks. They were warned not to because of two feuding families who would not hesitate to shoot anyone who interfered in their business. The girls waited and then felt compelled by God's Spirit to go. Eventually, the convicting power of the Holy Spirit fell on the families, and one-by-one their leaders cried out for forgiveness and were brought into the kingdom of God. Out of those two families came ministers, evangelists, missionaries, teachers, and college presidents. God helped them to reconcile their differences and see the light.

Dear Lord, may I move and speak in your timing, guided by the light of your Holy Spirit. Amen.

I Surrender All

> "A time is coming and has now come when the true worshipers will worship the Father in the Spirit and in truth, for they are the kind of worshipers the Father seeks."
>
> JOHN 4:23 NIV

The Aramaic word for "worship" means "to bow down" or "to surrender." Does it matter what stance we take when we pray or worship? Some feel bowing to their knees brings them closer to God. Some may lie on the floor in their room as David did when begging God for the life of his baby boy. Whatever position you may claim, it is the condition of the heart that God considers most. Whether you sit, stand, or lie down, let your heart be fully his and his alone. Let all that you are submit in complete abandonment to Jesus.

May we live out the words of Judson W. Van de Venter's beloved hymn, "I surrender all...All to Jesus I surrender. Make me, Savior, wholly thine!"

Dear Jesus, I desire to fully surrender to your lordship of my life. Amen.

His Presence Is Constantly Faithful

Now, may the grace and joyous favor of the Lord Jesus Christ,
the unambiguous love of God, and the precious communion
that we share in the Holy Spirit be yours continually. Amen!

2 CORINTHIANS 13:14 TPT

Jesus loves you. As his love pours into you, may it flow from you in word and deed.

Some of the last words Jesus spoke were, "I am with you always" (Matthew 28:20 NIV). When we have been sealed by the blood of Jesus, adopted into the family of God, his presence will forever be with us. We are prone to being lukewarm, making bad choices, indulging in self, and being rebellious. This can cause us to feel that our Redeemer does not love us or has forsaken us. If you feel as though God is absent, you must ask yourself, *Who moved?* We will always find that the answer to that question is that we moved, for God's presence is faithfully constant. Living without God's mercy and grace is a self-imposed prison. Go to him and leave your sin and resistance at his feet. The thrilling truth is that whatever the circumstances, our God will never leave us or forsake us. Hallelujah!

Father, may I never hide from you but confess and be restored to
relationship through your Son. Amen.

He Is More Than Able

A woman was there who had been subject to bleeding for twelve years, but no one could heal her. She came up behind him and touched the edge of his cloak, and immediately her bleeding stopped.

Luke 8:43–44 NIV

In today's verse, Scripture includes and honors a woman of faith for acting in secret and for having the faith of a mustard seed. She moved stealthily, wanting to steer clear of the hateful comments of those who blamed her for the disease. Hiding her face and her unclean condition, she determined not to make eye contact with the Man. She knew how important he was, and she believed if she could only grasp the hem of his garment, power would flow from him and heal her, which it did. The story continues by telling us that Jesus knew someone had touched him. Realizing she could no longer hide, the woman fell trembling at Jesus' feet.

While Scripture does not tell us what she said, it may have been something like, "I was desperate to touch you, Jesus, for I knew if I could just touch even the fringe of your robe, I would be made well." As verse 48 tells us, Jesus responded, "Daughter, your faith has healed you. Go in peace" (NIV). Place your faith in our great Savior and healer, for he is more than able.

Lord, give me faith to believe in your healing power. Amen.

Does He Care?

"Even to your old age and gray hairs I am he,
I am he who will sustain you.
I have made you and I will carry you;
I will sustain you and I will rescue you."

ISAIAH 46:4 NIV

From the formation of your first cell until the day when your weary and aged body will enter its final rest, God is the one who determines your steps. When you were a child, time seemed never-ending. In the midst of your adult years, you start to notice how fast time flies. When your hair is gray and your stance is shortened, you wonder where the years went. As you review your life, you may see a tapestry of beauty or a picture of pain. Those who see the latter may wonder, *Did Jesus care when my life was in despair? Did he hold me as he collected my tears? When my heart ached until I swore I physically felt it break, did he care?* Be assured, dear one, he cares.

Put aside your need to justify the path you walked and know that in his goodness, he gave you exactly what his loving wisdom knew you needed. Although your soul was touched by grief, your Savior never leaves your side. Trust him.

Lord, thank you for your perfect plan designed for me. Amen.

For the Love of Us

One Lord, one faith, one baptism; one God and Father of all,
who is over all and through all and in all. But to each one of us
grace has been given as Christ apportioned it.

EPHESIANS 4:5–7 NIV

Our greatest imaginings could never comprehend the gift of
love, mercy, and grace God freely gives to each of us. It is as if
he doesn't even notice how filthy we are, the most unworthy of
creatures, as he woos us to himself. Or is it the ability he has
to forgive and forget? Ah yes, because all our dirty rags and
our stench of sin were paid for by his precious Son. We, in our
infinite failure to please him, were made righteous because
Jesus was tortured, all for the love of us. We deserved eternal
punishment, but he wouldn't have it. His love is greater than our
depravity.

His provision is all we need, for his blood-stained cross
delivered us from death to life. Yet some ignore this greatest of
gifts. Those who accept his invitation for salvation in Jesus will
know the one true God. He is the Father of all, who gave all he
held dear to bring us near.

Jesus, thank you for your sacrifice, your death, so that I could
live. Amen.

Hope in Christ Alone

You have been my hope, Sovereign LORD,
my confidence since my youth.

PSALM 71:5 NIV

When a child is raised to know the truth of Scripture, realizing their worth in Christ in their early years, it brings wisdom. Believing God for all that he is and what he can do creates confidence, even in a young soul. Many, though, put faith in their own ability, only to fall prey to poor choices with disastrous consequences. They cavort with the wrong crowd. They take risks, thinking their youth makes them invincible. And for some, when it is too late, a thoughtless indiscretion changes the trajectory for their whole life.

Those who are trained to trust in Jesus, deciding to follow him from their childhood, grow in faith. They are certain of the future hope that is theirs in Jesus. Even if darkness looms, they know they will weather the storm with their Savior at their side. They are enabled by the power of the Holy Spirit to obtain victory in him, for their hope is in Christ alone. Raising our children to know the Lord must be our top priority.

Jesus, help me be a righteous example of you to young and old.
My hope is in you. Amen.

The Sweetest Aroma

We are hard pressed on every side, but not crushed;
perplexed, but not in despair.

2 Corinthians 4:8 niv

It may seem harsh, but we can only capture and preserve the
beautiful fragrance of the rose if we tear the flower apart, mix
the petals with pure oil, press them, set them aside, and press
them again repeatedly. The long and slow process brings the
greatest, sweet fragrance. Similarly, the sweetest aroma of Jesus
can be manifested in our lives as we are hard pressed. Perhaps
you have felt heartsick as you faced the sudden or painful deaths
of loved ones, agonizing illness, battles of depression, addiction,
the loss of a job or home, betrayal from family or friends, and
other kinds of crushing disappointments. You felt the difficult
times would never end.

As the pressing continued, though, you gained
endurance, character, and hope. In God's wisdom, he was using
hardship to transform you into the image of Christ. Now, you
have a different perspective, knowing that God is still refining,
allowing the pressure to bring out Christ's costly, precious
fragrance in your life. To allow that scent to have its fullest
perfume, you must trust in God's goodness and plan.

Jesus, if crushing me means that I will have your scent, your
appearance, and your heart, then press as hard as you must. I
trust you. Amen.

He Calms the Storm

He got up, rebuked the wind and said to the waves, "Quiet!
Be still!" Then the wind died down and it was completely calm.

MARK 4:39 NIV

The raging sea struck fear in the hearts of the disciples. "Where is he?" they cried. "Can't he save us?" And therein lies the problem…their lack of faith. They knew he was onboard. They had witnessed his powerful miracles, yet they still didn't believe what was right in their presence. The all-powerful Son of God can stop short any storm and any trial. However, our faith is key. Hebrews says that "without faith it is impossible to please God" (11:6 NIV). If the disciples had not awakened Jesus, do you think they would have perished? Apparently they thought so, for their faith was weak. We must remember we serve an all-knowing, ever-present God, who sees all and can do anything.

Let us walk in assurance, even in the dark, trusting that our mighty Savior will always settle the rocky waves of life. Today, no matter the circumstance, may he give us a glimpse of Sonshine through the storm.

Blessed Jesus, thank you for never leaving me or forsaking me
even in the darkest and most turbulent of storms. Amen.

Search Our Hearts

"I will sprinkle clean water on you, and you will be clean; I will
cleanse you from all your impurities and from all your idols.
I will give you a new heart and put a new spirit in you; I will
remove from you your heart of stone and give you a heart of
flesh. And I will put my Spirit in you and move you to follow
my decrees and be careful to keep my laws."

 EZEKIEL 36:25–27 NIV

God knows our hearts. He hears all that we think and feel. He
sees every pain, every desire, and every flaw—and because
we are human beings, there are many, many flaws. The good
news is that God sees us in all our sinfulness and still loves us.
Better yet, he can cleanse our hearts, stripping away the dirt and
leaving the goodness of his Spirit within us.

Only the Father can make us clean. He alone can
transplant a redeemed heart and pure spirit in us. Let us kneel
before God with humble attitudes, petitioning our Lord for
help to live holy, righteous, and victorious lives before men.
May we bring joy to our Lord and be credible witnesses of his
redeeming love.

Holy Spirit, search my heart! Lay before me those sins I have
committed and omitted and cleanse me by the blood of Jesus.
May I be reverent before you and not grieve you by having a
rebellious, unforgiving, or indifferent heart. Thank you, Father
God, for your pure and abiding love. Amen.

Forewarned with Assurance

"I have told you these things, so that in me you may have peace. In this world you will have trouble. But take heart! I have overcome the world."

JOHN 16:33 NIV

Wars and rumors of wars. Poverty, famine, destruction, and despair. Many ask where God is in these circumstances. Many turn their back on a loving and forgiving God because they wrongly place on him the blame for the actions of our sinful human race. Pray for his lost children so that their eyes are opened to who he is and how much he loves them.

Today's verse should give us all that we need to walk through life with full assurance that, no matter what, God's got us. Nothing can interrupt or destroy his plan. When trouble comes, we have been forewarned in his Word that if we only believe, he will help us be victorious. Jesus said we would have trouble. He also assured that he is the only answer to every hardship that comes our way. His peace and the hope he provides will strengthen us for any problem that will ever befall us. As in the words of Edward Mote's perennial hymn, "My hope is built on nothing less than Jesus' blood and righteousness."

Dear Jesus, thank you for not abandoning me in times of discouragement and doubt but overcoming them for me. Amen.

Go to Jesus

David said to Gad, "I am in deep distress.
Let us fall into the hands of the LORD, for his mercy is great;
but do not let me fall into human hands."

2 SAMUEL 24:14 NIV

David said a mouthful when speaking to Gad. It was an accurate depiction of the lack of mercy within the human race. Spend any time at a junior high school, and you will witness the horrid verbal attacks that some young girls spew onto their classmates, often without cause. The boys duke it out, but the girls have tongues that can set the world on fire. In our time of distress, to whom should we go first? We must go to Jesus. We should only seek human advice after asking the Lord in prayer for wisdom. Going to the wrong person to seek advice can open a barrage of gossip and dissension.

Cry out to Christ, and then listen for his direction. Seek God for wisdom about whom to trust with your heart. God means for us to be in a community that cares for concerns confidentially. As believers, we must strive to be the love of Jesus to our brothers and sisters, in good times and in bad.

Jesus, make my heart fertile ground to carry the burdens of others. Help me care for the concerns of my brothers and sisters. Amen.

Unquenchable Love

Many waters cannot quench love;
rivers cannot sweep it away.
SONG OF SONGS 8:7 NIV

You will not find the greatest love story ever told in your local theaters or on your favorite romance channel. It is only in one place. The Bible contains not only the greatest story ever told but the ultimate accounting of love given by the perfect Bridegroom. God intends this affection for every human ever born, yet only some will desire it. His adoration will never diminish, and he will never rescind it. He freely offers his love and mercy to sinners until the day of judgment begins. This is a love to die for, and that is exactly what Jesus did. He desired us and didn't want to live in his kingdom without us, so he gave his blood to buy us for his own. One day, we will celebrate this enormous love at the most magnificent wedding feast of all time. Will you be in attendance?

The Bridegroom will take his bride, his church, to be with him forever and always. If you have not accepted his sacrifice, won't you come to the altar today? The truest love of all awaits your decision to walk down the aisle into your Savior's arms.

Dear Jesus, my Bridegroom-King, birth anew within me a consuming passion to love you reverently and completely. Amen.

Holy as He Is Holy

Be very careful, then, how you live—not as unwise but as wise, making the most of every opportunity, because the days are evil. Therefore do not be foolish, but understand what the Lord's will is.

EPHESIANS 5:15–18 NIV

We often think that no one is watching what we do and that it really won't affect anyone if we make a small error in judgment. Who is going to care, right? When you profess to know Jesus, telling others of your transformation in Christ, there will be eyes on you. You might as well wear a neon sign. Some are interested in seeing what God can do with a person while some are eager to tear you down at the slightest mistake.

If you bear the name of Jesus, you carry a weighty responsibility. We must go into all the world and preach the gospel. We're to be ready with an answer. We are to be holy as he is holy. We can't play fast and loose with our actions, for time is short, and the commission is clear. Make disciples, for this was what Jesus asked of us, and it is his will for our service to him and others.

Dear Lord, help me live a holy life. Open my eyes to opportunities for sharing you so others may know you. Amen.

The Glory of God

Let us come before him with thanksgiving
and extol him with music and song.

PSALM 95:2 NIV

God deserves our praise and worship. We should never hesitate to raise our voices, lift our arms, and give him the greatest gratitude. He is *Elohim* (Creator), *Jehovah-Nissi* (the Lord is my banner), *Jehovah Jireh* (the Lord is my provider), *Jehovah Shalom* (the Lord is my peace), *El Shaddai* (the almighty One), *Jehovah Sabaoth* (the Lord of Hosts), *Jehovah Raah* (the Lord is my Shepherd), *Jehovah Tsidkenu* (the Lord our righteousness), *Jehovah Shammah* (the Lord is there). He is love, he is wise, he is merciful, he is faithful, he is the truth, he is righteousness, and he is holy.

There is no limit, no end to the glory of God, and our lips should proclaim his goodness with every breath we take. We should shout from the rooftops of his sacrifice for our salvation. We must love him with an undivided heart and surrendered soul and be willing to go wherever he leads. He deserves the best we can give him. He deserves our all.

Lord, give me a thankful heart that worships you. Help me spend my life glorifying your name and leading others to your Son. Amen.

Jesus Is the Only Way

> "I am coming soon.
> Hold on to what you have,
> so that no one will take your crown."
>
> REVELATION 3:11 NIV

Mankind has always struggled with the one thing God gave him to control: free will. God entrusted choice to us hoping we would choose him. Many do come to the Savior, but so many live empty, pointless, materialistic lives that have no benefit for eternity. The very thing that gives man his freedom is the door that can lead to his demise. Christians know that salvation in Jesus is the only way. God knows he must send to hell those who reject his Son.

Why then doesn't he make us love him? Scholars and theologians can only offer opinions to answer this question. As a statement of fact, there is no greater love, no grander future, and nothing worth anything at all unless Jesus Christ is at the center of it. Choosing him and the reward of a relationship with the one true God, he has left to our discretion. If only humanity would wake up before it's too late. Come to Jesus.

Jesus, I choose you because you loved me first. Help me to hold fast until you return. Amen.

Don't Grow Weary, Do Good

Love must be sincere.
Hate what is evil;
cling to what is good.

ROMANS 12:9 NIV

As long as we are on this earth, the Enemy will do his best to tempt us to sin. We must be vigilant to watch for his schemes, for he will appear as an angel of light, debating whether God really means what he says. Humanity has a propensity to see evil as good and good as evil.

Hate is a strong word, carrying murderous intentions, yet the Bible tells us to hate evil. Therefore, destroy any thought that would cause you to trespass against the goodness of God. Take every thought and action to the throne of grace, where you will find help and strength in your time of need. God has given us everything we need in Christ to deflect the flaming arrows of the Enemy that threaten to take us down. We can trust that the Lord will guide us as we walk in love. He will hold up our arms so that we don't grow weary in doing good. Surrender your heart and mind to Jesus Christ, determining to be sincere in continuing in righteousness.

Jesus, I know I can do nothing without you. Help my mind stay on what is lovely so I can sincerely display your goodness. Amen.

No Condemnation

"God did not send his Son into the world to condemn the world, but in order that the world might be saved through him."

JOHN 3:17 ESV

Why is it that our world tends to view God as a cosmic killjoy who is eager to lower the boom on any who cross him? The mindset is that God is not good, that he is a hard taskmaster who wants to make us all pay. Who perpetuated this myth? Scripture clearly states that God did not send Jesus to the cross to condemn us but to provide forgiveness and salvation to the world. When you consider how the Enemy has filled hearts and minds with this lie throughout the ages, it should move all of us to speak out and boldly tell the truth.

The verse preceding today's entry tells us that God loves the world so much that he sacrificed the life of his Son for the human race (v. 16). Who of us would give the life of our loved one for another? I doubt any hands are raised. It's time that the world sees God for who he is—always good, showering love on those who love him and to their descendants.

Father, help me speak the truth of your love and goodness to the world. Give me favor so others will believe. Amen.

Listen and Respond

"Behold, I stand at the door and knock; if anyone hears My voice and opens the door, I will come in to him and will dine with him, and he with Me."

REVELATION 3:20 NASB

A fun question we sometimes pass around at friendly gatherings is this: "If you could have dinner with anyone in history, who would it be?" Many at a Christian event will answer Jesus. Isn't it interesting that in Revelation, Jesus has the same desire about being with us? There he is, an absolute gentleman, standing at the door of our heart and tapping softly. He will never assume that he can just walk through the entry but will wait until we answer his request and extend a welcome. If the person on the other side of the door can see their need, they will answer the invitation to salvation. Once Jesus enters, a lifetime meal of relationship will begin.

For those who choose not to listen and do not respond with their invitation for Christ to enter, the future is grim. If you have not listened closely enough to hear his request, turn the ear of your heart toward heaven so that you can be assured a seat at the wedding feast with your beloved Bridegroom.

Jesus, being with you overflows my heart with joy. Thank you for your amazing grace and love. Amen.

Follow the Truth

Thomas said to him, "Lord, we don't know where you are going, so how can we know the way?" Jesus answered, "I am the way and the truth and the life. No one comes to the Father except through me."

JOHN 14:5–6 NIV

How desperately I feel my lack of faith this morning. At times, in prayer I feel like my words are bouncing off a wall. I don't feel a connection, and when I base my intercession on feelings, that is when my faith falters. We don't know God's specific plans for our day, yet we know we can safely follow wherever he leads. We can banish anxiety and follow the truth, our Savior. We should be giddy as we follow him knowing that, regardless of where we end up, it will be his best for us.

Whether it is a deep valley or a high mountain, the Father will be our companion. If Jesus is Lord of your life, you should have hopeful expectations for the days ahead. So go, even though you may not know where, and follow whether the road is smooth or rocky. Jesus is your guide and will ultimately deliver you safely home.

Dear Lord, help me move beyond my feelings and trust you, my perfect Savior, to fuel the embers of faith. Amen.

Agree in the Lord

Be kind and compassionate to one another,
forgiving each other, just as in Christ God forgave you.

EPHESIANS 4:32 NIV

"Life is short, and we have not much time for gladdening the hearts of those who are traveling the dark way with us," wrote Swiss philosopher Henri Frederic Amiel. "Be swift to love. Make haste to be kind."

In Philippians 4, Paul urges Eudodia and Syntyche to agree in the Lord. Here were two women who had labored side by side with Paul for the gospel, and now they were at odds with each other. Possibly there was offense and then gossip ensued. Maybe tongues were wagging as people witnessed the disgust each woman was exhibiting toward the other. The two women may have tried to gather allies, dividing the brethren. Undoubtedly their ministry was affected due to their poor attitudes. This is a situation where humility and forgiveness must take center stage. We must honor the Lord's command to consider others more important than ourselves. Put aside any sin that would hinder the gospel of Jesus as you shine for him in the world.

Lord, seal my lips from evil, open my heart, and bow my spirit in prayer. Amen.

Hands and Feet of Jesus

"The King will reply, 'Truly I tell you, whatever you did for one of
the least of these brothers and sisters of mine, you did for me.'"

MATTHEW 25:40 NIV

The Salvation Army began in England because one couple,
William and Catherine Booth, put legs on this verse. They
went to the poorest area of London and began sharing Jesus,
the answer to every need, whether body, soul, or spirit. As
their eyes were opened to the wickedness of slavery and the
trafficking of children, they put their lives and ministry in grave
danger to rescue vulnerable people. In the same period, George
Muller, walking in faith and never asking for contributions, was
founding orphanages for parentless, outcast, and abandoned
children. Warriors for Christ called to show God's justice,
mercy, and grace put their faith into action and became the
hands and feet of Jesus to those who were in need.

    We are called to act as the Booths and Muller did. Christ
calls believers to have their basin and towel ready, their five
loaves and fish at hand, and their sacrifice of love available to all.
We are the only image of Jesus some people will ever encounter.

*Dear Lord, you are Christ, the living, redeeming Savior and
deliverer. Help me be your hands and feet to those who are
suffering. Amen.*

The Unseen Savior

Though you have not seen him, you love him. Though you do not now see him, you believe in him and rejoice with joy that is inexpressible and filled with glory.

1 PETER 1:8 ESV

When a woman is pregnant, she has no idea what her child will look like and possibly doesn't even know the gender. She can't view their personality or hear what their voice will sound like. Yet she loves her unseen child with an intensity she has never known before. She believes her child will bring so much happiness to her life and that the world will be a better place because this child is in it. She has never held her child, yet her protective nature wraps her baby in her mind's arms. She is overflowing with love.

Is this how we feel about Jesus? We have never seen him, yet today's verse claims that those who know him love him still. We have no absolute picture of his appearance, but we know of his affection for us and the provision of his salvation. We believe with unwavering faith and are filled with joy at the thought of our King. His glory surrounds us as we place our faith in the unseen Savior.

Jesus, I haven't seen you, but I love you. My heart is filled with you. Amen.

February

He Will Walk with You

Trust in the LORD with all your heart; do not depend on your own understanding. Seek his will in all you do, and he will show you which path to take.

PROVERBS 3:5–6 NLT

Have you ever ruminated over a decision? Have you lost sleep because you did not know what the rewards or consequences of a certain choice might be? You can imagine what might happen, but there is no guarantee that your direction will be the wisest or the best. You can look at the pros and cons, but even those won't promise to turn out as you assume. You try to put stock in your own instinct, but you still have doubts, and it scares you.

Then you remember today's verse. Trust in God, for he alone can prepare and see the future. You might encounter a smooth road or one filled with potholes; nevertheless, he will walk with you. He will show you where to place your feet and how far to travel. As your trust increases, he will tell you great and magnificent things that you previously did not know. When tempted to go your own way, reign yourself back in and remember that his way is always best.

God, help me trust you with unwavering faith. May I never depend on myself but always follow you. Amen.

The Creator

In the beginning, God created the heavens and the earth.
GENESIS 1:1 ESV

Have you ever wished you could bring something into existence just by bobbing your head like Barbara Eden in the 1960s television show *I Dream of Jeannie*? Major Nelson, Jeannie's master, could have his heart's desire in the twinkle of an eye if he simply asked her for it. Most people don't believe anyone can make something materialize out of nothing. Those individuals don't know our Creator. God spoke everything into existence. He said, "Let there be light" (v. 3 ESV), and the light appeared. He saw the need for food and commanded vegetation, fruit-bearing trees, and all kinds of plants yielding seeds to grow. Out of the dust, he fashioned a man whose heart, brain, blood vessels, and organs are so intricate that it necessitates the existence of a divine architect. Yet many would prefer to believe that we evolved from apes.

When you look at the magnificent detail and design of the universe and everything in it, it is foolishness to think a monkey or a big bang brought these miraculous occurrences into existence. It was God who brought everything to life. He is the great Creator.

Father, help the world to open its eyes and admit that nothing comes into existence unless it is wrought by your miraculous hand. Amen.

Why Do We Fear?

"Do not fear, for I am with you; do not be afraid, for I am your God. I will strengthen you, I will also help you, I will also uphold you with My righteous right hand."

ISAIAH 41:10 NASB

As small children, we imagine all kinds of things that go bump in the night. The slightest sound of the furnace turning on can rattle us awake and cause us to think there is a monster under the bed. Whether we are young or old, fear can still threaten our sleep, our coming and going, or what we might attempt to achieve in life. If you belong to Jesus, you need never fear. In fact, he tells us that in today's verse. He is always present with us. His protection is over us. Nothing can enter or exit our lives without his approval.

Everything is under his control, and all of it is covered by his tender care. We need never fear, for our God is orchestrating our lives. So rest, knowing that your heavenly Father goes before, behind, and all around you, protecting you on every side with his steadfast love and almighty hand. He will never leave you or forsake you.

Father, please remove the spirit of fear from me and replace it with undeniable faith that never wavers. Amen.

The One and Only

As for God, his way is perfect: the LORD's word is flawless;
he shields all who take refuge in him. For who is God besides
the LORD? And who is the Rock except our God?

PSALM 18:30–31 NIV

There are few perfect situations in life. The ones we do
encounter are encouraging, possibly thrilling, and give us
confidence in the hope of similar future events. Still, there is no
guarantee of safety or even of tomorrow. We live in a desperate
world with sinful people who do thoughtlessly evil things. Many
live in anxiety, wondering what the future will deliver.

For those of us in Christ, we need never worry, for we
know our perfect Redeemer is our defender and shield. Our
Lord is the Creator, and he is in control. There is no other God.
He will never allow anything to cross our path unless he has
already given permission for it. His plans for us are perfect,
and we can safely rest in his protection. His promises are true,
for his Word is faithfully faultless. As we take refuge in Christ,
may our mouths sing his praise and our hearts be undivided in
allegiance to him.

God, thank you for the continual covering of your sovereignty.
I will sing your praise while I take refuge in you. Amen.

Heed His Warning

"Whoever has ears, let them hear
what the Spirit says to the churches."

REVELATION 3:13 NIV

What a magnificent gift our hearing is! Some sounds soothe
our souls, beautiful music, the laughter of a child, the voice of
that special someone. Some sounds can be disturbing. Screams
of "Fire!" or words spoken in anger. There are voices we tend to
ignore and some that we sit up straight to listen to. We must ask
God for discernment to know when he wants us to give heed
to spoken information and when he doesn't. We should always
have our ears open to God's Holy Spirit. Whether he speaks
through his Word or in the inner sanctum of our heart, we must
pay attention. In Revelation there are wonderful compliments
and stark warnings to the churches. As you read Revelation
3, do you recognize your church? If yes, then heed the Lord's
warning. We must correct our failings, realizing the time is
short. Jesus could return any day now.

May the Lord infuse us with strength, a heart of humility,
and a passion to follow him. May he open our ears to hear and
listen, mold our will to his, and help us to be true and obedient.

Lord, thank you, my Redeemer, for your Word and your will for
me. Amen.

Praise Him Continuously

You can pass through his open gates with the password of praise. Come right into his presence with thanksgiving. Come bring your thank offering to him and affectionately bless his beautiful name!

PSALM 100:4 TPT

Psalm 100 was my mom's favorite psalm. In a time of despair, pain, heartache, and temptation, she would practice and cling to the words of this uplifting psalm. She would also recite this verse in good times, times of blessing, and just ordinary days when no trouble darkened her doorstep. Why would she use the same verse for two opposite situations? Because God is always worthy of our praise. Whether we are in times of plenty or times of want, God is good. He always works on our behalf. We can't see the outcome of a trial, but we can look at God's character and promises and know that he is doing something beneficial on our behalf.

When the sun is shining and the birds are singing, many forget God because everything is sailing along. When times are dark, we fall silent. We must praise him continually. Determine to stop and thank him throughout the day and worship his great and holy name regardless of your circumstances.

Father, I praise your great and mighty name. Let me spend my life to glorify you. Amen.

Students of the Word

Jesus said to him, "Away from me, Satan! For it is written:
'Worship the Lord your God, and serve him only.'"

MATTHEW 4:10 NIV

If God himself, in the flesh, used Scripture to fight the battle of temptation, we must follow his example. We are to be students of the Word. Remember when you were in school and had to study for finals? Those were tests that resulted in mere grades that most of us don't even remember. On the other hand, having the memory of God's Word at your immediate disposal can keep you from sin. Knowing the truth of the Bible is a matter of eternal life or death. When you use God's Word against the Enemy, he cannot stand to continue in your presence.

Haven't you noticed that Satan shows up when you are weak? There is strength and power in Scripture. Know it and use it to shut down your enemy and avoid evil choices that will interrupt your relationship with your Savior. We should always be armed with the sword of the Spirit, which Ephesians 6:17 says "is the word of God" (NIV). Enter the spiritual classroom today and determine to be an A-plus student.

Lord, please help me retain all that I study in your Word. May reading your Word produce in me an understanding and obedient heart. Amen.

Great and Magnificent Things

The LORD is near to all who call on him,
to all who call on him in truth.

PSALM 145:18 NIV

The Lord invites us into his presence to call on him and ask him questions. As we listen intently, he will tell us incredible truths that we had no knowledge of. Think about that for a bit. The Creator, the one and only true God, wants to tell you his secrets, his plans, his purposes. This should make all those in Christ run to their prayer closet and cry out for this divine knowledge. More importantly, consider the fact that you are engaging in a private conversation with the Lord God Almighty and he asked for the appointment!

We are fools if we ignore this for one more second. Don't wait, but go to that special space you have created to spend time with the Savior. Pray, asking whatever you want to know, believing in his name, and he will be faithful to answer you.

Father, may I understand the gravity of coming to you to hear amazing things. I'm overwhelmed by the invitation. I will run to you. Amen.

Reveal Our Trespasses

Who can discern their own errors? Forgive my hidden faults.
Keep your servant also from willful sins; may they not rule over
me. Then I will be blameless, innocent of great transgression.

PSALM 19:12–13 NIV

The Lord forgives us our hidden sins. In fact, sometimes he
knows them long before we even realize they exist in us. Sin
can be so deeply hidden and our hearts so hardened to the little
foxes that have burrowed their way in. We know something
is amiss, but we give all kinds of excuses for our wrongdoing.
We witness a Christian we deem stronger in the faith doing an
activity we believed is wrong, but we figure if they engage in it,
why can't we? We find all kinds of justifications for the things
we watch, buy, or do. Yet if we're truthful, we know it's wrong,
for the spirit of God is pricking our heart with conviction.

We must go to him and ask that he reveal our trespasses,
remove the blinders from our eyes, and let us see clearly.
We must ask for forgiveness. The only safe place for us is in
relationship with our Savior. Don't break the connection by
allowing sin to control you. Be filled with the Spirit.

Lord, keep cleansing me, God, and keep me from my secret sins;
may they never rule over me. Amen.

Your First Love

Create in me a pure heart, O God,
and renew a steadfast spirit within me.

PSALM 51:10 NIV

Whenever we experience something good for a long period of time, we can start to become less enchanted by it. What was once beautifully magnificent soon becomes a bit mundane. Unfortunately, as Christians, we can start to feel this way about our relationship with Christ. To our shame, we take for granted the salvation and opportunities God has presented to us. Maybe God prompts our mind and asks us to minister to someone, but we hesitate because we had plans today.

We must ask ourselves: *Have we lost our first love?* If there is even an inkling of boredom with or disobedience to God, we need a heart and attitude check. When did our desires begin to usurp his? Ask, *When did I begin to place more importance on my menial wish list in place of fulfilling his purpose?* Seek his mercy, and he will forgive your foolishness. Request that he send his Holy Spirit fire to ignite your heart, returning it to the zeal of the day when you first received him. Tell him he is your greatest treasure and hold fast to your first love.

Lord, revive within my heart a passionate love for you, my God and Redeemer. May I never stray but always stay in intimate fellowship with you. Amen.

From Dry Bones

I prophesied as he commanded me, and breath entered them;
they came to life and stood up on their feet—a vast army.

 EZEKIEL 37:10 NIV

If there were ever any question of the extent of God's power, this account in Ezekiel gives the answer. This is one story in the Old Testament where God resurrected life from death. Dry bones with no flesh and no breath came alive at God's command and Ezekiel's prophecy. Where existence had vanished and hope had been lost, renewed life and an entire army was born. God breathed life as only he can so that many would know he is Lord. Any act, any miracle God may perform is in line with his perfect will and done for his glory.

One day, he will raise more of his people, and on that day, those who belong to him will meet him in the air. Believers in Christ will live with God in his kingdom for eternity. Dwell on this truth and see if your heart doesn't swell with wonder and anticipation of that great day. May the Lord's Holy Spirit infuse new, vibrant life into our dry spirits, making us his vessels.

Dear Lord, may I be a vessel, used by you, to bring your
redeeming life, hope, joy, peace, and love to others. Amen.

Judgment Is Coming

Not so the wicked! They are like chaff that the wind blows away.
Therefore the wicked will not stand in the judgment,
nor sinners in the assembly of the righteous.

PSALM 1:4–5 NIV

So often we look at the wicked and wonder how they get away with their evil deeds, from wondering when authorities will catch the murderer to bemoaning why there is no policeman around when someone is speeding past us. We fret over when God will move and strike down the perpetrators, giving them their just deserts. Instead, we should be praying for their salvation.

We must try to share the gospel on the streets and in the prisons. Don't mistake God's plan. He will punish the wicked. Those who do not seek God will be cast out of his presence, spending an eternity away from God. There is no greater punishment than being banished from his presence forever. So while there is time, share the gospel. You may be the one whom God has ordained to save a certain person from the fires of hell. The day of judgment is coming, and it may be closer than we anticipate. Be faithful to tell of the salvation of God.

Lord, no wickedness can stand in your presence. Help me share
the gospel so that many can turn from sin. Amen.

Obey God Immediately

It displeased Jonah exceedingly, and he was angry. And he prayed unto Jehovah, and said, I pray thee, O Jehovah, was not this my saying, when I was yet in my country? Therefore I hasted to flee unto Tarshish; for I knew that thou art a gracious God, and merciful, slow to anger, and abundant in lovingkindness, and repentest thee of the evil.

JONAH 4:1–2 ASV

Today's verse reveals Jonah's motive. He knew how good God was, how God would forgive and restore those who had wandered from their faith. Jonah didn't like it, so he tried to run from God. Landing in the belly of a fish gave him a few days to think and to remember the sovereignty of God. Once he came to his senses and agreed to obey the Lord, the fish spit him out to the shore. Yet when the Ninevites turned from evil and God spared them, Jonah still had a case of sour grapes. His despair became a desire to die. The Lord rebuked him, and the story doesn't tell us how Jonah reacted after that.

Our takeaway should be twofold: obey God immediately and forgive others as he has forgiven you.

Dear Lord, may I be ever mindful of your great love and mercy toward me and, like you, offer that to others. Amen.

Love in Action

"God so loved the world, that he gave his only Son,
that whoever believes in him should not perish
but have eternal life."

JOHN 3:16 ESV

Love in its divine origin is an action-producing noun. It was God's love that moved him to the action of giving his Son for our sins. Love is also a verb: love without action is just a word, but the motive for every action should be love. Scripture tells us to love our neighbors as ourselves, to care for the widows and the orphans, to feed the hungry, and to clothe the poor. We must be moved by care and selflessness to perform these acts of kindness. If you find this difficult, pray fervently that the Holy Spirit will fill you with a burning desire to love and serve.

The strength of Christianity is not outward laws but the outpouring of compassion birthed in Christ and the fulfillment of perfect love. May we be rooted in Christ so that our thoughts, words, and actions are in sync with his greatest will.

Lord, thank you for your love, mercy, and grace covering my failings. Fill my heart with your love so that loving actions will flow. Amen.

Jesus, Others, You

Blessed are the undefiled in the way,
who walk in the law of the LORD!
PSALM 119:1 NKJV

How can we, as sinful creatures, possibly be holy? Even once we are redeemed, we battle our sin nature. We are not slaves to it, but it does rear its ugly head in times of testing, temptation, and self-indulgence. We must pray to be filled with the Holy Spirit and meditate on God's Word day and night. Only an intimate relationship with Jesus will enable us to be blameless. The study of his Word will help us to walk according to God's law. If we do sin, we know we can come to him with our sin, and he will not only forgive but also forget our wrongdoing. He cleans our slate.

When you walk in total integrity, living in the light of God's Word and through his power, you will be exuberant. What joy overwhelms everyone who keeps the ways of God, seeking him continually! Those who dwell in the Almighty's shadow find their heart's passion.

J=Jesus
O=Others
Y=You

Jesus, fill me with your Spirit so I may live a blameless life before you. Help me memorize your Word to know your law. Amen.

He Calls Us Saints

He that searcheth the hearts knoweth what is the mind of the Spirit, because he maketh intercession for the saints according to the will of God.

ROMANS 8:27 ASV

Have you ever been at a loss for words? Have you been unable to speak your heart in prayer? Don't be discouraged, for when you can't verbalize the depths of your heart, the Holy Spirit prays for you. If that doesn't make you feel special, nothing will. Your God, who stepped in and saved you when you couldn't save yourself, who forgave you and made you joint heirs with his only Son, knows exactly what you need before you do. And on top of that, if you can't bring yourself to put it into language, he does it for you.

Our glorious Father has blessed us beyond imagination. We, as children of God, are so extravagantly loved. We have been given mercy and grace that we absolutely do not deserve. Yet it brings the one and only God pure joy to give us the kingdom. He even calls us saints. Praise him, thank him, and serve him with all your soul, heart, mind, and strength.

Lord, I'm overwhelmed by your goodness and that you have searched me and still love me. I will praise you forevermore. Amen.

This Little Light

The light shines in the darkness,
and the darkness can never extinguish it.

JOHN 1:5 NLT

Remember the Sunday school song "This Little Light of Mine"? When we have Christ within us, we are, hopefully, light bearers and light reflectors. Our light should shine so brightly that it is a beacon beckoning the lost to come to Jesus. Sadly, many times we hide the light, retreating in fear from the darkness—but Jesus came into this world to dispel the darkness of hopelessness and despair. When we remember that his power lives in us and that we have authority in Christ, we gain courage. We are shining stars in an evil generation. We must take the life of Jesus within us to the masses.

Do not belittle your responsibility or ability in Christ to reach the lost. He left us with the Great Commission, and we are to fulfill it. We know that the Enemy cannot make a move without God's knowledge and permission, so the devil will never win. Don't waste time. Rise up, warrior! Carry the torch of salvation to the lost and help them journey into the light of God's love.

Dear Jesus, may I be a conduit of your light into this dark and hurting world so that many can find you. Amen.

Come to the Water

> The Spirit and the Bride say, "Come." And let him who hears say, "Come." And let him who is thirsty come, let him who desires take the water of life without price.
>
> REVELATION 22:17 RSV

In Revelation, Jesus used his angel to speak to John and to present his comfort and his warning to the congregations. Jesus has given the invitation to come. He has given mankind more than enough years, decades, and centuries to respond. If we are thirsty, wanting to be cleansed, he offers his gift of the water of life. He has bid us partake, but are we willing to cast aside our dead works, lack of discernment, and attention to false teaching and to ask forgiveness for them all? The churches are forewarned, and we as the parishioners must make the changes necessary.

Come and cleanse your soul from any sin that may hinder you. Can't you hear Jesus calling you? *Come to the water, where you will find life in me. Come freely, for the price was paid by my body broken and blood poured out for you. You will find forgiveness, refreshment, and life eternal.* Let the Holy Spirit fill you and enable you to walk in a manner worthy of Christ.

Jesus, I hear your voice and desire to come to you. Take me to your cleansing water, wash, and fill me. Amen.

His Treasured Possessions

It is God who enables us, along with you, to stand firm for Christ. He has commissioned us, and he has identified us as his own by placing the Holy Spirit in our hearts as the first installment that guarantees everything he has promised us.

2 CORINTHIANS 1:21–22 NLT

When you think of how much God has done to make us worthy of Christ and how little we have contributed, we appear to be non-participants. It is God who initially draws us to Jesus through his Holy Spirit. It is the Holy Spirit that convicts us of sin. It is the story of the cross, an event entirely orchestrated by God for our salvation, that softens our hearts to the gospel. Without the Lord's action of bringing us to himself, we would never even come close to receiving the greatness of his gift.

We have been given a righteousness that is not our own but transferred to us through the sacrifice of Christ. His seal grants us security, putting his stamp of ownership on us. God has promised that on the day when he takes up his treasured possessions, we shall be his, belonging to him throughout all of eternity.

Lord, I am grateful that I'm "sealed" by you. Thank you for depositing your Holy Spirit in my heart to guide me. Amen.

Basic Instructions before Leaving Earth

The word of God is alive and powerful. It is sharper than the
sharpest two-edged sword, cutting between soul and spirit,
between joint and marrow. It exposes our innermost thoughts
and desires.

HEBREWS 4:12 NLT

You can visit all the libraries in the world and seek for all the
truth from philosophers, scientists, and the most educated men
and women, but you will come up short. There's no knowledge
that comes close to God's Word. You believe the words of
educated humans, but what about the one and only Book that
is actually alive? The words can jump off the page and into your
heart, bringing transformation to your soul. There is no other
book like the Bible, which is often said to stand for B-basic
I-instructions B-before L-leaving E-earth. If you ignore its
truth, you'll end up spending eternity away from God.

If you are wise, you will meditate on his Word day and
night. Holy Scripture has survived centuries and remained
on the best-seller list for ages, and its instruction will always
be completely correct. It's God's love letter to us. Study it,
memorize it, and live it.

Lord, help me crave your Word. May I be ready with an answer
for anyone who asks. Amen.

Trust in the Lord

Yes, my soul, find rest in God; my hope comes from him. Truly he is my rock and my salvation; he is my fortress, I will not be shaken. My salvation and my honor depend on God; he is my mighty rock, my refuge.

PSALM 62:5–7 NIV

When it seems like life can't possibly get any worse and you are at the point of losing hope, look to Jesus. Maybe you have been trying to handle your troubles on your own. Do you get impatient waiting for God to respond? Possibly there is some unknown sin that you need to identify. If you believe that to be true, ask God to reveal it, and then confess and receive his forgiveness. Then move forward in faith.

Don't let anything hinder you from clinging to Jesus. Acknowledge that you need the strength of your Rock. Cry out, and he will answer you. "Trust in the LORD with all your heart, and do not lean on your own understanding. In all your ways acknowledge him, and he will make straight your paths" (Proverbs 3:5–6 ESV). Turn your eyes to Jesus, and you will see him deliver you.

Jesus, may I be so attached to you that when I am plunged into the night of despair, I will press on through faith. Amen.

A Cheerful Giver

Glorify God with all your wealth, honoring him with your
firstfruits, with every increase that comes to you.

PROVERBS 3:9 TPT

When reading this verse, you might disqualify yourself,
thinking you are not wealthy. Maybe you earn a meager salary
and live paycheck to paycheck. You assume this verse doesn't
pertain to you, and you decide to let the offering plate sail past
you this Sunday. Then the pastor begins his sermon. He directs
you to Mark 12:41–44, the account of the poor widow who put
two small coins in the offering while the rich threw in large
amounts. Jesus explained that the widow had put in more than
all the others. Where those with money gave out of their wealth,
she gave out of her poverty.

Regardless of what our income is, God has graciously
gifted it to us. We must follow the example of the poor widow
and give sacrificially. God promised that if we bring the whole
tithe, he will open his storehouse and pour out on us an
overflowing blessing. He knows what we need and has promised
to provide. Trust him and be a cheerful giver.

Lord, I am rich in you. Help me be faithful in tithing from your
provision for me. May I rejoice in giving my offering. Amen.

Access to Grace

Being therefore justified by faith, we have peace with God through our Lord Jesus Christ; through whom also we have had our access by faith into this grace wherein we stand; and we rejoice in hope of the glory of God.

ROMANS 5:1–2 ASV

At one time, we were estranged from God due to unbelief. We were in chains as prisoners to sin. Then we were introduced to salvation in Jesus, and once we made him Lord of our life, we gained access to grace. Christ transformed us by the renewing of our mind and the filling of the Holy Spirit (see Romans 12:2). We were on a mountaintop with our first love. As time progressed, trials brought on by spiritual warfare and the struggles of earthly life made our faith wane. We became unsteady, losing our hope. We groped about, wondering what went wrong and how to get back to the mountaintop.

In our searching, God spoke gently, *Trust me.* And with our yes, faith mounted and peace quieted our troubled soul. Next, praise flowed from our mouth, and we couldn't wait to shout his worship from the rooftops. Let our song bless and glorify our almighty God.

Jesus, thank you for the grace I have received through my faith in you. I will always boast of your great salvation. Amen.

God Is Love

Whoever confesses that Jesus is the Son of God, God abides in him, and he in God. So we know and believe the love God has for us. God is love, and he who abides in love abides in God, and God abides in him.

1 JOHN 4:15–16 RSV

Our almighty God is the definition of love. We are only able to come to his love because he loved us first. Once we put our trust in Jesus, testifying that he is the Son of God, he lives in us, and we live in him. What an incredible act of care and provision by our heavenly Father. We entered this world as sinners, yet for our entire stay in the womb, he molded us. We went our own way, rejecting his purpose, yet he continued to woo us. We had no possible chance of saving ourselves, so he sent his own Son to die on our behalf. He wanted to have us so much that he allowed Jesus to be nailed to a cross in our place.

The Father and the Son walked this path so that we could belong to them and spend eternity with them. Truly, God is love.

Lord, thank you for sending Jesus to die in my place. Thank you for salvation and the hope of eternity. Amen.

Good News of the Gospel

That which we have seen and heard declare we unto you,
that ye also may have fellowship with us: and truly our
fellowship is with the Father, and with his Son Jesus Christ.
1 JOHN 1:3 KJV

When the apostles shared the good news of the gospel, they
were fulfilling the instructions Jesus left with them before
his ascension. He said, "Go therefore and make disciples of
all nations, baptizing them in the name of the Father and
of the Son and of the Holy Spirit" (Matthew 28:19 ESV). As
people were saved, they became part of the early church. The
community shared with each other everything they had. They
prayed for and supported each other. They had such strong
fellowship that the numbers of those coming to Christ started
to soar.

Some were persecuted and some martyred for the sake
of the gospel. Yet nothing could stop their surrender to the cross
and their desire to see the multitudes come to Christ. God and
his Son, in relationship with them, called them, as he calls us,
to tell of his salvation. We're to help new believers grow in the
faith, and as we do, we have fellowship together with God as the
body of Christ.

God, help me feel an urgency to go and make disciples. Amen.

Seek Peace and Pursue It

Whoever desires to love life and see good days, let him keep his tongue from evil and his lips from speaking deceit; let him turn away from evil and do good; let him seek peace and pursue it.

1 PETER 3:10–11 ESV

"It is appointed for men to die once, but after this the judgment" (Hebrews 9:27 NKJV). Some of us imagine our whole life playing out on heaven's theater screen, and we shudder. All those private moments we never wanted anyone to know about, all the unkind words we spoke on display for all to see. When we awake from that momentary nightmare, we are assured by his Spirit that we will not be judged, for believers are not appointed to wrath (see 1 Thessalonians 5:9). Our works will be put to the test, but we will be saved.

While we are on this earth, however, if we want to live a good long life, the recipe for doing so is in today's verse. Do not lie, gossip, or do evil. We should not only desire peace with all men but also run after it with all our energy. We must strive to do good to all, love our neighbor as ourselves, and put the needs of others ahead of our own.

God, help me treat others with love and respect and never to do another harm. Amen.

Don't Be Shocked

Beloved, do not be surprised at the fiery ordeal among you, which comes upon you for your testing, as though something strange were happening to you.

1 PETER 4:12 NASB

"To the degree that you share the sufferings of Christ, keep on rejoicing, so that at the revelation of His glory you may also rejoice and be overjoyed" (v. 13 NASB). Jesus said we would suffer for his name, and he lets us know we should not be surprised when it happens. In fact, we are to face it with joy. The New Testament is full of examples where Christ's followers were beaten, imprisoned, and faced worse for the sake of the gospel.

We must ask ourselves: If Jesus suffered, why shouldn't we? We will never be afflicted to the extent Christ was. We are told not to see this as strange but to receive it with joy. In fact, we are to be over the moon with joy about being persecuted for our precious Savior. His will is for us to rejoice always, pray continually, and give thanks in all circumstances. When struggles come, don't be shocked, but submit yourself to the Lord and let his strength carry you through to victory.

Father, strengthen me when the fires of trial burn. Help me rejoice that you count me worthy to suffer for Jesus. Amen.

Christ's Righteousness

We are all like an unclean thing,
and all our righteousnesses are like filthy rags.
ISAIAH 64:6 NKJV

Even in the times when we feel most pure, filled with good thoughts and goodwill, we are not. God sees us as we really are. We are still sinful and self-centered, even though we have salvation in Jesus Christ. As long as we remain on this earth, our sin nature will be present. It will only be when we see Jesus and are in eternity with him that we will be like him. Now, he lives in us and has forgiven us all our sins, but we still fall into temptation. Knowing this should never be a reason to excuse our actions but should encourage us to draw even closer to God.

We must train ourselves to know his character, obey his statutes, and surrender to his purpose for our lives. We must pray for his power to fill us and anoint us to do his will. We must be students of the Word so that we walk a straight and narrow path, being careful to follow God's instructions. It is only the blood of Jesus that will make us righteous.

Jesus, thank you for the cross, for without your sacrifice, I'd be lost for eternity. Wash me in your blood and make me clean. Amen.

Without Fear or Trembling

The LORD is my light and my salvation—so why should I be afraid? The LORD is my fortress, protecting me from danger, so why should I tremble?

PSALM 27:1 NLT

Most of us have experienced a time when we were afraid of the dark. Little noises and shadows cast on a wall through a window by a wind-blown tree can strike fear in our hearts. We might find ourselves hiding under a blanket or even under the bed. It is at a time like this that we must remember how big our God is.

Does that mean that danger will never darken our door? No, not at all. But it does mean that God is with us in all situations, and it is he who will allow or disallow an event. You can trust that nothing will come near you that he does not see and cannot change if it is within his will. As a believer, you are sealed for eternity. You're a child of God, and your heavenly Father will one day carry you safely home to live with him forever.

Father, I know not what tomorrow holds, but whatever comes across my path, I know you will be my Rock and my shield. Amen.

March

Come Confidently

The LORD God called to the man,
"Where are you?"
GENESIS 3:9 NLT

Have you ever felt like hiding from our holy, righteous God? (Ridiculous, of course.) Perhaps you uttered an unkind thought. You engaged in a harmful deed, told a lie, or invited lust into your heart. Then there's pride, covetousness, bitterness, fear, unforgiveness—on and on the list could go. The Enemy is quick to accuse us, conniving to discourage and defeat us. He whispers, *He'll never forgive you. You have sinned beyond what his forgiveness will allow.* He twists the words of God, but it is our choice whether to believe him. Turning your face from God will only lengthen the time of your broken relationship. Instead, show yourself to the Savior and seek his pardon. He will welcome you with loving, open arms and bring restoration.

We need never try to hide; in fact, because of Calvary, we can come confidently into the presence of a holy, loving, merciful God. He loves us, desires to spend time with us, and is always ready to forgive. Thank you, almighty, loving God.

Father, as you continue to cleanse me, may I grow deeper and deeper in love with you. Bind me in relationship with you. Amen.

Lose and You Will Find

"Whoever wants to save their life will lose it,
but whoever loses their life for me will find it."
MATTHEW 16:25 NIV

We are born selfish creatures. We learn the word *mine* as an infant and desperately attempt to avoid sharing. We grow into a sense of self-preservation even if it means someone else suffers loss. We hold on to what is best for number one, striving to make our lives as profitable to ourselves as possible. This is completely the opposite of how Christ told us to live.

Jesus explained that when we put others ahead of ourselves and lose our life for his sake, we will find it. When we are merely seeking our own advancement and pleasure, our actions are void of heavenly benefit. We must choose to lay ourselves on the altar for Jesus, being broken bread and poured out wine for his service. Living a selfless life on earth as we store up our treasure in heaven will lead to reaping rewards for eternity. Don't think this will mean that your existence here will be lacking, for when you surrender your life to the will of God, it is then you begin to live abundantly.

Jesus, help me to be committed to your plan and never to go back to living for myself. Fulfill your will in and through me. Amen.

God's Perfect Justice

The LORD has made Himself known;
He has executed judgment.
A wicked one is ensnared in the work of his own hands.

PSALM 9:16 NASB

God's eyes roam throughout the earth looking for those whose hearts are faithful to him. There is not a single thing God does not know, whether we do it in public or secret. There is no intent of the heart that God cannot read. He knows those who desire to live righteously, and he sees the minds of those whose feet run to do evil. Because he is holy, he must judge the acts of those who reject him. He has tarried and been patient more than any other would have been so that many could come to him for forgiveness. The ones who will not seek him give him no choice.

A sovereign God cannot allow rejection of the salvation provided by his Son's death to go without punishment. He desires for all to come to him to find forgiveness. We are in a season when there is still time. Help those who are lost come to Jesus, find redemption for their soul, and live for eternity. Today is the day of salvation!

Jesus, make me a bold mouthpiece for the gospel. Break my heart for the lost and open my mouth to share salvation in Christ. Amen.

My Portion

The LORD's loyal kindness never ceases; his compassions never end. They are fresh every morning; your faithfulness is abundant! "My portion is the LORD," I have said to myself, so I will put my hope in him.

LAMENTATIONS 3:22–24 NET

Do we truly comprehend the relief of knowing that if we confess, God will not hold our sins against us? Every morning, his compassion waits to greet us. He does not want us to faint under the heaviness of our trespasses but to come to him for forgiveness. He will never bring it up again, nor should we, for he forgives and forgets.

God is our portion, our everything, and there is nothing we need but him. There is no one else who can save us or provide for us as he can. His comfort calms our heart while his desire for us bids us to come and sit at his feet. Once there, we are still as we wait for his voice. We pick up his Word, and his great love is spoken from the pages. There is nothing this world can offer and nothing another person can do or be to us that comes anywhere close to who our God is in our lives.

Dear Father, praise to you, my Lord, for you are the strength of my heart, my portion forever. Amen.

God's Call

The eunuch asked Philip, "Tell me, please, who is the prophet talking about, himself or someone else?" Then Philip began with that very passage of Scripture and told him the good news about Jesus.

ACTS 8:34–35 NIV

An angel of the Lord told Peter to take a trip down the road that goes from Jerusalem to Gaza. Peter did not ask why but obeyed and went. There he saw an Ethiopian man who was a eunuch, a court official of Queen Kandake of Ethiopia. He had taken personal time off to come to Jerusalem to worship the God of the Jews. Peter saw the man sitting in his chariot reading from the writings of the prophet Isaiah.

When Peter approached, asking if the man understood what he read, the man replied that he did not and needed help. Peter explained that the silent sheep led to the slaughter about which Isaiah wrote was Jesus, the Son of God. Peter shared the gospel with the man, who then responded to God's call. As they continued on their way, the eunuch saw a body of water and asked to be baptized. God, who desires us, is ecstatic when we hunger and thirst for him. He fulfills our longings and sends just who we need to encourage us.

Father, put a fire within me to know you. I ask this in your holy name. Amen.

He Provides

"Look at the birds of the air; they do not sow or reap or store away in barns, and yet your heavenly Father feeds them. Are you not much more valuable than they?"

MATTHEW 6:26 NIV

You are not a reservoir with a limited number of resources; you are a channel attached to unlimited divine resources. Does that ignite a desire in you to ask for the luxuries of this life? Are you hoping to increase your worldly goods, keep up with the Joneses, and get the latest and greatest model of everything? Have you gotten trapped in the vicious cycle of working longer hours just to get that new toy?

When God sees a heart that prioritizes its own kingdom of goods, he will gently prick at that person to get them to take their eyes off themselves. Once that person is humbled, the Enemy may tempt them to fret over what they don't have, but God shows them a better way. He provides. We never need to worry or strive, for our Father will care for all our needs. As our faith builds, the importance of material things diminishes, and the desire to build his kingdom with our finances becomes our main goal.

Father, all I acquire here will burn one day. May I be gratefully content with your provisions. Amen.

Jesus at the Core

"Therefore, everyone who hears these words of Mine, and acts on them, will be like a wise man who built his house on the rock."

MATTHEW 7:24 NASB

A home where Jesus Christ is Lord is filled with wisdom, discernment, and love. Homes where the inhabitants lean on their own understanding may find themselves splitting apart. Currently, some surveys claim that 50 percent of all marriages end in divorce or separation. It breaks God's heart when two people give up after they have pledged themselves to one another in his sight. When selfish desires overrule placing your spouse's needs ahead of the things you want, over time it wears away at affection and commitment.

In God's Word, we learn to always place the concerns of others ahead of our own. Marriages that go the distance have Jesus at the core of their relationship. Those spouses know that without Jesus in control, chaos will eventually ensue. They place a priority on praying together, studying the Word together, and worshiping together. If these activities are missing from your marriage, it's not too late. You can start today to repair the foundation of your union. Study Scripture, apply it to your lives, obey God's Word, and speak the truth of it to one another.

Lord, I pray that you would establish our home on the solid Rock, Christ Jesus. Amen.

Our Heart's Desire

Take delight in the LORD,
and he will give you your heart's desires.
PSALM 37:4 NLT

What do you delight in? Is it a person, a favorite sport, or a possession? What do you run to when you need to be filled up, encouraged, or just to feel alive again? Do you binge a feel-good movie or gather with other believers to fellowship in the Lord's name? It's good to take inventory of our choices and look at where our love may lie. If our delight is not first and foremost in the Lord, we need to determine why. Our heart's desire should, in all honestly, be Jesus. If you are not quite there yet, you need to know it takes attention.

You don't build intimacy in a relationship unless you spend time with the object of your affection. You must be intentional, and as you engage more and more with the Lord, reading about him, praying to him, and envisioning him in all his glory, you will find pure delight in his character, his Word, and his love for you. Make a regular date to get alone with the lover of your soul.

Lord, may I be willing to surrender my thoughts, choices, and activities to you. Cause me to desire you more than anything else. Amen.

His Watchful Protection

The LORD watches over the way of the righteous,
but the way of the wicked leads to destruction.

PSALM 1:6 NIV

We live in a chaotic world. It's not *Happy Days* from back in
the fifties, when kids respected adults and you could watch
any show on TV and not be embarrassed by the content. Yes,
since the beginning of time, there has always been evil. Today,
however, it seems as though society has accepted it. Evil is on
a rampage in today's world, and what people have deemed
"decent" is far from it. The Bible says in Isaiah, "Woe to those
who call evil good and good evil" (5:20 NIV). A woe in the
Bible is usually tied to those who rebel against God. The way of
the wicked is a sure road to ruin.

Yet for the righteous, their way is always under God's
protective eye. He not only guides those who do good, but he
also provides his best plan for their life and is the one who
gives them exactly what they need. What joy and comfort you
can have in knowing that if you obey God, he will never stop
joyfully watching over you. Your way will be straight and your
victory secured.

Father, help me obey and please you by always choosing good.
I want to live to glorify your holy name. Amen.

Deserving of Praise

Yet you are holy,
enthroned on the praises of Israel.
PSALM 22:3 NLT

Great is the Lord and worthy to be praised! People in Scripture sang about the majesty of the Lord in all kinds of situations and places. Some in synagogues and some as they marched to battle. I can imagine a certain young mother in a stable lifting her voice in thanksgiving. No doubt Mary was filled with joyous worship as she held the Savior of the world. God is always good, and for that we must praise him. It is an absolute that he is all powerful, and for that he deserves our esteem. It is truth that Jesus is the only way of salvation, and for those who believe, they are joined with his church as his bride. He is holy and righteous, and the heavenly beings cry his accolades day and night.

Scripture reminds us that exaltation brings us into God's presence, and he, the Creator, our holy, all-knowing, all-powerful God, is enthroned in our praises. This act also sends your enemy running, for he cannot listen to us worship our Lord. So enter his gates with thanksgiving and his courts with praise.

Heavenly Father, no matter the circumstance, may I never cease to praise you with a worshipful, contrite, and thankful heart. Amen.

Peace Gives Life

A sound heart is life to the body,
but envy is rottenness to the bones.

PROVERBS 14:30 NKJV

The green-eyed monster has tripped up many people over time. Why is it so easy to fall into envy? What is it so easy for us to ignore the plenty we have and to want what our neighbor possesses? Why do we hate those who are more lovely than we are, as if it were they who created their beauty? We should praise the one who blesses others and be grateful for his goodness to all mankind. The Bible says that when we stress, when we are jealous, when we gossip to try to elevate ourselves over another, our bones rot. Our mental health is affected, and we become angry or depressed.

Medical science reports that hatred, jealousy, and all types of ill will can make you sick. God's desire for us is that we live a life of peace. The only way we can do that is to be filled with his Spirit and obedient to his Word. In Scripture, he gives us every strategy we need to live a calm and contented life. Rejoice over God's blessings for you and others.

Jesus, help me have a thankful heart, full of joy for all you have given me and all you have given others. Amen.

Neglecting the Tithe

"You have planted much, but have harvested little. You eat, but are never filled. You drink, but are still thirsty. You put on clothes, but are not warm. Those who earn wages end up with holes in their money bags."

HAGGAI 1:6 NET

Even those in the days of Haggai were living paycheck to paycheck. They had sown plenty but had nothing much to show for it. Nothing they did seemed to move the needle toward a life of financial success. It was as if all that they held simply slipped through their fingers. The people were living unto themselves and their own desires and pleasures. They never had enough while spending it on themselves, so they neglected the giving of tithes and offerings.

The Lord says, "You earn wages, only to put them in a purse with holes in it" (v. 6 NIV). They produced excess, but due to their neglect of God's house, he blew it all away (v. 9). God will provide for all our needs when we provide for the church and for those less fortunate. Store up your treasures in heaven. Be sure that you bring the whole tithe into his house, and he will surely provide all that you could ever need.

Lord, help me to look honestly at the way I live and make changes where necessary. Amen.

Lights that Shine for Him

"I have come as a light to shine in this dark world, so that all who put their trust in me will no longer remain in the dark."

JOHN 12:46 NLT

Those who do not believe in the Son of God for salvation walk through life with blinders on the eyes of their heart. They continue in the dark, foolishly thinking that the reason they are here on earth is for their own pleasure. Jesus looks upon those individuals and his heart yearns to see the scales fall off their eyes so that they can gaze into the face of the one who died for them. He left heaven, a place referred to as *paradise*, to save all who have chosen to follow a spiritually destructive path. He shines as the brightest light, hoping to lead to the grace of his salvation all those who are lost.

If they would only believe, they would be saved. We must take up the charge to share the gospel boldly and broadly throughout the world. We are the lights that shine here on his behalf to lead as many to him as possible.

God, enlighten my soul so that I may know that the whole purpose of my being is to love you and love others through you. Amen.

Pray for Israel

Let Israel hope in the LORD: for with the LORD there is mercy,
and with him is plenteous redemption.
PSALM 130:7 KJV

We who live in the United States often have no idea what it is
like for our persecuted brothers and sisters in other parts of the
world. We shudder at the thought of being arrested or killed
for our faith. We can't imagine seeing our believing family
members martyred for Jesus. Oh, we say we would die for him,
but we do not face that possibility day in and day out. Yet there
are stories of praise and adoration coming from the lips of those
facing their executioners. In all truth, it would be an honor to
die for Christ, and if that moment should come, he will give us
what we need to withstand it.

When you remember God's people, Israel, pray for them.
Pray for those who don't know him so that they realize that
the Savior has come. May they know the name of Jesus and his
desire for them to have his salvation. May they accept his love
and redemption.

Father, fill the persecuted with your presence, where there is
hope and joy, which is their strength. Amen.

Enjoy the Still Waters

He makes me lie down in green pastures.
He leads me beside still waters.

PSALM 23:2 ESV

Oh, how it must pain our heavenly Father when we scurry around frantically, allowing fear and stress to control us. For our part, it is a lack of knowing his character and his care and a lack of trust that he can handle whatever is affecting us. If we would only trust that he can do what his Word says he can do, we would have peace that passes understanding. We would skip through our days with no concerns for we would know our God holds the solution to every problem. We would go directly to him when we are distressed instead of ruminating day and night over offenses and troubles. We would enjoy the still waters of his grace, compassion, and presence, for we would have no need to rush and fix things on our own.

Read his Word, and you will find it is replete with proof of his power, sovereignty, and love. Take time to bask in his presence, study his Scripture, and then live what you have read. Believe him and all the miracles he can do.

Jesus, I pray today for those I know who are in distress. I pray that they find solace, peace, hope, love, and faith in your presence.
Amen.

Into His Arms

His massive arms are wrapped around you, protecting you. You
can run under his covering of majesty and hide. His arms of
faithfulness are a shield keeping you from harm.

PSALM 91:4 TPT

As we visualize the mighty arms of our heavenly Father
embracing us, we may feel humbled and the greatest sense of
security. Saying it is a privilege to be under his covering does
not come close to adequately describing this interaction with
God. Our Father loves us more than we can ever understand.
When we consider the lengths he allowed his Son to go for us to
be saved, we should feel astounded.

As we absorb the truth of what has been done for us
and what he continues to do in his faithfulness, we should
fall on our faces in worship. He bids us to run to him, to hide
confidently in the strength and refuge of his heavenly hug. If
you are hesitating, ask yourself why. We need never fear, for
he is our safeguard, our deliverer, and our Abba. He is always
available and waiting for his dear children to come to him, for
he loves us with an everlasting love.

Abba, I have no fear. You are my protector, my Father who will
faithfully surround me until the day I come home to you. Amen.

Rest in Him

Those who trust in the LORD will find new strength.
They will soar high on wings like eagles.
They will run and not grow weary.
They will walk and not faint.

ISAIAH 40:31 NLT

We live in a fast-paced world full of demands. Between relentless advertising messages and pressures of social media, the stress can feel overwhelming and insurmountable. You may experience sleepless nights, plotting your next business presentation or juggling your bills in your head until you can think of nothing else. You wonder how in the world you will make the bake sale cupcakes, clean the house, taxi the kids to activities, lead the Bible study, and maintain your sanity.

You need Jesus; you need his strength. Go to God. Admit that you are in over your head and ask for wisdom and guidance. Pray for more trust in him and less dependance on yourself. Ask for discernment for when to say no. If you petition the Lord for the ability to run and not get weary, he will hear you, answer, and provide what you need.

Jesus, help me believe that you will equip me with all I need to carry on. Amen.

What a Glorious Creator

"Worthy are You, our Lord and our God, to receive glory and honor and power; for You created all things, and because of Your will they existed, and were created."

REVELATION 4:11 NASB

If you can try to imagine what total darkness, lack of life, and nothing in existence would be like, you might feel deep sadness. God made us to be loved. He created us to be in relationship. If it were not for the purposes of God, there would be nothing. So many fight the concept of an intelligent creator, but the intricacy of the human body alone is beyond understanding. God meticulously fashioned every cell, every strand of DNA, and every organ and made them all work together in harmony. He placed every mountain in the perfect spot, made every flower grow in its season, and planted seeds that would bear food.

Instead of trying to explain him away or replace his great work with some ridiculous theory, we should be praising him. Because of his power and love, we have life, we have salvation, and we, as believers in Christ, have a future in heaven with him. Give him glory, sing his praises, and do it continually.

Lord, I praise you, magnificent Creator. Thank you for making me and everything around me. Amen.

He Will Complete It

The one who calls you by name is trustworthy
and will thoroughly complete his work in you.

1 THESSALONIANS 5:24 TPT

What strikes me about today's verse is the fact that God has called each of us by name. Let's consider all that the Creator has done for us poor, sinful people. He chose us before the foundation of the world. He loved us before we loved him. He created us in our mother's womb and breathed life into us. Since we could never save ourselves, he sent his sinless Son to die on our behalf.

He has forgiven us all our sins and does not condemn us. He fills us with his Spirit. He created works in advance that we would do for him. He desires time with us, hears our prayers, and answers them. He sings over us. He protects, provides, and delivers us from the Evil One. He tells us to call to him and he will tell us great and unsearchable things we do not know. He has made a covenant with us, made us heirs with Christ, and promised us eternity. He is faithful to complete all he has promised. What a glorious Lord and Savior.

Father, you are eternally faithful and true to your promises.
I trust you to complete all that you created me for. Amen.

To Be Saturated in Prayer

Don't be pulled in different directions or worried about a thing.
Be saturated in prayer throughout each day, offering your
faith-filled requests before God with overflowing gratitude.
Tell him every detail of your life.

PHILIPPIANS 4:6 TPT

We spend far too much time fretting over things that are
completely out of our control. It is human nature to worry,
but this type of behavior never profits us. It's honestly a lack of
faith. If we believe that God is who he says he is, that his Word
is truth, we will follow the instructions in today's verse. At the
first sight of trouble, we should drop to our knees, pour out our
heart, and then thank God in advance for how he will step in
and handle it all.

If we ask in faith, he will equip us with wisdom and
discernment, guiding us to something good from the various
trials. Allowing ourselves to continue under stress never
accomplishes anything but heartache and frustration. Let's
determine now to never handle anything without going to his
throne of grace, laying it at his feet, and then praising him as he
works for our good.

Lord, forgive me for being indifferent in my times of prayer. Give
me a dedicated heart that yearns for oneness with your Spirit.
Amen.

Opposition from Sinners

Let us...[fix] our eyes on Jesus, the pioneer and perfecter of faith. For the joy set before him he endured the cross, scorning its shame, and sat down at the right hand of the throne of God. Consider him who endured such opposition from sinners, so that you will not grow weary and lose heart.

HEBREWS 12:1–3 NIV

We think our life is so hard, and for many, that is true. But we must stop and consider the one who suffered with us and for us. Jesus knew all too well his purpose for coming to earth, what his life would be like, and how it would end. Even though he would encounter rejection, have the life of a wanderer who lived solely for others, and eventually meet a torturous death, he faced it with joy.

He may have prayed in Gethsemane for God to remove his journey to the cross if possible, but he also said, "Not my will, but yours be done" (Luke 22:42 NIV). He went to the cross forgiving those who killed him. If we are to share in the sufferings of Christ, we must remember his sacrifice and not grow weary in our trials.

Jesus, may I face your purpose for me with rejoicing. Amen.

Dress in the Spirit

Put on truth as a belt to strengthen you to stand in triumph.
Put on holiness as the protective armor that covers your heart.
Stand on your feet alert, then you'll always be ready to share
the blessings of peace. In every battle, take faith as your wrap-
around shield, for it is able to extinguish the blazing arrows
coming at you from the evil one!

Ephesians 6:14–17 TPT

We have an enemy who is diligently out to steal, kill, and destroy
(John 10:10). He is coming after us, our spouses, our children,
our family, and our friends. We must go to the Lord for strength,
donning the armor that he has provided for us. As we trust in his
power to fight the battle for us, we can confidently go forward to
the front lines. Have courage as you march into victory, for the
Lord goes before you. Rejoice as you see the enemy of your soul
grow weaker at the sound of your worship to the King. Dress
daily in the battle gear that God has provided: the belt of truth,
the breastplate of righteous, shoes sharing the gospel of peace,
the shield of faith, the helmet of salvation, and the Sword of the
Spirit, which is the Word of God.

Dear Lord, remind me daily to dress defensively with your
protective armor. Amen.

Choices Made in Love

Jesus answered, "the foremost is, 'hear, israel! The LORD is our god, the LORD is one; and you shall love the LORD your god with all your heart, and with all your soul, and with all your mind, and with all your strength.'"

MARK 12:29–30 NASB

God's love for us is the compelling force behind this command. He was perfect and complete before he created us. It was for our good that he desires our love. Would we ever have come to adore him if he hadn't cared for us first? We may have stayed lovers of self, but he saved us by pouring out his affection on us. When we enter a relationship with him through Jesus and love him passionately, we know a supernatural fulfillment. We make choices that enhance our spiritual lives through the influence of his Holy Spirit. We walk through our sorrows, trials, and difficulties with hope as we keep our minds stayed on him.

Placing all our emotional and intellectual strength into loving him, we learn to know him better. As we remain fixed on his Word, we hear him speak. He must always be our first love, the number one priority in our lives.

Father, may my love for you and your commands flourish, knowing they are all for my good. Amen.

Abiding in the Word

Jesus was saying to those Jews who had believed Him,
"If you continue in My word, then you are truly My disciples."

JOHN 8:31 NASB

Most Christians will admit that they have experienced doubt.
They wonder whether they were sincere enough, humble
enough, when they accepted Christ and whether they are really
redeemed. The Bible makes it clear that if we believe in the
Lord Jesus, we will be saved. If you want to test where your
commitment stands, though, you can measure it against today's
verse. Jesus said if we obey his Word, we can be sure we are his
disciples.

We must be honest. How important is the Word of God
in our lives? Do we hunger for it? Do we go to it when we have
a crisis of faith or a decision that requires wisdom from God?
When Jesus was tempted in the desert by the devil, Jesus used
Scripture to refute him. We should be able to do the same. If we
can't declare God's Word when we need to do spiritual battle,
fend off discouragement, or get a chance to share the gospel,
then we need to spend more time in Scripture.

God, help me hunger for your Word, memorize it, and readily give
an answer to anyone who may ask. Amen.

Old Testament Saints

> Therefore, since we are surrounded by such a huge crowd of witnesses to the life of faith, let us strip off every weight that slows us down, especially the sin that so easily trips us up. And let us run with endurance the race God has set before us.
>
> HEBREWS 12:1 NLT

If you ever had stage fright about standing in front of a crowd to speak, this verse may cause you concern. There are actually a couple of interpretations of this verse, but Bible scholars and theologians have not reached a definitive conclusion. Some portions in Scripture will remain a mystery until we have the chance to ask a few questions in heaven. One thought is that this verse means exactly what it says: that the Old Testament saints and others are watching our lives from heaven.

Another more-favored interpretation says that the Old Testament saints witnessed to their faith by their service to the Lord while on the earth. Either way, we have the patriarchs' lives that we should study and their good works that we should emulate. This will aid us as we represent Jesus for younger believers in the faith who will view what we do, good or bad. We always want to encourage them toward growth in Christ.

Jesus, may I always remember that I may be the only example of you that some people ever see. Help me live a holy life. Amen.

Diligence

I have competed well;
I have finished the race;
I have kept the faith!
2 TIMOTHY 4:7 NET

It is easy to understand that great accomplishments take more effort and time than good accomplishments. However, much of how people conduct themselves regarding work or other responsibilities is a reflection of their upbringing. Did their parents teach them any work ethic? Were they allowed to try tasks and fail, or did their parents figure a child's project would only be done right if the parents did it for them?

If your parents did not train you to work hard and persevere, you can still get there. Jesus said that whatever we ask for in his name, we will receive (John 14:14). Christ can birth a new passion in you and place you where you will thrive. Wherever you struggle and whatever you don't know or comprehend, ask God to equip you with it. With Christ you can do anything. Remind yourself that it is God you are working for, not man. And when it comes to finishing well with faith, trust in him who predetermined what you would do for his kingdom. He will make you victorious.

Jesus, help me to work as unto you. May I, with all my heart, run the race you designed for me and finish well. Amen.

God Gives Gifts

He gave some as apostles, some as prophets, some as evangelists, some as pastors and teachers, for the equipping of the saints for the work of ministry, for the building up of the body of Christ.

EPHESIANS 4:11–12 NASB

When God formed you in your mother's womb, he did so with forethought, planning, and predestination. He knew who you would be in his kingdom, and he gave you the gifts you would need to accomplish his purpose. Of course, those abilities needed to be developed in you, and God orchestrated the events in your life that would bring about that development. The only thing that will sidetrack those talents is if you refuse to use them.

Maybe like Moses, you are uncomfortable speaking in front of others…but do you trust God to speak through you? Possibly, like the rich young ruler, you are wealthy and aren't very generous when it comes to supporting your local church. If you grasp that this is the only life you have to use the abilities the Lord has given you for his honor, knowing the outcomes will last for eternity, you may find yourself eager to participate. Honor what God has given you by willingly doing whatever he asks.

Father, energize my faith to be willing to serve you with my gifts. Amen.

Do Whatever Is Needed

Ye know that because of an infirmity of the flesh I preached
the gospel unto you the first time: and that which was a
temptation to you in my flesh ye despised not, nor rejected;
but ye received me as an angel of God, even as Christ Jesus.

GALATIANS 4:13–14 ASV

How often do we cancel plans because we might have an ache or
the sniffles? Obviously this didn't stop Paul. We don't know the
details of Paul's illness while he was in Galatia, but his suffering did
not deter him from going out to the people and sharing the good
news of Jesus. There are so many reports of dire circumstances
surrounding Paul, but he never quit. His love for Christ and his
desire to see others come to salvation motivated him.

It may not be a sickness, but maybe we just don't want
to serve in the nursery on Sundays or greet people at the door.
"We aren't called to that," we say. Shouldn't we do whatever is
needed for the cause of Christ? Paul used every opportunity to
share the good news, whether ill, in prison, or standing before
kings. Shouldn't we be willing to go outside our comfort zone
for Jesus?

Lord, help me to not live with excuses but to be faithful to share
your gospel in all circumstances. Amen.

God's Will for Us

He hath showed thee, O man, what is good; and what doth
Jehovah require of thee, but to do justly, and to love kindness,
and to walk humbly with thy God?

MICAH 6:8 ASV

Some people spend anxious hours wondering whether they are
in God's will. They have prayed but heard nothing from God.
They have received counsel from friends, but the advice didn't
bring any answers. If only we would search God's Word, we'd
eliminate worrisome moments. God gives us in Scripture all
the instructions we need to be in his will. There are the Ten
Commandments, the words of Jesus, the teachings of the apostles,
and today's verse among other admonitions from the prophets.

What a different world it would be if we all adhered to
Micah 6:8. Doesn't everyone want to be treated with justice?
Don't you feel great when you are kind or when someone is
kind to you? Wouldn't you much rather converse with a humble
person than a proud one? If we'd just concentrate consistently
on the Word and what God expects from us, it would eliminate
all the guessing. Of course, we won't ever be perfect this side
of heaven, but if we insert the actions of justice, kindness, and
humility in our lives, we can be assured of pleasing the Lord.

Father, help me to show justice and kindness in humility. Amen.

His Powerful Spirit

He would grant you, according to the riches of his glory,
that ye may be strengthened with power through his
Spirit in the inward man.

EPHESIANS 3:16 ASV

To be strengthened with God's power through his very own spirit…let that sink in. The very spirit of the living God, all powerful and all knowing, can live in us. It is almost incomprehensible; in fact, it is impossible to really grasp. Scripture says we are dust, yet God offers us the same power that he exerted when he raised Jesus from the grave (Ephesians 1:19–20). God, through the riches of his glory, desires to impart his power to us. Our spiritual inner man must have the faith to believe he will do it. Without faith, we can't please God, so if we ask him something in prayer, we must thank him in advance for what he will do.

Ask God to glorify himself through the strength he will give you. Leave your prayer closet with hopeful expectation and determine to watch for how the Spirit's power is evident in your life. And when you receive what you have asked for, give your testimony of God's goodness. Praise his name to all you come in contact with.

Father, what a privilege to be filled with your Holy Spirit. Thank
you for imparting your power to me. Amen.

Temptations

We do not have a High Priest who cannot sympathize with
our weaknesses, but was in all points tempted as we are,
yet without sin.

HEBREWS 4:15 NKJV

When Jesus walked the earth, he was subject to temptation
just as we are. The only account recorded in Scripture is his
temptation by Satan in the desert. This temptation came after
the Holy Spirit led Jesus away into the wilderness to endure
forty days of fasting, so obviously Jesus was feeling weak. Still,
he resisted the devil and remained sinless. He used Scripture to
refute the devil, and eventually, the devil fled.

Jesus understands the gravity of sin's consequences
because that is what he faced on the cross. This perfect God as
man, who never even for a moment entertained a sinful act,
died in the place of all mankind. We can't begin to understand
the magnitude of the weight of that sin he carried. Jesus, our
compassionate King-Priest, sympathizes with us as we battle
with temptation. He understands our humanity and always
provides a way for us to escape.

Jesus, I am thankful that you understand my struggles. You don't
condemn me, but you help me resist temptation. I am so grateful
you paid for my sin. Amen.

April

The Depth of His Affection

Know this love that surpasses knowledge—that you may be
filled to the measure of all the fullness of God.

EPHESIANS 3:19 NIV

God's longing and desire for us, his children, is that we would
comprehend and accept his great love. Knowing that this love
surpasses our knowledge means that we need the Holy Spirit
to even begin to interpret the depth of this affection. Can you
imagine giving yours or your child's life for that of another? Yet
that is exactly what God did. He allowed his one and only Son
to be killed in a merciless way so that we, as sinners, could be
forgiven. It is far beyond what we would have ever conceived
of, let alone agreed to do on anyone else's behalf. It took this
extreme act to bring us into the kingdom.

The cross and our acceptance of Jesus' death for us
enable God's Spirit to dwell in us to the extent that we have
all his fullness. This is the greatest gift and most extravagant
affection that has ever existed. He has given everything to have
us. We must give him our everything in return.

Father, thank you for being willing to sacrifice your Son for me.
Thank you for your great love. I give you my life for your purpose.
Amen.

He Bore Our Cross

According to the law, I may almost say,
all things are cleansed with blood,
and apart from shedding of blood there is no remission.

HEBREWS 9:22 ASV

Christ came down as a servant to a world that he knew would reject, revile, and hate him. He showed perfect love through the testimony of his teaching and sacrifice of his life for us. The suffering of his horrific death we cannot, in our wildest imaginations, fathom. The decision to go to the cross he made with full knowledge of what he would suffer. He knew this was the only thing that would provide forgiveness and salvation for creation.

Perhaps the foreknowledge of what this would entail is why he was disturbed to the point of sweating blood as he prayed in the garden of Gethsemane. Without the obedience of Jesus to bear our cross, we would have no remission of our sins and no hope of salvation. Oh Savior, cleanse us with the beauty of your blood shed for all.

Blessed Redeemer, bathe me in your blood, dear Jesus. May my heart ever praise you, my Savior. Amen.

Our Sins Are Forgiven

He saith unto them, Be not amazed: ye seek Jesus,
the Nazarene, who hath been crucified: he is risen;
he is not here: behold, the place where they laid him!
MARK 16:6 ASV

Peter had cursed and denied ever knowing or having anything to do with Jesus. Realizing what he had done, his heart was shattered, and he sobbed with bitter tears. Now, upon hearing that the tomb was empty and that an angel had declared Jesus was alive, Peter had to face the one whom he had seen suffer beyond comprehension and had denied ever knowing. Imagine all that went through his mind. *How can I face him? Will he condemn, rebuke, show his disappointment, or turn away from me?*

When Jesus met up with Peter, he said, "Do you love me?" Then, after asking Peter that same question three times, Jesus commissioned Peter to feed and care for his sheep (John 21:14–17). No disgust, rebuke, or condemnation, only tender love and a belief and confidence in Peter. Despite Peter's utter failing, God used him mightily for the kingdom. Though we may fail the Lord at times, his indescribable love constantly calls us to fulfill the high purpose for which we were created.

Lord, may I humbly accept your forgiveness and embrace the purpose for which you created me. Amen.

After His Resurrection

Behold, the veil of the temple was rent in two from the top to
the bottom; and the earth did quake; and the rocks were rent;
and the tombs were opened; and many bodies of the saints
that had fallen asleep were raised.

MATTHEW 27:51–52 ASV

What must the Roman soldiers have thought when the earth
quaked and the veil tore? Did they recognize right at that
moment what a massive mistake they had made. Imagine their
thought process. *If this was truly the Son of God, am I responsible
for his death?* What did the crowd who begged for Barabbas
think? Did they, at that moment, realize the enormous error
of their choice? There must have been cries of anguish as they
considered the possibility that this was the Messiah whose death
they had just called for.

As these miraculous events erupted after Christ died,
no doubt people ran for cover, hiding from God. Yet what Jesus
had just done demonstrated how great God's love is and his
desire to save, not condemn. When the people who witnessed
the crucifixion came upon the saints who were raised from the
grave, they all surely declared, "This was the Son of God."

Dear Lord, help me to live in the fullness of your resurrection
power. Thank you for not condemning. Amen.

Recognize Our Savior

When day was now breaking, Jesus stood on the beach:
yet the disciples knew not that it was Jesus.

JOHN 21:4 ASV

Have you ever said of someone, "I barely recognized them"?
Sometimes because of sadness, weight loss, or illness, a person's
appearance changes dramatically. Those who had been intimate
friends with Jesus did not recognize him after his resurrection.
Yet he was not a spirit or ghost but flesh and blood. I wonder
if, perhaps, carrying the weight of the sin of the world was
reflected in his appearance. We know that the scars on his hands
and feet were still present. Or maybe he glowed with the power
of new life. Scripture says Christ was not handsome; he was a
man of sorrow acquainted with grief (Isaiah 53:3).

He was constantly aware of his mission to earth—of the
cross and bearing upon himself all the sins ever committed by
mankind. After the resurrection, his mission was completed.
He had rightly fulfilled the purpose he had come to accomplish.
It was finished! The ecstatic joy that love had prevailed must
have radiated from his appearance. Was it a wonder they didn't
recognize him?

Jesus, thank you for the cost you paid for my sins and the
grandeur of the love that propelled you to redeem me. I will praise
and love you for eternity. Amen.

A Promise

By two immutable things, in which it is impossible for God to
lie, we may have a strong encouragement, who have fled for
refuge to lay hold of the hope set before us: which we have
as an anchor of the soul, a hope both sure and stedfast and
entering into that which is within the veil.

HEBREWS 6:18–19 ASV

There are situations in life about which our skeptical soul would
like to have an ironclad guarantee. We want a promise, totally
foolproof and delivered exactly as we were assured. Unfortunately,
human beings, at times, do not honor their word, and they
stretch the truth into full-fledged lies. It's just the sin nature of the
creature. For our God, it is impossible for him to utter anything
that is not entirely truthful. Every word that proceeds from his
mouth is trustworthy. "All Scripture is breathed out by God and
profitable for teaching, for reproof, for correction, and for training
in righteousness" (2 Timothy 3:16 ESV).

We know that what God has promised, he will definitely
deliver. We have hope, and we have certainty that, due to
Christ's sacrifice, we can come boldly before the Father's throne.
The Lord has promised that through the blood of Jesus, we are
one with him for eternity.

Father, thank you for being completely trustworthy. Amen.

Hard to Love

"If you love those who love you, what benefit is that to you? For even sinners love those who love them."

LUKE 6:32 ESV

If you have ever had a person in your life who just grates on your nerves, you probably had a hard time being around them. At times, we might also come across strangers who look different or act oddly, and we want to turn and go the other direction. What would happen in either of these scenarios if we reminded ourselves that those people are made in the image of God?

Remember, Jesus died for the sins of the world, and he loves us all. If you find it difficult to reach out and care for anyone who crosses your path, then you might find it helpful to dwell on today's verse. When we love the unlovely, we are doing what Jesus does. When we show kindness, whether it's offering a smile or buying a homeless person a meal, we do it for Jesus. Remember Matthew 25:40 (NKJV): "The King will answer and say to them, 'Assuredly, I say to you, inasmuch as you did it to one of the least of these My brethren, you did it to Me.'"

Jesus, may I love as you love and give as you gave, sacrificially and for the good of others. Amen.

Obey or Don't Obey

Let your conversation be gracious and attractive so that you will have the right response for everyone.

COLOSSIANS 4:6 NLT

We always want to speak to people as we would like to be spoken to. Usually, that is not a big issue, but once in a while, someone will make a comment in your direction that makes your blood boil. That is when it is truly hard to hold your tongue. Scripture suggests that we season our conversations with salt. Make them tasteful and appropriate so that we avoid any offense. If we desire to do this, then we must work on it in advance. Memorizing today's verse will make it available to recite in those trying discussions.

We must draw closer to Jesus so that we find it more important to please him than to get the last word in. It comes down to either obeying Scripture, which is for our good and the good of others, or not obeying. The choice is up to us, and depending on what we choose, the rewards or negative consequences will follow. Choose words that are loving and life giving so that you may please your Father who is in heaven.

Father, help me choose to obey your commands about the way I should use my words. May they bless others and honor you. Amen.

Pray in This Way

"Our Father in heaven, hallowed be your name, your kingdom come, your will be done, on earth as it is in heaven. Give us today our daily bread. And forgive us our debts, as we also have forgiven our debtors. And lead us not into temptation, but deliver us from the evil one."

MATTHEW 6:9–13 NIV

In all the religions of the world, prayer is an integral part of trying to reach, find favor with, and connect with a deity. Many religions demand penance or great ritual; in the past, some even demanded human sacrifice. What does the Bible say about prayer to the one true God? In Luke 18, Jesus says humility of spirit, persistence, and expectancy are the keys to prayer. Then he gives us the perfect prayer pathway in Matthew 6:9–13. God hears all our prayers.

If we are ever short on words, we can always use today's verse as a starting place to get us going. We can also ask the Holy Spirit to help us pray, and he will, for he intercedes for us. The Lord desires that we come to him with praise and our requests. Prayer is a wonderful gift from our heavenly Father that we must engage in continually. Don't hesitate but run to your place of prayer.

Lord, help me meet with you in prayer consistently. Amen.

God Will Establish It

He spake before his brethren and the army of Samaria, and said, What are these feeble Jews doing? will they fortify themselves? will they sacrifice? will they make an end in a day? will they revive the stones out of the heaps of rubbish, seeing they are burned?

NEHEMIAH 4:2 ASV

Nehemiah is a great book of the Bible (as, of course, all are), and the prophet's fervent prayers, humility, courage, tenacity, hard work, and utter dependance on God's mercy are amazing. Sanballat, one of the governors serving the Persian king, was not happy about the wall the Jews were building in Jerusalem, so he mocked them. In fact, he insulted them in front of the whole army of Samaria. Obviously Sanballat didn't know that God's plans cannot be thwarted and that God would empower his people to complete their task. Even though it was done with much opposition and plots of war by Sanballat and others, the wall was built.

What God determines, he will establish. It may not be an easy path, but when God is on your side, nothing can alter his plan for you. Continue to trust him and work for his kingdom, and he will make sure that whatever your wall is, it will come to pass.

Dear God, give us the faith to know that you make beauty out of ashes. Amen.

Revere the Sabbath

Ye shall keep my sabbaths, and reverence my sanctuary:
I am Jehovah.

LEVITICUS 26:2 ASV

This is the fourth commandment. It is not a suggestion as are none of the commandments. Even though we don't live under the law, we must still adhere to the words on the tablets Moses carried. According to those tablets, the Sabbath day is to be observed in commemoration of God creating the world in six days and resting on the seventh. God blessed the seventh day and made it holy. No one was to do any work on the Sabbath, and instead, we are to spend it in worship, receiving renewal from the week's tasks.

There are numerous things that God commanded in the Old Testament that many people don't follow today. Search the Scriptures and ask God for wisdom about how he wants you, in particular, to respond to these laws. Seek the counsel of your pastor. May the Holy Spirit be upon those who bring forth the truth of God's Word, whether in sermon or song. May we rejoice that we serve a God who knows we need rest and time to reflect upon his goodness.

Lord, show me your will for your Sabbath. Give me the desire to meditate on all that you are and all you have done. Amen.

A Light in the Storm

Seeing them distressed in rowing, for the wind was contrary unto them, about the fourth watch of the night he cometh unto them, walking on the sea; and he would have passed by them: but they, when they saw him walking on the sea, supposed that it was a ghost, and cried out; for they all saw him, and were troubled. But he straightway spake with them, and saith unto them, Be of good cheer: it is I; be not afraid.

MARK 6:48–50 ASV

Jesus had slipped away from his disciples to Bethsaida to pray and meet with God. It was dark, and a storm had come up, and the disciples were struggling and afraid. This is when Jesus came to them, walking on the water. Pastor and Bible teacher Tony Evans said, "It often takes the darkness of a storm to show us the light of God's presence."

Don't fear when you can't see what's ahead; keep going, for he has promised to never leave you or forsake you. God will always create illumination when and where you need it. Our almighty God exchanges light for darkness, joy for sorrow, hope for despair, peace for fear, courage for weakness, and truth for lies.

Lord, as you are my light, let me be a light to others, leading them to you. Amen.

The Day of Salvation

The Lord is not slack concerning his promise, as some count slackness; but is longsuffering to you-ward, not wishing that any should perish, but that all should come to repentance.

2 PETER 3:9 ASV

We long for the return of Jesus. We look at this weary, mixed-up world and think, *If only we could be in paradise with him today.* We could escape all the politics, turmoil, and personal struggles and be in a place of perfection. We wonder why he doesn't come back and how much worse this earth can get. Don't ever think his tarrying isn't due to his great love for mankind. He delays so that as many people as possible come to know him. He beckons the multitude to be washed in the blood of Christ.

Now is the day of salvation, but one day it will be too late. Be thankful, for the sake of your unsaved friends and loved ones, that God in his kindness leaves us all here while he woos his unbelieving children to him. We are blessed with the Lord's tender mercies as he continues to draw people to him. He is eager to forgive and save the lost.

Lord, thank you for your kindness in wanting many to come to know you personally. Let hearts be quick to repent and seek your mercy. Amen.

Believe and Be Saved

They said, Believe on the Lord Jesus,
and thou shalt be saved, thou and thy house.
ACTS 16:31 ASV

Some people say it's too simple, can't be real, and sounds like a fairy tale. Forgiven, just by asking forgiveness of your sins and professing your belief in Christ…they just don't buy it. But it's truer than anything else in existence. The truth about what is at the center of our lives and our history is that Jesus was crucified on the cross for our sins and raised from the tomb for our salvation. We can participate in new life as we believe in him, accept his mercy, respond to his love, and attend to his commands. We leave the old sinful self behind and are transformed, a new person in Christ.

As we walk in this new life, we must share the good news with our own family and with others. Eugene Peterson, author of *The Message* version of the Bible, said, "God loves you. He's on your side. He's coming after you. He's relentless."[1] Be the one today who helps a lost soul realize that God wants to save them.

Jesus, thank you for your cross. It is the reason I am set free and joined with you for now and throughout eternity. I am forever grateful. Amen.

---

1   Stoyan Zaimov, "Eugene Peterson's Son Reveals His Father 'Fooled' Everyone, Had Only One Real Sermon for the World," The Christian Post, November 5, 2018. www.christianpost.com.

Rejection

Blessed are you when people hate you, when they exclude you and insult you and reject your name as evil, because of the Son of Man.

LUKE 6:22 NIV

When you come to faith in Jesus, many who knew your past life will question it. Family members might be put off by it. Friends may look for new people to hang with, at least until you come to your senses. This may cause you great pain at first. Yet when you consider what you lost compared to all you have gained by coming to Jesus, it is well worth it.

Don't fret over those who will walk away but rejoice over the many new brothers and sisters in Christ you will gain. These will be relationships like you have never known before, for you are bonded with one another in love and through faith in the Savior. You are children of the King, and together, you will live forevermore. Remember, our battles are not against flesh and blood but principalities, demons, and the Enemy himself. Pray for the salvation of those who persecute you. Continue to love those who give no love in return.

Jesus, help me not to hold offense against anyone who belittles me for following you. Let your light shine through me and attract them to you. Amen.

Exemplify the Love of Christ

In love of the brethren be tenderly affectioned one to another; in honor preferring one another.

ROMANS 12:10 ASV

Remember that it is not our brothers and sisters who come against us but Satan and his army. We must remember to place the blame where it belongs. "Resist the devil and he will flee from you" (James 4:7 NKJV). Start praising and worshiping, and the old snake will slither away. Don't let disagreements or petty actions drive you away from fellowship but exemplify the love of Christ by offering pardon and acceptance.

Love is seeing the flaws and the scars and caring for each other despite them. Love is what rushes in to say, "I'm sorry," and to reply, "I forgive you," when a wrong is suffered. Love works around bad habits and mannerisms. Love puts itself last and others first. Love speaks life. Love is recognizing all the fears and insecurities and knowing your role is to comfort. Love is working through the challenges of the valley and celebrating the mountain tops. Love is strong, and it strengthens with time because it is real. Love one another as he has loved us.

Jesus, help me forgive as you do. May I recognize that all battles originate from the pit of hell. May I always be quick to offer mercy and love. Amen.

Enemies of God

If we deliberately keep on sinning after we have received the knowledge of the truth, no sacrifice for sins is left, but only a fearful expectation of judgment and of raging fire that will consume the enemies of God.

HEBREWS 10:26–27 NIV

The title for today's reading sends chills down my spine: Enemies of God. Who in their right mind would ever want to be an enemy of God? Yet our world is full of them. So many live foolishly for self and ignore the great salvation that our precious Savior offers. Evidence of our Lord is everywhere. Who can look at a newborn baby and not see God's handiwork? Who can explain the intricacy of the human body and honestly believe it just evolved? How can anyone view a starry sky and not believe that Christ's hand placed each one there?

Oh, how blind the world is to the truth. They remain enemies of God, walking in ignorance and sin, continuing to their death as days pass. Pray intensely for the lost. Their future is dim and will be full of judgment and a blazing, all-consuming fire unless they believe in the one and only Son of God.

Jesus, let my heart burn for the lost. Loosen my tongue to preach the gospel. Open their eyes so that they may see you. Amen.

Longing for Peace

Behold, how good and how pleasant it is
for brethren to dwell together in unity!
PSALM 133:1 KJV

Either in the human family or the family bonded together by our Savior, harmony is a precious gift. Many try to achieve tranquility in relationships, but it evades them. As the body of Christ, we will find that it is only possible to experience this as we submit ourselves together in love, honoring each other above ourselves. As the bride of Christ, we are responsible for showing the world the beauty of his love. There is such a stark contrast between how the church exists together so beautifully and the drama the world lives in.

For the unsaved, there is so much hate, anger, and striving for revenge. Turmoil mounts, and things get out of control quickly where there is no knowledge of the truth. There is a longing for peace, but no one knows how to really attain it. That is because we can only receive that comfort from God. This world needs Jesus, and we must be the means through which they hear the good news.

Dear Lord, help me to look through eyes of love for the salvation
of others—family, friends, or any who cross my path. Amen.

Delight in His Commands

Give me understanding, so that I may keep your law and obey it with all my heart. Direct me in the path of your commands, for there I find delight. Turn my heart toward your statutes and not toward selfish gain. Turn my eyes away from worthless things; preserve my life according to your word.

PSALM 119:34–37 NIV

Don't you have admiration for the person who wrote this psalm? They are completely committed to following and obeying God, as we all should be. We must ask ourselves if we feel this strongly about turning our heart toward his statutes, avoiding selfish gain, and becoming blind to things that have no value. Yet how often do we spend time watching worthless things on our screens?

These verses should lead us to pray to have an undivided heart toward our Father in heaven. Do you delight in his life-giving commands? Do you crave time in his Word? If you're struggling in this, ask the Holy Spirit to give you an insatiable craving for the Word of God. Ask him to direct you to live righteously and help you avoid evil. Pray that your life will be sustained by gaining wisdom from the Bible.

Father, help me desire to be a student of your Word and then to apply what I learn to every area of my life. Amen.

Keep Hope Alive

As for me, I watch in hope for the LORD,
I wait for God my Savior; my God will hear me.
MICAH 7:7 NIV

The prophet Micah said these words just after stating the distressing and depressing conditions of the days in which he lived. He said that the godly had disappeared from sight and that not one righteous person was left. Members of one's own family were enemies, and Scripture describes the situation as hunting one another with a net (v. 2). These were dysfunctional, sinful people, much like many today.

Micah had the right perspective though. He knew the character of his God, and that gave him hope. He had confidence through faith that the Lord would hear him, answer, and judge fairly. He stood firm, believing God when others didn't. He praised the Lord for being a God who pardons iniquity. He understood firsthand that the Father delights in giving his steadfast love to his children. If life isn't going the way you hoped, turn your eyes to the Savior and believe that he is working for good on your behalf. He is trustworthy. As you watch for him, believe he will fulfill his purpose in your life.

Father, our world and sometimes my personal life are so messed up. Help me draw near to you. Increase my faith and give me hope. Amen.

Wait and Don't Worry

Be still before the LORD and wait patiently for him;
do not fret when people succeed in their ways,
when they carry out their wicked schemes.

PSALM 37:7 NIV

Nothing takes God by surprise. Just when we thought life was just going swimmingly, the Lord knew there was a storm ahead. Maybe he beckoned you to spend some quiet time with him because he knew you would need his strength. Possibly, you decided you would rather engage in some other activity and would catch up with him later. Then it hit; someone purposely said something evil and untrue about you, and it spread like wildfire. Suddenly, you made time to meet with God and pour out your heart. You begged him to fix things. As you sat there in his presence, he stilled your heart and said, *Wait and do not worry, for this is my battle.*

Nineteenth century evangelist and missionary George Müller said, "The beginning of anxiety is the end of faith, and the beginning of true faith is the end of anxiety." May we find comfort and calm in God through our faith and keep our eyes fastened on God, knowing he will never forsake us and always defend us.

Lord, help me focus on you, not on the troubling conditions in my life. Help me rest and trust that you will be victorious on my behalf. Amen.

God's Love

*All Scripture is breathed out by God
and profitable for teaching, for reproof, for correction,
and for training in righteousness.*

2 TIMOTHY 3:16 ESV

The Bible says that God himself is its author. The Creator of the universe commissioned these life-giving words with his breath. What Scripture contains can leap off the page and become part of your mind and heart, training you toward righteousness. Can a book that has existed for centuries still be completely applicable today? Only this Book. Its words, statutes, commands, and promises open our eyes to God's magnificent will.

Every day, believers are reading its contents over and over again, memorizing its words, preaching its message to massive crowds, and speaking it over the airwaves. The Bible contains concepts that help us become the followers of Christ that God intended us to be. Its pages are full of power to cut straight through to our hearts and lead us to a personal relationship with the Creator. Its stories tell of the time our Savior walked the earth, spoke to the multitudes, sought the lost, and gave his life on our behalf. The Bible is God's love letter to us.

Dear Lord, stir in me an insatiable desire for your Word. May it draw me closer to your heart of love. Amen.

Come to the Table

You prepare a table before me in the presence of my enemies;
you anoint my head with oil; my cup overflows. Surely
goodness and mercy shall follow me all the days of my life, and
I shall dwell in the house of the LORD forever.

PSALM 23:5–6 ESV

Talk about the ultimate host! In this psalm, the Lord is showing us how he honors the guests he brings to his table. Not even the greatest foe can interrupt in his presence. To anoint one's head with oil has many health benefits and can be quite costly. It is an honor to have the King of kings pour oil on our heads as a way of consecrating us to him. He can bring healing to a sick body. He is calming and peace-giving.

Pouring oil is a sign of greatest hospitality. He has extended an invitation to all humanity to come to the table. Do not allow the enemies of busyness, anxiety, disappointment, anger, lust, unforgiveness, hurt, pride, and the many struggles of life keep us from his bountiful table. There is an abundance of joy, peace, forgiveness, and love in his presence.

Lord, anoint me with your oil, cleanse me, and feed me from your
Word. I'm honored to be at your table. Amen.

Prayer Warriors

From the day we heard, we have not ceased to pray for you, asking that you may be filled with the knowledge of his will in all spiritual wisdom and understanding, so as to walk in a manner worthy of the Lord, fully pleasing to him: bearing fruit in every good work and increasing in the knowledge of God; being strengthened with all power, according to his glorious might, for all endurance and patience with joy.

COLOSSIANS 1:9–11 ESV

Prayer warriors are precious and incredibly valuable people. They intercede on behalf of others, taking concerns, hopes, and struggles before the Lord for sisters and brothers in Christ. They are fervent in prayer, continuing until they see God move. They are an encouragement and a source of comfort to us, for we know we are not the only ones seeking God for our needs. When they are given a prayer request, they take it to God immediately and passionately pursue his answers for others.

Prayer warriors are a gift from God. If you have never supported someone in this way, ask God to open an opportunity for you to serve him by becoming a prayer warrior. There is nothing better you can do for someone.

Father, help me be proactive about praying for people. May I offer to support others in prayer. Amen.

No More Tears

"He will wipe away every tear from their eyes, and death shall be no more, neither shall there be mourning, nor crying, nor pain anymore, for the former things have passed away." And he who was seated on the throne said, "Behold, I am making all things new."

REVELATION 21:4–5 ESV

This verse sounds too good to be true…but it is true. Those who believe in Jesus for salvation will one day live with him forever in heaven. Scripture says when we see him, we will be like him. Can you imagine? What a glorious day it will be when he wipes away all our sadness, for we will never cry again. It is an incredible relief to know that the aches, pains, and diseases we suffer from now will not exist anymore.

Nothing will be like before, for our Father will make all things new. The same God who dwells in us now will dwell with us on the new earth throughout all of eternity. What we think of as the most "perfect" relationship, place, and time will pale in comparison to what the new heaven and earth will be like in his presence.

Father, thank you for preparing a place for me in your kingdom. I will praise you forevermore as I gaze on your glory. Amen.

Don't Sell Your Soul

"What will it profit a man if he gains the whole world and forfeits his soul? Or what shall a man give in return for his soul?"

MATTHEW 16:26 ESV

We witness some people scratching and clawing their way to the top. They will step over anyone, even their own mother, to gain riches. Yet many wealthy people report that their riches do not make them happy. Life is so short. Trading what you will have in eternity for the here and now is a deadly mistake, so don't sell your soul!

Recently, the name of Elizabeth Taylor came up in a conversation. Some young ones may not remember her, but she was a very famous actress, considered the most beautiful woman in the world, and adored by millions. She had wealth untold and many lovers. Yet her last years were spent in great distress, agony, depression, and poor health. I pray somehow she didn't lose her soul; only God knows. But the Scriptures are clear that striving for the treasures, pleasures, and power on this earth can cause us to ignore salvation and end up without God for eternity.

Dear Lord, may our eyes be on you and your kingdom, surrendering lordship to the only one who can give us abundant life here and in the everlasting. Amen.

Wisdom and Understanding

"He said to man, 'Behold, the fear of the Lord, that is wisdom, and to turn away from evil is understanding.'"

JOB 28:28 ESV

The book of Proverbs instructs us to get wisdom and get understanding. Wisdom, according to Scripture, is better than gold. We are told that, even if it costs us everything, we must get understanding. The Bible says those who get wisdom find life and receive favor from the Lord (Proverbs 4:5–8). Wisdom will protect you because your feet will run from evil. Understanding will guide you to the proper form of humility, not a fake one, honestly placing others before yourself and working for their benefit first and foremost.

We must note that, as today's verse says, fearing the Lord is the beginning of wisdom. Does that mean we should be afraid of God? No, not at all, but we must hold a reverent respect and awe of our God. He is holy and righteous, and our righteousness is as "filthy rags" (Isaiah 64:6 NIV). Yet through the blood of Christ, we have been washed clean. Believing in the one and only Son of God for your salvation is wisdom and understanding. If you don't know him, show yourself to be wise and accept him today.

Jesus, thank you for my salvation in you. Help me desire wisdom and understanding so I can be an example of you to others. Amen.

God Living in Us

Whoever keeps his commandments abides in God,
and God in him. And by this know that he abides in us,
by the Spirit whom he has given us.

1 JOHN 3:24 ESV

To have the one true God living in us is the most magnificent thought. To know it is actual fact is beyond amazing. Yet there is a stipulation, a requirement that we must fulfill. We must live day in and day out by his commands. Do we do this out of duty or just to receive the desired result? No, we do it out of love, gratitude, humility, and surrender to our Lord and Savior. What we receive in return is much greater than anything we could ever offer. Knowing what Jesus did for us on the cross makes us want to obey, fanning the flames of our love for him.

Realizing that his Spirit has been gifted to us and lives within our very soul should make us fall on our knees in praise. The truth of his residence in our heart should make us erupt with joy, fill us with peace, and motivate our hope. Praise his holy name!

Father, abide in me and never leave. To you alone I want to cleave. Thank you for your faithfulness, for in you I have full peace and rest. Amen.

We Are Witnesses

"God exalted him at his right hand as Leader and Savior, to give repentance to Israel and forgiveness of sins. And we are witnesses to these things, and so is the Holy Spirit, whom God has given to those who obey him."

ACTS 5:31–32 ESV

The apostles testified that they had seen the Son of God, who came to offer forgiveness and salvation. And after an angel of the Lord freed them from prison during the night, the angel commanded the apostles to preach in the temple. Disturbed by this, the high priests and captain of the temple quietly removed the apostles, fearing the crowd might retaliate if they used force. Standing before a council, the apostles then testified to the life of the Savior. It enraged the council, but the apostles were set free and didn't cease teaching and preaching of the Messiah.

Like the apostles, we, too, must spread the news. We are witnesses of all God has done for us, from the sacrifice of Jesus to the work God does in our lives today. Because we are witnesses, we must then bear witness until everyone has heard the good news of Salvation.

Jesus, I pray this world will believe in you and surrender to your salvation. Amen.

He Will Never Forsake Us

Gideon said to him, "Please, my lord, if the LORD is with us, why then has all this happened to us? And where are all his wonderful deeds that our fathers recounted to us, saying, 'Did not the LORD bring us up from Egypt?' But now the LORD has forsaken us and given us into the hand of Midian."

JUDGES 6:13 ESV

In the beginning of Judges 6, it tells that "the children of Israel did evil in the sight of the LORD" (v. 1 NKJV). So the Lord delivered them into the hands of the Midianites. The Midianites terrorized and oppressed the people of Israel. What happens next in chapters 6–8 is an amazing story of God's love, mercy, grace, and deliverance. Sin carried a cost, which at this point in time, had not yet been paid by Jesus.

The consequences of Israel's evil brought judgment on them, but it was for their good. The pain would draw them back to God, and eventually, he would deal with their enemies and bless his children. Even in seasons of distress, God will not forsake those who belong to him. His plan, time, way, and purpose are always kind, perfect, and for our victory.

Lord, I will praise you and give thanks to you, my Redeemer and Savior, who will never forsake me. Amen.

May

Presents in the Present

I don't mean to say that I have already achieved these things
or that I have already reached perfection. But I press on to
possess that perfection for which Christ Jesus first possessed
me. No, dear brothers and sisters, I have not achieved it, but
I focus on this one thing: Forgetting the past and looking
forward to what lies ahead.

PHILIPPIANS 3:12–13 NLT

As one matures in age, it is easy to want to live in the past.
A little of this is good, as we remember with praise and
thankfulness God's love, mercy, and grace. We recall his
provisions in times of need, his comfort in times of sorrow, his
strength when we were weak, and his compassion when we fell.
May we use our memories to propel us on with passion and
purpose, making each day count for God and his kingdom.

Regardless of your age, don't slow down or grow weary
of doing good. May we focus on the Lord, our source of power,
instead of idly waiting to become perfect so that we will not let
the good deeds go undone or the songs remain unsung. God
will work through us and equip us for his glory.

Father, please help me not to focus on my failures and weaknesses
so that each day, I will please you in thought and action. Amen.

Mending Our Broken Pieces

My brothers, if anyone among you wanders from the truth and
someone brings him back, let him know that whoever brings
back a sinner from his wandering will save his soul from death
and will cover a multitude of sins.

JAMES 5:19–20 ESV

When a person returns to the divine master of mercy and grace
for forgiveness, redemption, and healing, they are beautifully
and marvelously made new. When brothers or sisters in Christ
aid someone in getting right with God, they are saving that
person from destruction. How wonderful it is to be someone
trustworthy enough to be allowed into someone else's mess to
help them find forgiveness.

In humility, recognizing our many errors and
weaknesses, may we be God's instrument of love,
understanding, and compassion to those who have lost their
way, faith, or belief. Help me speak words of truth and healing
into the lives of my brethren, Father.

Lord, thank you for mending people, including me. Please help
me share your love and grace with my brothers and sisters and see
them restored in their relationship with you. Amen.

Increasing Faith

Cast your burden on the LORD, and he will sustain you;
he will never permit the righteous to be moved.

PSALM 55:22 ESV

Why would we ever want to be anywhere other than in the secure care and control of our heavenly Father? As children of the King, we are made righteous through the blood of Jesus.

Today's verse says that when we hand our troubles over to the Lord, he will take care of us. He won't let us fall, so we have nothing to fear. Seems like it should be so easy, but it's not. Sometimes a lack of faith on our part affects the outcome. Remember the woman with the issue of blood in Luke 8? She boldly cast her burden on Christ by touching the hem of his robe in the belief that she would be healed. Jesus said that her faith had made her well. Can God work even when we have no faith? Of course, he can. Does our faith influence God? Yes. Hebrews says that without faith it is impossible to please God (11:6). Nothing is impossible for God, but he wants our faith to grow. He wants our complete trust in his ability. Put your faith to work.

Father, increase my faith, and if that requires that I go through
hardships, give me courage to trust you. Amen.

We Didn't Know Him

You, who once were alienated and hostile in mind, doing evil deeds, he has now reconciled in his body of flesh by his death, in order to present you holy and blameless and above reproach before him.

COLOSSIANS 1:21–22 ESV

There was a time in each of our lives when we were enemies of God. We didn't know him, we didn't want him, and we lived for self. Maybe we engaged in little white lies because we figured everyone does it. Possibly we took something that didn't belong to us because we felt it was owed to us. We might have spoken carelessly, more concerned about spouting out our opinion than anyone else's feelings. Perhaps we even committed more serious sins that caused others to suffer.

The day we confessed our sin and came to know Jesus, all that was erased. God tossed our evil deeds to the bottom of the ocean, never to be dredged up again. The stain of our sin turned white, and God now views us as though he were looking at Jesus. The weight of our wrongdoing fell off our shoulders, and we could start fresh, for God makes all things new. What a glorious truth, a blessed act by our Father, who sacrificed what meant most to him in order to save us.

Lord, stamp your image deep on my heart and my life. Amen.

God Gives Rest

It is useless for you to work so hard from early morning
until late at night, anxiously working for food to eat;
for God gives rest to his loved ones.

PSALM 127:2 NLT

Man has always wanted more. "Keeping up with the Joneses"
is a familiar phrase that says it all. If someone else has it, we
want it too. So many work long hours, neglecting family and
ministry, just so they can earn more money. They worry that
it is never enough and look for every possible way to increase
their income. Then, just when they feel like they are getting
somewhere and can enjoy the fruit of their labors, they realize
the anxiety has made them ill.

Without your health, it is hard to have a good time.
What is the solution? Depend on God and be content. He alone
owns the cattle on a thousand hills (Psalm 50:10), and he alone
chooses what we have and what we don't. That is why Paul
encourages us to be content in any circumstances. When we
place our lives in God's hands, he will provide all that we need,
even the sleep that revives us. Stress less and put your trust in
your heavenly Father.

Father, forgive me for not trusting you to provide. I place all that
I am and desire into your hands. Amen.

Expansive Grace

"Do not fear, for I am with you; do not be dismayed,
for I am your God. I will strengthen you and help you;
I will uphold you with my righteous right hand."

ISAIAH 41:10 NIV

Whatever predicament you are in, however dark the outlook,
never underestimate the expanse of his grace or the extent of
his power. So many times in the Old Testament, God told his
people not to fear because the battle was his. Just think of how
the Israelites felt, terrified as they fled Egypt with the Pharaoh
and his army in pursuit, then later arriving in Jericho, where
they again faced enemies they believed were unbeatable.

How often do we try to fix things ourselves? How long do
we ruminate over troubles in the middle of the night? We must
spend time in the Word and at the feet of Jesus, asking for help
to relinquish control, and wait for him to defend and deliver us.
When we know who our God is, we have nothing to fear.

Lord, remind me that you are my God, my Savior, my deliverer,
my defender, and my reason to live. May I find rest in your
presence. Amen.

God Must Be First

He said to him, "You shall love the Lord your God with all your heart and with all your soul and with all your mind. This is the great and first commandment. And a second is like it: You shall love your neighbor as yourself."

MATTHEW 22:37–39 ESV

We are to love God with all our strength, and we are to prefer nothing to him. God wants our affections fixed upon him—heart, soul, and mind. Many people choose not to have a relationship with God because they have the wrong impression of him. They think his commands make him a cosmic killjoy. They are blinded by the god of this world, choosing to give their lives to idols, chasing after worthless things.

The truth is that our heavenly Father deserves all our undistracted affection. When it comes to our Lord, we are to have an undivided mindset. It is not a suggestion but a command. Remember always that he loved us first and that he gave his Son so that we could be saved. We wouldn't have breath in the morning if he didn't supply it. We are to put him first in our heart and then love our neighbor as we love ourselves.

Lord, help me always keep you first in my life. Keep my heart fully yours. Amen.

Gain Wisdom

The fear of the LORD is the beginning of wisdom,
and the knowledge of the Holy One is insight.
PROVERBS 9:10 ESV

Wisdom is a great treasure, more so than even gold.
Understanding who our God is helps us respond to him with
awe and respect. Fearing God does not mean we are to be
afraid but that we are to reverence him. Gaining insight helps
us stay on the straight and narrow, avoiding the need for God's
discipline. When we study this verse, "The fear of the LORD is
the beginning of wisdom," we can see a parallel between it and
the way we teach a child to fear fire. We are not withholding
pleasure but desiring to keep them from harm. Would you allow
your child to play in a busy street just because they wanted to?
They may cry, thinking they are being kept from having fun, but
the parent knows they are saving their little one's life.

God's rules are for our safety, not to limit our enjoyment.
Proverbs warns us to gain wisdom because it is better than
life. Wisdom and the knowledge of who our God is and what
he requires of us will actually save our life and make it blessed
abundantly.

Lord, give me a clearer understanding of the fear I am to have for
you. Amen.

It's All about God

Jesus answered, "It was not that this man sinned, or his parents, but that the works of God might be displayed in him."
JOHN 9:3 ESV

Our Lord always has a purpose that was determined long before man entered the scene. See, we make the mistake of thinking everything is about us when it is solely about our great Creator. God deserves honor and glory, for nothing would exist—the earth, our lives, or even the concept of love—without him. We are created for God's pleasure, not our own, yet he desires to give us his kingdom. We should be willing to suffer if it means that God will receive glory.

If we are ill, whether he heals us this side of heaven or not, we must testify to his compassion from a sincere heart. He is always good. God's ways are always best, designed with his glory in mind. He has given us life, salvation, and a future with him for eternity. Let's not look at the difficulty of the issue but instead keep our eyes on the only one who can bring victory from any circumstances and give him praise.

Lord, may I not be so quick to place blame on myself, others, or you when difficult and life-wrenching events happen. Help me see your purpose in all things. Amen.

Growth in Christ

Like newborn infants, long for the pure spiritual milk, that by it you may grow up into salvation—if indeed you have tasted that the Lord is good.

1 PETER 2:2-3 ESV

Is your Bible sitting on a shelf collecting dust? While it bids you come and learn, are you busy joining the newest streaming channel so you can devote your time to binging new content? What good will you gain and what will you add to your life by engaging in various frivolous activities? When will we understand that only God's Word can show us the best way to live and how to redeem our time?

We must turn away from those things that would eat away at and seek to distract us from our sweet fellowship with God. We need to deafen the wrong voices that say, *Come away and seek your own pleasure…that Book will always be there.* We will only experience growth in Christ if we spend time as a student of the Scripture. Pray for an unquenchable thirst for spiritual milk. Ask God to help you gain understanding and develop a true desire to be in the Word. You won't find a better way to spend your time.

Lord, may I grow in ways that glorify you. May your Word penetrate my life and the fruit of the Spirit be evident. Amen.

God's Indwelling Spirit

I say, walk by the Spirit,
and you will not gratify the desires of the flesh.
GALATIANS 5:16 ESV

How can we walk by the spirit if we are not committing time, energy, and attention to learning God's Word? The world and the flesh make sure that they keep our attention in their direction. It is so easy to be drawn away and led into all types of sinful behavior. The only way to avoid that is to remain on our knees. We must also commit time to working on our walk with Christ. We have been given all that we need for faith and salvation. If we are missing the mark, it is because we choose to.

Sin eventually leads to death, and it can make our stay on earth incredibly miserable. We must decide if we are for God or against him. To continue in sin means that we love ourselves more than we love our Savior. Our flesh will fail us no matter how much we long to live victoriously. We must seek God continuously. We must ask the Spirit to indwell us, and may God use us as we make the decision to kill our flesh and live for Christ.

Lord, I need your help to surrender control of my body, mind, and soul to your Holy Spirit. Please make me more like Jesus. Amen.

A Life of Gratitude

Awake, my glory! Awake, O harp and lyre! I will awake the dawn! I will give thanks to you, O Lord, among the peoples; I will sing praises to you among the nations.

PSALM 57:8–9 ESV

Whether in good times or bad, we are to live a life of gratitude. First Thessalonians 5 says we are to rejoice always, pray continually, and give thanks no matter what we are going through, for that is God's will for us in Christ (vv. 16–18). It can be difficult to worship when we are suffering through trials, but that does not excuse us from lifting our voice and hands. If we believe who our God is, we will trust that he is bringing good on our behalf even though we don't know the outcome yet.

Remind yourself that he is at work in unseen places. We can be in the midst of the hardest situation, but if we think about our God's power, deliverance, plans, and love for us, we will endure with joy. We can remain assured he will continue his good work in us and that we will experience maturity in the process.

Father, thank you for always working for my good. Your desire is for me to be conformed to the image of your Son, and that is my hope as well. Amen.

The Price

We have beheld and bear witness that the Father
hath sent the Son to be the Saviour of the world.

1 JOHN 4:14 ASV

Have you ever sent a loved one on an important errand? If you
have, you probably needed to give them instructions for the
task. There might have been some warnings involved with your
plan of action. Maybe there was a fork in the road they needed
to watch for so that they stayed on the right path. Possibly
they'd have to deal with a difficult person to fulfill the duty.
Maybe there were consequences or rewards, depending on their
performance.

Imagine the conversation God had with his Son before
sending him to earth. Did they talk about the Twelve whom
Jesus would choose? Did they converse about the questions the
Pharisees would ask? Did Jesus inquire about where he would
lay his head at night? Was the conversation about the cross one
that brought tears to their eyes and joy at the same time because
of what it would accomplish? Out of love, God sent his Son to
be the Savior of the world. They both knew what that would
cost, and they paid the price for us all.

Father, thank you for sending Jesus to die for me. I don't deserve
your grace, but I am so thankful. Amen.

Open the Door

"Those whom I love, I reprove and discipline, so be zealous and repent. Behold, I stand at the door and knock. If anyone hears my voice and opens the door, I will come in to him and eat with him, and he with me."

REVELATION 3:19–20 ESV

The Word says that we have a day, appointed by God, on which we will die. If you have not accepted the free gift of grace Christ offers before that day is completed, you will face judgment. That judgment will lead to a sentence of eternity away from God. There is nothing worse. Yet that day hasn't arrived, so the good news is that today, right now, is the day of salvation.

Do you hear the knock on the door of your heart? Your beloved is whispering in your ear to come. Will you answer his call and welcome the Savior in with open arms? He promises once you do that, you will become a new creation in Christ. He will never leave you, and he will count you as his treasured possession. If you haven't decided, don't wait until it is too late. Open the door today.

Lord, may I be humble, tender, and quick to open the door for you, inviting you into my heart to be Lord of my life. I thank you for your sacrifice. Amen.

When Trouble Comes

"I will return to my place until they admit their guilt
and turn to me. For as soon as trouble comes,
they will earnestly search for me."

HOSEA 5:15 NLT

Have you ever noticed that when life is rolling along smoothly, many people seem to grow away from God? Some become more involved with all the material possessions they are accumulating than they are with the faith they claim. Others still talk the talk, but the walk is limping along. But let the roof cave in, and all of a sudden, they need God. Where were they when his blessings were pouring out? Did they think all the good in their lives was from their own doing?

Can you count yourself in this scenario? If you can, then maybe you feel God is far away during your present difficulty. He didn't move away; you chose to distance yourself. Yet because of his faithfulness, he will hear your cry, and he will answer. He will move heaven and earth to come to the child who needs him. Seek him with a humble heart, ready to commit yourself to him regardless of your circumstances.

Father, forgive me for ignoring you and your goodness to me. I confess the ways I have turned from you and lay myself on your altar to use as you will. Amen.

A Joyful Noise

Make a joyful noise unto the LORD, all ye lands. Serve the
LORD with gladness: come before his presence with singing.
PSALM 100:1–2 KJV

Have you ever known someone who wasn't the best singer but
would proclaim that when they sang to the Lord, they were
making a joyful *noise*? You may laugh, but God is smiling from
ear to ear. It blesses our Father's heart when we cheerfully
come before him and sing his praises. When we are glad in his
presence, it pleases him beyond measure. When we sing, it is
beautiful to him, and remember that you are singing for an
audience of One. Even if you hit some bad notes and the person
in church next to you puts in their ear plugs, know that you are
bringing pleasure to your King. It is the condition of the heart
God looks at, not the perfection of the vocals. So belt it out!
Let heaven hear your voice and rejoice with the angels at the
goodness of your Savior.

On a sentimental note, this was my mom's favorite
psalm, and I can still hear her reading it in the King James
translation. What a precious memory!

Father, I pray that my voice, my smile, and my heart warm yours
as I sing your praises. You deserve glory and honor. Amen.

A New Creation

I have been crucified with Christ; and it is no longer I that live, but Christ liveth in me: and that life which I now live in the flesh I live in faith, the faith which is in the Son of God, who loved me, and gave himself up for me.

GALATIANS 2:20 ASV

If you have ever watched a butterfly emerge from a chrysalis, then you have seen a complete transformation. What once was is no more, and something absolutely beautiful has appeared in its place. When a person seeks forgiveness for their sin and asks Jesus to be their Lord and Savior, a new creation is born. No longer is the unregenerated soul alive in that person, but the life of Christ is now its resident. It is a new life, one that is defined by faith in the one who died to save sinners.

The one and only Son of God is alive in the believer, changing their heart from hard to soft, a fertile place for God's Word to take root and grow. The Holy Spirit has filled God's child and will encourage, convict, and guide. All this takes place because the greatest love of all was offered to mankind.

Jesus, thank you for making all things new. Fill me and use me for your glory. Amen.

Godly Correction

The LORD is slow to anger and great in power,
and the LORD will by no means leave the guilty unpunished.
In the gale and the storm is His way, and clouds are the
dust beneath His feet.

NAHUM 1:3 NASB

Have you ever known a truly patient person? Think about times (maybe when you were a child) when you frayed your parents' nerves. Were they understanding, or did their temper flare? Did they allow you to be a terror and get away with everything, or were you reprimanded? If they did correct you, did they come at you as a fairy godparent or a raging bull? Hopefully, their correction was godly and not done in anger.

We can be certain that when we sin, God will not explode in fury, but he will lovingly discipline. He is almighty, and Scripture says it is a fearful thing to fall into the hands of the living God. Even though his punitive measures may not be pleasant, they are for our good. He wants us to be more like his Son, and if that requires a little discipline, he will do what it takes to mature us in Christ.

Father, forgive me for disobeying you. I am ashamed and deserve your correction. Help me be wise and make righteous choices from now on. Amen.

The Path of Life

You make known to me the path of life; in your presence there is fullness of joy; at your right hand are pleasures forevermore.
PSALM 16:11 ESV

Having a relationship with God is incredibly fulfilling. In fact, life is empty and void without it. The future doesn't look so great without God, for it eventually ends in death and separation from him. God created us for relationship. He wants to walk through life with us as he did with Adam and Eve in the garden. Sin entered and ruined that, until Jesus came and was the solution for our sin. The cross of Christ gave us the offer of new life, and when we accept him, we start on the path God prepared for us in advance. The old life is gone, and a life of joy, peace, and hope begins, for we now know whom we have believed in.

We must do all we can to stay in relationship, rejecting the lure of sin and keeping our eyes on Jesus. Make a regular appointment daily to spend time in God's Word. Pray throughout the day and if you wake up during the night. Stay on his path of life for you.

Jesus, may I ever stay united with you, my Redeemer. Amen.

Restoration

Restore unto me the joy of thy salvation;
and uphold me with thy free spirit.
PSALM 51:12 KJV

David penned this psalm after Nathan the prophet came to confront him about David's relationship with Bathsheba. Nathan's words convicted David, and even though he had blatantly sinned against God by committing adultery and murder, he confessed immediately. He fasted and prayed, asking forgiveness for his sin, and pleaded with God for the life of his son, whose life God required as a consequence of David's transgressions.

David humbled himself before the Lord, and then the news came that his baby had died. Hearing this, David got up, cleaned up, worshiped God, and ate. Many thought this odd, but David took responsibility for his transgressions, and when God had done what he said he would, David thanked him even though it included the painful loss of his son. He asked God to purge him of his sin, to create a new heart in him, and to restore the joy of his salvation. Then David declared God's praises. He asked to teach transgressors God's way so sinners would return to him. His love for and repentance to God brought him back into right relationship with him.

God, please help me be filled with your Holy Spirit. Amen.

Turn to God

Yet even now, saith Jehovah, turn ye unto me with all your heart, and with fasting, and with weeping, and with mourning: and rend your heart, and not your garments, and turn unto Jehovah your God; for he is gracious and merciful, slow to anger, and abundant in lovingkindness, and repenteth him of the evil.

JOEL 2:12–13 ASV

What an amazing God we serve. He explains all that we need to do to make things right with him and backs it up with his beautiful response when we do. He doesn't want a showy display of ripped robes and crying out in the city square. He wants to see deep into our hearts to determine if we are truly sorry for our sins. Our soul should be desperate for him and his pardon.

Knowing his character, we should run as quickly as possible to receive restoration. He will be gracious and merciful and receive our cry for forgiveness. He's not one with a quick temper but considers our condition and keeps his anger at bay. He is compassionate, filled with lovingkindness for us. Even when we have come to him for forgiveness one million times, he will never turn us away or tire of saying, "Welcome back, my child."

Father, forgive my sins. I want to rest in the shelter of your arms. Thank you for restoring me. Amen.

God Is Our Protector

The angel of Jehovah came again the second time,
and touched him, and said, Arise and eat,
because the journey is too great for thee.
1 KINGS 19:7 ASV

Elijah had just proven to the prophets of Baal that their god
was a phony and that his God was real. Not only that, but he
also killed all the prophets of Baal with the sword. His enemy
Ahab was not happy about this and made his way to Jezebel to
report the account. Jezebel was furious and vowed to kill Elijah
within the next twenty-four hours. Although Elijah had just had
a major victory, he considered Jezebel a formidable opponent
and was filled with fear. His despair led him to ask God to let
him die.

Instead, God sent his angel to minister to Elijah, leading
him to a cave where God would address the issue. Elijah
thought he was the only one left who honored God and that he
would be killed for it. God reminded Elijah that seven thousand
men of Israel had never bowed to Baal, and they would be
spared. That story encouraged me this morning as I awoke
feeling really down. God is our defender, always just, and he will
honor those who honor him. His faithfulness never ends.

Father, thank you for encouraging me through the living Word.
Amen.

Easily Offended

*Good sense makes one slow to anger,
and it is his glory to overlook an offense.*
PROVERBS 19:11 ESV

We live in a world that is easily and deeply offended. The cancel culture, social media slander, and road rage are just a few examples of society's current state of mind. Anger, distrust, and suspicion are rampant. People take matters into their own hands, seeking revenge and harming the innocent. When we think about God looking down on his creation behaving this way, we know he is saddened. His desire is that we love one another as we love ourselves, and there is little to no understanding of that.

God's Word says that if we have good sense, we will not erupt in anger easily. The Bible also states that we will pay no attention to a slight toward us. Carrying anger and offense makes us more miserable than the one who caused it. God tells us how to respond to hurt and rejection for our good. If someone scorns you, let it roll off your back and pray for them. Ask God to love them through you. You will find freedom, peace, and joy as you forgive and forget.

Father, help me forgive when someone hurts me. Help me remember that my battle is not against man but against the Evil One. Amen.

Overflowing Goodness

May God, the fountain of hope, fill you to overflowing with uncontainable joy and perfect peace as you trust in him. And may the power of the Holy Spirit continually surround your life with his super-abundance until you radiate with hope!

ROMANS 15:13 TPT

Today's verse carries the promise of wonderful things if we will only trust in God. The adjectives that precede some of these promises fill our thoughts with awe. They produce a fountain of hope, confidence overflowing, rejoicing that has no boundary or limits, and peace that passes any kind of understanding. This world cannot offer anything close to this. The world presents itself as something fabulous and fulfilling, but in the end, if we love the things of the world, we cannot love God.

Trusting in anything outside of God is pure foolishness. It can bring no benefit. However, as we place our faith in the Lord, through the power of his Holy Spirit, our lives will be filled with all good things, and we will shine like the sun with hope. All joy and blessings are gifts from our heavenly Father, for these good things we can only attain by his magnificent grace.

Holy Spirit, please give me the gift of faith. I want to radiate joy and hope so that the world sees Jesus in me. Amen.

Accept "No"

God was very angry when he went, and the angel of the LORD stood in the road to oppose him. Balaam was riding on his donkey, and his two servants were with him. When the donkey saw the angel of the LORD standing in the road with a drawn sword in his hand, it turned off the road into a field. Balaam beat it to get it back on the road.

NUMBERS 22:22–23 NIV

When we have the wrong heart motive for our actions, it impairs how we see the plan of God for our lives. God had already told Balaam not to curse the people who had come out of Egypt as King Balak of Moab had requested. Balak didn't want to take no for an answer. Balaam waited to hear from God again even though God had said no. God knew Balaam was going to Moab for his own gain and not to do God's will. God let Balaam go, but he was angry. He sent his angel to stop Balaam, but only his donkey saw the heavenly being. Finally, God opened Balaam's eyes to see the angel, and God let Balaam know that he opposed Balaam's plan.

Aren't we that way sometimes? We have an answer from God, but we still want our own way. We must accept it when God says no.

Lord, I surrender. Amen.

Constant Companion

Nevertheless I am continually with You.

PSALM 73:23 NKJV

We often have times in life when we feel all alone. Maybe a close friend is estranged from you. Possibly family members that lived close have moved away. Perhaps you lost your job, and with it went the community you have been with day in and day out for several years. Yet there is one who is always with us, never takes his eye off us, never tires of our presence with him. Our almighty God, our kind Abba, is constantly by our side. He desires our company. When he looks at us believers in Christ, he sees us as he sees his Son.

There is no better friend and no greater ally. He protects us with his mighty arm. He has given us love that is everlasting. He offers deliverance, salvation, and all that we could ever need. Wherever we travel on earth, he guides our way. He has promised us a home with him in heaven. Remember, you are always on his mind, written on the palm of his hand, and loved deeply within his heart. What more could we ever want?

Abba, I am overwhelmed by your great grace and love. I am filled to overflowing with joy. Thank you for always keeping your eye on me. Amen.

Going before Him

As it is written in the book of the words of isaiah the prophet:
"the voice of one calling out in the wilderness, 'prepare the way
of the LORD, make his paths straight!'"

LUKE 3:4 NASB

Like a band leading a parade or a bridesmaid processing down
the aisle before the bride, John the Baptist prepared the way for
the Messiah by going before him. He told of Christ's coming
and baptized those who believed. John was chosen to be the
mouthpiece, the representative, for the Son of God. He had
spent his adult life traveling the wilderness and telling anyone
who would listen that the Savior of the world was coming. Some
people thought John was crazy. Some hung on his every word.

Then one day, it happened. Jesus appeared on the scene
and wanted John to baptize him. As John did, heaven opened,
and the spirit of God descended like a dove on Jesus. A voice
from heaven said, "This is My beloved Son, in whom I am
well pleased" (Matthew 3:17 NKJV). Can you imagine the
excitement John felt as he saw and experienced what he had told
others about? How wonderful to fulfill God's purpose for your
life by representing his one and only Son.

Jesus, help me know your purpose for me. I give my life to
represent and glorify you. Amen.

Give Thanks

Oh, that men would give thanks to the LORD for His goodness,
and for His wonderful works to the children of men!
PSALM 107:8 NKJV

Doesn't it make you sad when people say bad things about our
God? They blame him for all that goes wrong in the world, not
realizing that it is sinful man who is the cause. They completely
neglect thanking him for the beauty of his creation and instead
applaud mother earth for it. They ask where God is when a
tragedy strikes instead of looking at the person whose hand
caused it. They ask why there is poverty and hunger, yet didn't
he call the church to care for those in need?

Instead of finding fault, all mankind should fall on their
face to honor and praise the Lord. He deserves our gratitude for
his love, his salvation, and the goodness of his grace. Not one
single person on earth would see the light of another day if God
did not allow it. We could never have made restitution for our
sin; only Jesus could. We could thank God all day, every day for
the rest of our lives and never exhaust the list of his merciful
gifts to us. Give thanks.

Father, I thank you for all your good gifts and your everlasting
love. Amen.

Walk Carefully

Look therefore carefully how ye walk, not as unwise,
but as wise; redeeming the time, because the days are evil.
EPHESIANS 5:15–16 ASV

Many people are people watchers. You never know how intently someone is eyeing your behavior. Can they tell you are a Christ follower by your actions? Do the words that proceed from your mouth honor God or display that you aren't truly who you say you are? One way to ensure that you are representing Jesus well is to seek wisdom. Be aware that life is short and that the days go by quickly, and before you know it, Christ will return. Will what you did and said on this earth draw people toward heaven or not make any difference at all? Will you stand out as a shining light for the gospel?

Your actions could bring someone to the Savior. God tells us to be holy as he is holy. There is an old saying from missionary C. T. Studd that says, "Only one life, 'twill soon be past, only what's done for Christ will last."[2] Make your days count for your Savior and for eternity. Don't fit in; stand out for Jesus and do it wisely and righteously.

Jesus, I want to glorify you with my life so that when I stand before you, I will hear, "Well done." Help me walk in a manner worthy of your name. Amen.

---

2   C. T. Studd, "Only One Life," Tony Cooke Ministries, www.tonycooke.org.

Glory Revealed

I consider that the sufferings of this present time are not worth comparing with the glory that is to be revealed to us.

ROMANS 8:18 ESV

Some of us have trouble dealing with setbacks. Many moan when they have the common cold. We really don't like to be delayed, contradicted, or inconvenienced. Waiting in long lines is not our thing. We want quick service, and we want it now. So most likely, we groan when considering that Jesus said we would share in his sufferings. Most of us have never encountered horrific times. We live pretty blessed lives. We will never be tormented as Jesus was.

Have you been homeless, rejected, asked to leave a city, questioned, beaten, whipped, or nailed to a cross? Jesus was perfect, yet he suffered all this and more. We should realize that if God asks us to endure hardships for the sake of the gospel, then we are blessed. It is an honor to share in adversity as our Savior did. Keep your eyes on the prize, for one day, the glorious reward for a sacrificed life lived for Jesus will make your suffering more than worth it.

Jesus, thank you for all you went through while on this earth to save me. Help me rejoice as the disciples did when I am mistreated for your name. Amen.

Unseen Wars

Now war arose in heaven,
Michael and his angels fighting against the dragon.
And the dragon and his angels fought back.

REVELATION 12:7 ESV

We watch TV shows and movies that feature fantastic creatures, world wars, angelic beings, and otherworldly things. Even if it unnerves us, we think, *It's just a show*. As believers, all we need to do to substantiate that there is a realm where angels and demons are fighting spiritual battles is to open our Bibles. It's all around, above, and below us, but these battles are hidden from our eyes, and we can be sure God's reason for that is in our best interest. We have a hard enough time with invisible enemies.

We all need to be aware that Satan has also been known to use believers to do his dirty work. He is just waiting for the chance to make a weak Christian say or do something to harm another, but our battle is against Satan not our brethren. Read Scripture and know your enemy's tactics. Wear your armor and don't let him get a foothold. Pray to be filled with the power of the Holy Spirit.

Father, thank you for protecting me from wars in the heavenlies. Give me the power of your Spirit to fight off the evil advances of Satan. Amen.

June

Trust Him

What time I am afraid, I will put my trust in thee.
In God (I will praise his word), in God have I put my trust,
I will not be afraid; What can flesh do unto me?
PSALM 56:3–4 ASV

There's a legend of a little girl who was abducted. The abductor later phoned the child's parents, told them where they could find her, and said he could not harm her because she kept singing, "Jesus Loves Me."

Oh, the faith of a child! Conquering fear takes trust and praise. Trusting God is only possible if you know him and believe he is who he says he is. Can you sing hymns of praise to him? Can you quote Scripture that will make your heart swell with belief in the Savior? Do you understand that man is without power unless God gives it to him? There is nothing a mere human can do to us, for God is in control. We are always under his care and predetermined purpose. So the next time fear threatens to keep you from going where God wants you to go, shut it down. Tell anxiety to leave. Believe God's goodness and trust him without any doubt.

Lord, when fear lurks, may my quivering lips be quick to praise you, knowing trust will well up within me. Amen.

Get Right with God

Are ye so foolish? having begun in the Spirit,
are ye now made perfect by the flesh?
GALATIANS 3:3 KJV

You were going along so well, following Jesus, staying in the Word and prayer. What happened to derail you? Where did the disconnect happen? Was it unconfessed sin? Did you ignore the prompting of the Holy Spirit to *not* utter that unkind comment and feel no regret? Did you give time to other activities and neglect spending time with Jesus? Have you foolishly allowed yourself to make close friends with those who don't know or honor Christ? Have you let some offense or hurt from a person control your every thought? Are you distancing yourself from God's goodness because you feel offended that he wanted to make you more patient by placing you in a time of waiting?

These are all situations that we need wisdom to avoid. Any of these are dangerous roads to take that have the potential to lead us away from God. Don't give place to anything that would prevent you from being in a close relationship with the Father. If you are struggling in any of these areas, don't wait. Get right with God today.

Lord, thank you for longing to continually restore my brokenness
as I relinquish the shattered pieces to you. Amen.

Every Morning

In the morning, LORD, you hear my voice; in the morning
I lay my requests before you and wait expectantly.

PSALM 5:3 NIV

Every morning, we should immediately open our mouths to praise God for putting breath in our lungs and blessing us with another day. We must remember that his mercies are new every morning. He has kept watch over us all night and now desires to stir our spirits to use our day to bring him glory. To honor him with our actions, we need to start our new day with a quiet time with him.

If you are not doing this regularly, let's discuss a few things to do during that time. Thank him for all he has done and given you. You can begin with praise music and join in song to worship him. Have your Bible, journal, and pen ready so as you study the Word, you can record things he reveals to you. Go to him in prayer with faith, believing that when you ask according to his will, you will receive what you need. Thank him for hearing you and let him know that all your hope is in him. Determine not to miss a day of communing with your Lord.

Father, I dedicate my waking moments and early morning to you.
Amen.

The Power of the Cross

For he has rescued us from the dominion of darkness and
brought us into the kingdom of the Son he loves, in whom we
have redemption, the forgiveness of sins.
COLOSSIANS 1:13–14 NIV

We need to remember how lost we were, without hope or any
chance of redemption if not for Jesus. Our sinful souls would
continue to run to evil and destruction if not for the love and
transformation God has done in our hearts. Imagine how
hopeless, how incredibly doomed a life without Christ would
be. We were dead in our trespasses, and the Lord lifted us out
of the pit by sacrificing his sinless Son. It should humble us all,
knowing how destitute and corrupt we were, that our Father
would even want to save us, let alone give his Son for us.

May we ever be mindful of and thankful for the price
and power of the cross. May our lips never cease to praise him
continually for the Lord's grace, mercy, and lovingkindness
toward us. May we remember how extravagantly he loves us.
May we worship our deliverer every moment of every day until
we go to the reward of living in his presence for eternity.

Lord, help me praise you continually for the cross. Saturate me in
your love and grant me your joy. Amen.

Peace Be with You

Hath now been manifested by the appearing of our Saviour
Christ Jesus, who abolished death, and brought life and
immortality to light through the gospel.

2 TIMOTHY 1:10 ASV

When I was young, I loved to hear my folks sing. They vocalized
with gusto and great joy, proclaiming Christ's salvation. What
eternal assurance! Our desire to rejoice should not be governed
by our circumstances but by absolute confidence that Christ
dwells within us, that we are loved by him completely, and that
we have the assurance of eternal life with him.

When Jesus took his last breath on the cross, many who
knew him were confused, thinking all was lost. They wanted
to continue to believe as they had when they walked the earth
with him, but he was now lifeless. After the shock, his apostles
finally gathered in the upper room to console each other and
try to understand what had just taken place. It was a few days
since his crucifixion. As they saw him appear and heard the
words, "Peace be with you," they were awestruck. As he showed
them his hands and his side, they humbly cheered (John 19–20
ESV). Jesus had conquered death, and the Savior they had been
mourning was alive as their heavenly King.

Father, I am grateful that, though the world constantly falls short
of its promises, Jesus never does. Amen.

Walk Humbly

Don't be selfish; don't try to impress others.
Be humble, thinking of others as better than yourselves.
PHILIPPIANS 2:3 NLT

"Don't toot your own horn!" "Let another praise you, not yourself!" These are just a couple of phrases you might have heard at some point in your life. How do you feel when someone commences sharing all their great qualities and why they are so successful? Does someone's puffed-out chest and talk about their own material possessions turn you off?

Turning the tables, do you put others first? What about that one slice of your spouse's favorite pie in the fridge? Do you eat it or save it as a treat for them? Unfortunately, we often tend to favor ourselves; that is just our human nature. God's way is different and much better. When we walk humbly with the Lord, quelching our pride and putting others ahead of ourselves, we are living righteously, and the Father will bless us. Our example is Jesus, who, although he was God, surrendered himself to death on a cross so that we could live. Aren't you thankful he wasn't selfish but put us first? Be like Jesus.

Jesus, thank you for your humble sacrifice that saved me from being lost for eternity. Amen.

Come before Him

Let us therefore come boldly to the throne of grace, that we may obtain mercy and find grace to help in time of need.
HEBREWS 4:16 NKJV

Sometimes we are timid about expressing what we need. Maybe we don't want to burden anyone else, or we are embarrassed that we can't provide what is necessary for ourselves. Could it be we are just shy or possibly that we fear man's response? *What if no one wants to help me?* we think. *What if I meet with a lack of compassion and feel judged?*

We may have to suffer such reactions from mortal man but never from our God, whose steadfast love endures forever. The Lord encourages us to come before him with courage and to be bold and receive his assistance in our time of need. He is ready to listen and, actually, already knows what you are going to ask for. He is eager to supply your needs because you are his beloved child. He rejoices in the fact that you trust him and believe he will take care of your necessities. He even wants to bless you beyond what you could hope or imagine. Don't hesitate…go to your loving heavenly Father.

Father, thank you for always hearing and answering me. Thank you for your generous love and gifts. Amen.

Believe as a Child

Jesus called them unto him, saying, Suffer the little children to come unto me, and forbid them not: for to such belongeth the kingdom of God. Verily I say unto you, Whosoever shall not receive the kingdom of God as a little child, he shall in no wise enter therein.

Luke 18:16–17 ASV

During the time in history when Jesus walked the earth, many adults perceived children as more of a burden than a blessing. Children only had value once they were able to contribute to the workload, so the disciples thought the little ones were disturbing Jesus, and they rebuked those mothers who brought their kids to him. The Messiah then proceeded to tell his followers to let the children come. He said if people couldn't receive the kingdom with faith like a child, they would not be able to enter it.

Jesus turned the society's idea of a child's value on its head. Can you imagine being beckoned to climb into the lap of the Savior? We may not be able to do that physically, but we can ask God to gather us up in his wings to hold us close. We'll feel his presence within our soul, warming us spiritually from head to toe.

Jesus, help me hurry to you with the faith of a child. Amen.

He Knows Us

The heart knoweth its own bitterness;
and a stranger doth not intermeddle with its joy.
PROVERBS 14:10 ASV

Even at our "best," we often fail at understanding and sharing another's sorrow, heartache, or bliss. We can falsely base our compassion on who the person is and whether we have a sincere hope for their best. If we don't have truthful concern for others, we need to pray for it.

Proverbs 14:10 says that no other human can fully understand both the bitterness and the joy of all your circumstances in life. Jesus—a Man of sorrow acquainted with grief and a servant of all, who was reviled and betrayed—is the one who knows and understands all. There is nothing we could ever face that he hasn't faced already. Remember, he was tempted yet without sin. There is no one who can give us better advice on how to avoid temptation. We may not find anyone on this earth who can provide what we need in certain situations, but Jesus will always have the solution. He is the answer to everything in life, in good times and bad. He is the one who sticks closer than a brother, and he will never leave or forsake us. He knows us better than anyone else and loves us more too.

Jesus, I want to become more and more like you. Amen.

Live a Godly Life

Grace and peace be yours in abundance through the knowledge of God and of Jesus our Lord. His divine power has given us everything we need for a godly life through our knowledge of him who called us by his own glory and goodness.

2 PETER 1:2–3 NIV

Sometimes life seems like a Rubik's Cube that is almost impossible to put together successfully. Try as we may, we find ourselves stressing, striving, and getting exhausted in the process. Whenever we try to figure out or fix things on our own, we are probably headed for defeat. The only one who can orchestrate the right outcome is God. He is all powerful, all knowing, and a very generous Savior.

Have you been anxious lately? Peace and grace can be yours when you take the time to consider whom you belong to and what he is capable of. Gain knowledge of him from his Word. Do you struggle making the right choices? His power gives you everything you could ever require to live a godly life. All that we could ever need is freely offered to us by our good God to display his glory. What a wonderful Savior we serve!

Lord, let faith rise up within me to see your purpose accomplished in me and my loved ones who know you. Amen.

Mary Magdalene

After He had risen early on the first day of the week,
He first appeared to Mary Magdalene,
from whom He had cast out seven demons.

MARK 16:9 NASB

They showed her no mercy. Seven demons had relentlessly tormented Mary Magdalene. The community shunned her. Parents would shelter their children from her as she walked by. She wasn't a leper, but she might as well have been. When Jesus met her, he cast out all the demons, and she became one of his most faithful followers. Mary Magdalene followed him throughout his ministry, supporting all that he did. She dedicated her life to him. When many of the disciples had left Jesus as he hung on the cross, Mary stayed by his side. She knew the gravity of what he had saved her from, and there was nowhere else she would ever go. When Jesus was placed in the tomb, she was there. On the day he was resurrected, she was there. She even ran to tell the disciples that the Savior had risen.

We may not have had seven demons, but we were dead in our sins and trespasses. Jesus saved us and made us new. Let's follow Mary's example of dedication to him.

Jesus, out of my immense gratitude I give all that I am to you…
forever. Amen.

Prayer Partners

Brothers, pray for us.
1 Thessalonians 5:25 ESV

It is such a privilege to pray for one another—during prayer meetings, in prayer closets, at friends' homes, and at our church. It is our greatest weapon against the Enemy, and there is nothing better we can do for others than to lift them up in prayer. There is an issue, though, that I don't think we Christians discuss enough. It is that we often say this phrase so flippantly: "I'll pray for you." As soon as the person we offered to pray for walks away, we, unfortunately, forget that promise. The other person's need doesn't hold the importance with us that it should, so we neglect to be faithful to our promise.

If we realize that God hears the commitment we made to pray for our brother or sister in Christ, then maybe we would be more inclined to follow through. If you don't think you will remember to pray later, offer to pray with the person immediately. What joy there is in sharing in a prayer partner's struggles or requests. Ask God to bring to you someone you can pray for.

Lord, please impress upon my heart the importance of being faithful in praying for others. Amen.

Search Me, God

Create in me a pure heart, O God, and renew a steadfast spirit within me. Do not cast me from your presence or take your Holy Spirit from me.

PSALM 51:10–11 NIV

Early in the morning before we start our day, we should make sure that we spend time with the Lord and examine our hearts. Any unknown sin will come to light when we ask the Lord to reveal it. Then we can start fresh and walk in righteousness before our God.

What a privilege and comfort to know that all we need to do is confess our sin and he will forgive us. He will forget our sin ever happened. We are free from any condemnation. Not only will he absolve us of our sin, but he'll renew our heart and place an unwavering spirit in us. All we need to do is ask for his gracious forgiveness, and he will be faithful no matter how many times we transgress.

Father, please reveal my sin to me so that I can be cleansed by the blood of Jesus. Thank you, Abba. Amen.

A Jealous Heart

Do you think Scripture says without reason that he jealously longs for the spirit he has caused to dwell in us? But he gives us more grace. That is why Scripture says: "God opposes the proud but shows favor to the humble."

JAMES 4:5–6 NIV

Humility carries with it promises of God's favor. We should all be looking at Jesus as our example, for "being found in human form, he *humbled* himself by becoming obedient to the point of death, even death on a cross. Therefore God has highly exalted him and bestowed on him the name that is above every name" (Philippians 2:8–9 ESV, emphasis added). Someday, every knee in heaven and on earth will bow to Christ.

Why does God oppose the proud? They choose to follow the ways of this evil world by exalting self over the Lord. They run after worldly pleasures, rebelling against the purpose God designed them for, to be holy as he is holy. It's this behavior that makes him jealous because he wants so desperately to save them. We were created for his pleasure, to worship him within the most intimate relationship. His jealous heart longs for his created ones to give him their love, adoration, and all their being.

Father, thank you for your jealous heart that desires all to come to salvation. Amen.

Whom Will You Serve?

"If serving the LORD seems undesirable to you, then choose for yourselves this day whom you will serve, whether the gods your ancestors served beyond the Euphrates, or the gods of the Amorites, in whose land you are living. But as for me and my household, we will serve the LORD."

JOSHUA 24:15 NIV

We serve a God who is true gentleman. He does not force us, threaten us, or bribe us to come to him for salvation. He gives us free will to choose or reject him. To be given this privilege to decide is a gift, but choosing wrongly leads to separation from God. The Israelites struggled to stay faithful to the Lord. They rebelled and chose to follow after foreign gods. With their own hands, they made idols of wood to worship.

Can you imagine how God felt? His children he created and loved rejected him for some toy they carved and named their god. He showed them tough love, causing them to suffer hardship in hopes that they would return to him. When they asked for forgiveness, he forgave, blessing their previously rebellious hearts. Use your freedom to choose wisely. Proclaim with Joshua, "As for me and my household, we will serve the LORD."

God, please help me to choose wisely, for serving you is a privilege with eternal consequences. Amen.

At the Feet of Jesus

"Martha, Martha," the Lord answered, "you are worried and upset about many things, but few things are needed—or indeed only one. Mary has chosen what is better, and it will not be taken away from her."

LUKE 10:41–42 NIV

Looking at Martha and Mary, we see two different personalities. Martha appears to be type A, and Mary is a bit more laid back. One is determined to be the hostess with the mostest, and the other is a devoted listener. Martha stresses over serving those in attendance, working to provide for Jesus and others. She has a pity party over the fact that no one is helping her. Does she even know that she is missing pearls of wisdom from her Savior as he teaches?

Mary, on the other hand, is all ears. She is filled with wonder as she sits at the feet of Jesus. She commits his words to memory and savors every moment with him. When Martha complains, Jesus tells her that she has chosen wrongly. This is causing her tension when she could be experiencing the joy of being with her Savior. Don't be so busy for the kingdom's sake that you forget to spend intimate time in prayer, in the Word, and with our Savior.

Lord, may my daily choices bring me closer to you. Amen.

Don't Drink the Kool-Aid

Therefore, dear friends, since you have been forewarned, be on your guard so that you may not be carried away by the error of the lawless and fall from your secure position. But grow in the grace and knowledge of our Lord and Savior Jesus Christ. To him be glory both now and forever! Amen.

2 PETER 3:17–18 NIV

Jesus warned that false prophets would come. This passage is a reminder to Christ's followers not to be swayed by wrong doctrine. When we are not in the Word, walking closely with Christ, we can be influenced by the wrong words, motives, and voices. We have to be vigilant to remain in intimacy with the Lord so that we can spot a phony a mile away. Otherwise, we are placing ourselves in danger of believing something that is in total opposition to Scripture.

It has happened many times as a new cult pops up proclaiming to be Christian, and before you know it, everyone involved is drinking deadly Kool-Aid. Be on guard and know God's truth so you can boldly shut down any lies or imposters. Yield to God with a burning passion to know him intimately and to avoid imposters.

Lord, give me wisdom to discern truth from lies. Help me fill my heart and mind with your Word. Amen.

Our Great High Priest

Therefore, since we have a great high priest who has ascended into heaven, Jesus the Son of God, let us hold firmly to the faith we profess. For we do not have a high priest who is unable to empathize with our weaknesses, but we have one who has been tempted in every way, just as we are—yet he did not sin.

HEBREWS 4:14–15 NIV

Much of Hebrews chapters 3–4 deals with unbelief and doubt. We fail, fall, and become discouraged. But then Hebrews 4:14–15 (TPT) ignites our hearts with faith for: "We have a magnificent King-Priest, Jesus Christ, the Son of God, who… sympathizes with us in our frailty. He understands humanity, for as a man, our magnificent King-Priest was tempted in every way just as we are, and conquered sin."

When the Enemy whispers in your ear that no one before has ever been tempted as badly as you, realize it is a total lie. If you've sinned, remember that confession clears the path to forgiveness and restores your relationship with God. So now, go "freely and boldly to where grace is enthroned, to receive mercy's kiss and discover the grace we urgently need to strengthen us in our time of weakness" (v. 16 TPT).

Abba, help me come to you freely and boldly in times of weakness. May I remember Jesus understands and has been tempted as I have. Amen.

God Does Not Hide

Verily thou art a God that hidest thyself,
O God of Israel, the Saviour.
Isaiah 45:15 KJV

At times, it seems as though God is "hiding" from us, but we need to remember that he has promised to never leave us or forsake us. God does not hide, and even when we feel deserted, he is near. We are the ones who, through disappointment, anger, or feeling neglected, turn away from the Father. We get offended when we feel God has not answered our prayers or when the outcome of an answered prayer doesn't turn out as we wanted. We forget all his blessings and focus on what we didn't receive. So we hide, but God doesn't. We have sin in our heart, and we don't want to admit it or face God.

God declares that all who seek him shall find him. Even when God seems to be the most distant and we feel deserted, God is by our side. Check your heart for any unknown or hidden sin, and once you find it, go in humility to God, confess, and obtain his forgiveness and love. He is right there, fully available and waiting for you. He will rejoice in your return, giving you a fresh start as he offers his grace and mercy.

Jesus, thank you for always being by my side. Amen.

Refiner's Fire

"I have refined you, but not as silver is refined.
Rather, I have refined you in the furnace of suffering."
ISAIAH 48:10 NLT

When looking at the definition of *refine*, it sounds wonderful
to be brought "to a fine or a pure state; free from impurities."[3]
When we read today's verse and realize the method that God
must use for our refinement, it can be daunting. We want to
mature and grow in Christ, but we aren't thrilled that it involves
suffering. We should be comfortable leaving ourselves in the
Savior's hands, but we give in to fear. When we prayed that God
would use us, we didn't expect that it would include hardships.
However, we've already committed to lay ourselves on his altar,
so we steady ourselves, waiting for the boom to drop.

Our attitude should instead be one of faith, knowing that
whatever we walk through, our Savior is present. We are only
a prayer away from telling him we are weak and receiving his
strength. He will go with us. In fact, he has already been where
we are going and has prepared the way. Don't be afraid but allow
him to bring beauty from the ashes in your life. You will come
out looking more like Jesus.

Jesus, I surrender all that I am to you. I trust you to walk with me
through the fire. Amen.

---

3   Dictionary.com, s.v. "refine." www.dictionary.com.

Yoked with Jesus

"Take my yoke upon you and learn from me, for I am gentle
and humble in heart, and you will find rest for your souls.
For my yoke is easy and my burden is light."
MATTHEW 11:29–30 NIV

Can you picture a wooden frame with a place for two to be
joined in a singular task? The apparatus is heavy, worn by the
weather, and even has a few splinters. There is hesitation in
your spirit to put it on due to the unknown of what it will feel
like or restrict you from. Wouldn't it be better if you just took
things into your own hands and went your own way? You are
exhausted, but at least you will still maintain control.

Then you hear the gentle voice of Jesus inviting you to
join him. He says he will bear the weight; he just wants to be
with you and work toward lightening your load. He knows you
are weary, and he desires to lift your spirits. What now seems
like a burden too heavy to carry, he will absorb by his strength
and great love for you. Go with him, for there you will find rest
for your soul.

Jesus, thank you for taking the load of my stress and troubles.
I trust you. Amen.

Unattainable Thoughts

"My thoughts are nothing like your thoughts," says the LORD.
"And my ways are far beyond anything you could imagine. For
just as the heavens are higher than the earth, so my ways
are higher than your ways and my thoughts higher than your
thoughts."

ISAIAH 55:8-9 NLT

We have all run into someone in life who thinks they know
everything. Even if you know the person is wrong, you don't
dare say anything. The response would be a diatribe of why *you*
are mistaken, backed up with even more false facts. We can read
every book and study every "-ology," and we will never come
close to thinking how God does.

As believers, we are transformed in mind and heart, but
we do not have the intellect or motives for our thoughts that the
Lord does. He is holy; we are on the road to holiness with the
help of his Holy Spirit. He is all-knowing, and our brains have
limitations. Yet doesn't it give you great comfort to know that
he has thoughts that surpass everyone else's? He knows all and
is working on your behalf. Find relief in the confidence that his
ways are the best ways. He is for us, not against us.

Father, I worship your knowledge. I praise you for your ways.
Amen.

Choose Your Words Carefully

Do not be rash with your mouth or hasty in your heart to bring up a matter before God, for God is in heaven and you are on earth! Therefore, let your words be few.

ECCLESIASTES 5:2 NET

In troubled times, many people offer to do certain things for God if he will only answer their prayers. They plead, beg, and assure God that if he will only perform this for them or give them what they are asking for, they will follow through on their promise. Unfortunately, they often say this type of prayer with little forethought, uttering it in a time of distress and not considering it carefully.

Before we ever give our word to God or man, we should think about what that entails and what our capacity is to fulfill it. Is it even something we truly are open to doing, or are we just in a desperate moment? Are we promising God something that is within our reach or out of our hands? Do not be flippant with your vow, for once you say it, God expects you to follow through. Be assured, though, that God is gracious and forgiving, and remember that if we fail him, he won't fail us.

Father, help me to consider and choose my words carefully, to know what I am promising, and to be ready to follow through. Amen.

None Like Him

Who is a God like you, who pardons sin and forgives the transgression of the remnant of his inheritance? You do not stay angry forever but delight to show mercy. You will again have compassion on us; you will tread our sins underfoot and hurl all our iniquities into the depths of the sea.

MICAH 7:18–19 NIV

Micah said these words just after stating the distressing and depressing conditions of the days in which he lived. Micah knew the heart of his Lord and that God would always love his children even though they had sinned. God's people had become disloyal, were disobedient, and rejected godliness.

God may be angry for a while with his own children, but he will never stay that way. He proves the extent of his great grace and mercy by pardoning and delivering his people. The second chances are endless for those who belong to him. His mercy has nothing to do with us and everything to do with him. He desires to bless us because of his steadfast love that endures forever. And once we ask for forgiveness, he stamps out our sin, throwing our iniquities to the very bottom of the sea, never to be dredged up again.

God, I am grateful that your anger expires and is replaced with your great love and protection. Amen.

Jesus Forgives

Jesus said, "Father, forgive them, for they do not know what they are doing." And they divided up his clothes by casting lots.

LUKE 23:34 NIV

Jesus gave us an example to follow when he asked God to forgive those torturing, spitting on, beating, and nailing him to a cross. He said they didn't know what they were doing. Does it seem far-fetched to think they were blind to their actions? Since God is all knowing, he understood that they really didn't get the gravity of the actions they took, but don't take that as license to sin and use the same excuse. Those who tortured Christ really didn't believe he was the Messiah but thought he was just some crazy imposter. So as Jesus hung broken and bloodied on the cross, from the depths of his heart he asked his Father to pardon those who killed him ignorantly.

Have you been hurt, offended, or worse? How easy would it be to say the same words as Jesus? Would they flow off your tongue or choke you? Pray for mercy and grace in your heart so that you can forgive as he does. Remember, if we don't forgive those who sin against us, our Father in heaven won't forgive us.

Lord, give me your heart of forgiveness so that I may glorify, imitate, and radiate you. Amen.

The Deliverance of the Lord

Many fell, because the war was of God.
1 CHRONICLES 5:22 ESV

Have you faced a confrontation that you wanted to run from? Most of us have. It's not easy to be in conflict. In fact, it's something many of us avoid like the plague. When we attempt to do battle on our own and move forward out of irrational emotions and hurt feelings, we usually don't proceed in a God-honoring manner. This can lead to greater conflict and a failure to resolve anything.

When we take our situation to God, he takes us on a whole new path forward. Even if we have begun to take things into our own hands, if we cry out to God, he will take the lead. The Lord in his wisdom knows just what battle strategy will win the day, and he will always claim the victory. What a comfort to know that when we surrender all to him, he fights on our behalf. He advises us to stand still and watch the deliverance of the Lord. How fearful it would be to think we are left to our own devices in this life. Praise God that he will never stop defending and delivering us.

Father, thank you, my champion, for saving me, fighting for me, and delivering me. Amen.

Sanctification and Inheritance

"Now I commit you to God and to the word of his grace, which can build you up and give you an inheritance among all those who are sanctified."

ACTS 20:32 NIV

Oh, the comfort of being owned by the God of creation. There is nothing we have done or could ever do to adequately repay him for his grace, his salvation, and his constant care. The love letter he left to instruct us, the Bible, teaches us how to live in a manner that will honor him. It is the word of his knowledge, his gospel, and his plan for those who believe and will follow him into eternity.

We so completely do not deserve salvation, yet God freely and fully gives it to all who call on his name. Not only do we receive sanctification and inheritance but also oneness with Christ, becoming heirs who will receive our portion as children of the King. He encourages us with the assurance that we will live abundantly if we surrender our lives to Jesus. He blesses us with gifts to represent him while we are on earth. He will deliver what he promises, for our God is faithful.

God, you have extravagantly forgiven my sins, sanctified me, and made me one with Christ as a joint heir. Your grace and mercy are overwhelming. I give you my praise. Amen.

Share the Message

Consequently, faith comes from hearing the message,
and the message is heard through the word about Christ.
ROMANS 10:17 NIV

If people don't hear the Word of God, how will they be saved?
If they don't know the story of the one who came to earth to die
so their sins would be forgiven, how can they live eternally with
God? I heard a parable once about a man who went through
many phases of life with his best friend. His best friend was a
closet Christian and never shared the good news with the man.
The tale finds the unsaved man at the judgment seat asking his
friend why he never told him about salvation. As the believer
hung his head in shame, the unbeliever said, "I can never again
call you my friend." Their friendship was fatally flawed, and one
man's soul was lost forever due to the other's indifference about
sharing Christ.

It is the Word of God and the Holy Spirit that awakens a
response of faith within people, but they may never experience
that if no one shares the message. Oh Jesus, help us pull our
loved ones back from the fire!

Jesus, burden my heart for those who don't know you. Open my
mouth with boldness to share your message of salvation. Amen.

He Disciplines with Love

Whom the Lord loveth he chasteneth,
and scourgeth every son whom he receiveth.
HEBREWS 12:6 ASV

Would a good parent allow their toddler to run into a busy street or even to rip up books just because it seems fun to do? Would they react if their child threw a major tantrum out in public, or would they just accept it? A good parent will deal with all these scenarios in a way that discourages their young one from ever doing it again. As moms and dads, we read in God's Word that sparing the rod leads to spoiling the child. You better believe if God recommends this to us, he subscribes to it for his own wayward and disobedient kids.

Does God discipline us because he is mean or doesn't like us? Just the opposite. He disciplines out of his great love and concern that we live obedient lives and become righteous. His kindness won't allow him to leave us as we are, but instead, he will do what it takes to transform us into his righteous children. When he does offer correction, receive it from your Father who loves you and only does what is best for you.

Lord, help me accept your discipline so that I will grow into the likeness of Christ. Amen.

Our God

The earth has yielded its produce;
God, our God, blesses us.

PSALM 67:6 NASB

God has promised to supply all our needs. He allowed his
Son to carry and pay the price for our sins. He has blessed us
with every blessing he could possibly offer. He loves us with
an everlasting love. He promises that if we seek him, we will
find him. He tenderly hides us under his wing. He counts the
number of hairs on our head. He sings over us. He listens to
our prayers and answers them. He even knows what we will ask
before we reach our knees. He calls us the apple of his eye and
his treasured possessions.

He's created a home for us in heaven, where we will live
with him for eternity. He never gives up on us, always forgives
us, never abandons us, and entrusts us to share the good news
of salvation with the world. He left us his Word so there would
no mistaking how much he wants us and how we can best follow
him. This is God, our God. The Creator of all is ours, and we are
his. There is no greater joy, no greater news, no other God.

God, you are almighty, holy, and loving, and you are mine. Thank
you. Amen.

July

Meditate on the Word

"Keep this Book of the Law always on your lips; meditate on it day and night, so that you may be careful to do everything written in it. Then you will be prosperous and successful. Have I not commanded you? Be strong and courageous. Do not be afraid; do not be discouraged, for the LORD your God will be with you wherever you go."

JOSHUA 1:8–9 NIV

What wonderful instruction and promises are in today's verse! If we follow it closely, we will prosper. There are a few stipulations, however. Consider what it will entail to keep God's law on your lips, to review it every moment throughout the day and night. This doesn't mean you have to sit still and repeat Scripture over and over and do nothing else. However, you will need to know the Word well enough to bring the right verses to mind when you need them.

You will have to make choices so that you can retain his truth. Turning the TV off so you can read your Bible could be one of them. Meditating on and following the Word will make you confident and unafraid. You will go forward with hope because you will have the wise instruction of God's Word in your heart and on your tongue.

God, help me remember your Word. Amen.

Resurrected

Jesus saith unto her, Mary.
She turneth herself, and saith unto him in Hebrew,
Rabboni; which is to say, Teacher.

JOHN 20:16 ASV

From the day that Jesus commanded seven demons to leave Mary's body, she followed him. She witnessed him preach to the masses, she experienced miracles, she stood by him at the cross, and then she searched for him at the tomb. When she saw the stone had been rolled away, she assumed that his body had been moved. She ran to tell the disciples, who traveled to the tomb to see for themselves. Discouraged and confused to find his body missing, they returned to their homes.

Then two angels met Mary as she was weeping at the tomb. She told them she was distraught because someone had taken her Lord's body. Soon Mary heard the voice of her beloved Savior. When he said her name, all her fears and despair dissipated, and joy flooded her soul. Her Jesus was resurrected! She ran to tell the disciples that she had seen the Lord. The grave was defeated, redemption had come, and the Savior was and is alive. If Jesus could cast out demons and defeat death itself, imagine what else he can do in our lives.

Jesus, you defeated sin and death. I long for the day you will return. Amen.

Obedient Children of God

The fear of the LORD is a fountain of life,
by which one may avoid the snares of death.
PROVERBS 14:27 NASB

Early in your faith, this verse may have confused you. You had
heard that God is love, so why are you supposed to be afraid
of him? The Bible states in Psalm 34:11–14 NASB, "Come, you
children, listen to me; I will teach you the fear of the LORD.
Who is the person who desires life and loves length of days,
that he may see good? Keep your tongue from evil and your lips
from speaking deceit. Turn from evil and do good; seek peace
and pursue it."

We should not be afraid of God, but we are to reverence
and respect him. We are to obey his Word and believe in his Son
for our salvation and to escape destruction. When we adhere
to Scripture, we're filled with joy, peace, and purpose for God's
kingdom.

As obedient children of God, if we give him control and
follow his statutes, we experience abundant life. His ways are
not intended to restrict us but to lead us to life everlasting in
him. Fearing God leads to life.

Father, help me revere you and stay true to what your Word says.
I want to obey and live. Amen.

In God We Trust

Blessed is the nation whose God is the LORD,
the people he chose for his inheritance.
PSALM 33:12 NIV

Our nation was founded on faith in God. Our forefathers
created the laws this country would follow prayerfully. For
decades, prayer was a staple in schools. Church was an event
that entire families of believers attended and participated in
consistently. It was evident that God was continually blessing
America. I think the patriots of old would roll over in their
graves if they could see what is happening in our country today.
Ungodliness is rampant. Sinful beliefs that are in complete
opposition to God's Word are destroying lives. New beliefs are
warping and distorting God's design for creation. God's plan for
marriage is perverted. Satan is having a heyday as he seeks to
steal, kill, and destroy.

Change can come if we humble ourselves, confess our
country's sin, and turn from wicked ways. We desperately
need Jesus; otherwise, our nation will fall. We'll only remain
independent if we throw ourselves on the dependency of God.

God, forgive me for my heinous beliefs, evil acts, and rejection of
you. Please bring revival and healing to our land. Amen.

No More Yoke

It is for freedom that Christ has set us free.
Stand firm, then, and do not let yourselves
be burdened again by a yoke of slavery.

GALATIANS 5:1 NIV

When you consider all that Jesus suffered to bring us to
salvation, you would think we would avoid sin like the plague.
How can we say we love him when we continue to give in to
temptation? Jesus said if we love him, we will obey him. How
often do we confuse his generous grace with a license to sin
because we can confess later. He sees our hearts, and he knows
our motives.

We can't stick one foot in the world and the other in
God's realm. We will live a divided life and give ourselves over
to the possibility of leaving the faith. Scripture says that in
the end times, many will fall away. To avoid being one of that
number, be committed and surrendered to Jesus in every way.
Don't let the devil get a foothold in your life. Sin leads to death,
but Christ offers freedom. Hold fast to the eternal life he offers.

Dear Lord, may your Holy Spirit dominate and completely fill me,
that I may choose life so that I can represent you well and live. No
more yoke of sin for me. Amen.

Christ as Savior

Many are the woes of the wicked, but the LORD's unfailing love surrounds the one who trusts in him. Rejoice in the LORD and be glad, you righteous; sing, all you who are upright in heart!
PSALM 32:10–11 NIV

It is hard to understand why anyone reading these verses would want to do anything other than trust the Lord and live righteously. Anytime Scripture uses the word *woe*, you know bad times are coming. If you have not made a decision for Jesus, he is waiting, desiring to have you as his own. Don't let shame stop you. He'll forgive and never condemn.

Make your eternal position secure. Don't let this day pass without laying your sins at Jesus' feet and inviting him to be your Savior.

Won't you come to him now? Simply pray, saying, *Jesus, I believe you are the Son of God. Thank you for dying for my sin. I humbly ask your forgiveness. Please come into my life and be my Lord and Savior. I give myself completely to you.*

Jesus, thank you for coming into my heart and saving me. I am yours. Amen.

Pray in Faith

> Without faith it is impossible to please God, because anyone who comes to him must believe that he exists and that he rewards those who earnestly seek him.
>
> HEBREWS 11:6 NIV

Have you ever felt like your prayers were bouncing off the wall? If you have prayed a specific request for a long while with no answer, it might be that you are still waiting on God's timing. Or it could be that you are asking for a miracle but that once you say "amen," you take matters back into your own hands. God as our Father wants us to ask him and then let go of our requests, trusting him with the outcome. We should be waiting patiently in hopeful expectation.

Search your heart and mind. Do you really believe that God can and will do what you are asking? If you ask without faith, then your lack of faith could be hindering your prayer. Oh, God can answer even if we have no trust, but will he? He will definitely not be pleased with our lack of faith. Today's verse says he rewards those who believe in his ability to grant their requests and that he will answer those who passionately seek him. When we pray in faith, God honors those prayers and will not hesitate to give us his very best within his will.

Dear Lord, help my faith increase as I pray to you. Amen.

Stay Dependent

I keep my eyes always on the LORD. With him at my right
hand, I will not be shaken. Therefore my heart is glad and my
tongue rejoices; my body also will rest secure.

PSALM 16:8–9 NIV

Do you ever get out of step with God? So often, we tend to run
ahead, side-step, or lag behind him. It can be due to worry, fear,
or self-will. We get anxious about the outcome of something
and think that maybe God is too busy and that we should just
step up to the plate. We tell ourselves that even if we mess
up, he'll come in and do the cleanup. We fool ourselves into
thinking that God is in heaven cheering us on because we are
being proactive.

 Our Lord wants us to stay dependent on him, not strive
to be independent. He wants us to trust his timing, not set the
clock ahead. If we need help, he'll come to our rescue, but he'd
much rather we follow his lead. Don't step in front of God, or
you may then find yourself dangling on a cliff. Stay in lockstep
with Jesus. When we do, we will find the way smooth and the
path straight, and victory will always be the result.

Father, help me keep my eyes fixed on you so that I follow your
lead continuously. Amen.

His Time, Not Ours

Do not overlook this one fact, beloved, that with the Lord one
day is as a thousand years, and a thousand years as one day.
2 PETER 3:8 ESV

Just as God's ways are not our ways and his thoughts are not our
thoughts, we also know we live on separate timetables. We live
in a culture that expects instant gratification, whether it be fast
food or an immediate response online. God's timeclock moves
differently than ours. We think he is tarrying when, in his
wisdom, he is waiting for the perfect moment to fulfill his will.
He is sovereign and all-knowing, and we cannot expect him to
bow to our schedule.

Are you desperately wanting him to return to take his
church home? He longs for you as well, but he still wants to give
as many people as possible time to accept his gift of grace and
eternal life. Are you getting on in years and wondering why he
hasn't answered that prayer yet? Maybe in his wisdom, he will
answer it once you leave this earth. Is that door you want to
walk through still closed? Wait for him to fulfill his plan; don't
force your way in. Find peace in knowing that he will do what is
best when the timing is right.

Father, help me trust your perfect timing. Amen.

No Other God

"I have not spoken in secret, from somewhere in a land of darkness; I have not said to Jacob's descendants, 'Seek me in vain.' I, the LORD, speak the truth; I declare what is right."

ISAIAH 45:19 NIV

In the Old Testament, Israel had a history of leaving their first love, namely God. They dabbled in all kinds of sin, including idol worship, and suffered the consequences. Can you imagine the sorrow the Lord felt as he watched his children worshiping a piece of wood they carved themselves? Think of his frustration as they cried out in vain to something that had no breath and could never answer. There he was, wooing them to come to him, delivering them time after time, only to have them eventually run back to their false gods.

Graven images have no life, existing in darkness without a voice. The one true God calls us to seek him, promising that we will find him. Every word that proceeds from his mouth is truth. There is no other way, and there is no other God. If we surrender to him, he will come and fellowship with us. He'll never leave us, guiding us through life until, one day, he leads us home.

Father, you alone are God, mighty to save and always faithful and true. I praise you! Amen.

Jesus Chose to Come

The Word became flesh and made his dwelling among us.
We have seen his glory, the glory of the one and only Son,
who came from the Father, full of grace and truth.

JOHN 1:14 NIV

Imagine heaven the way the book of Revelation describes it.
Streets of gold, gates made of beautiful gems, a city that looks
like pure glass, and, in the center, the throne of God. Why
would anyone ever want to leave? Especially to be beaten and
killed by God's creation?

Jesus chose to come to earth with his Father's plan in
his heart. He would become a man, live, suffer, and die at the
hands of the people he made, and as a result, he would bring
salvation to those who killed him. He died for all mankind, so
we're all responsible. We're also the recipients of his great gift of
forgiveness and eternal life. Let it sink in. He left paradise, came
to earth, suffered man's insults and rejection, and then gave his
life in our place. There is no greater act of love.

*Jesus, I bow to you in humble gratitude for your sacrifice. Thank
you for your gift of salvation. Amen.*

Victory over Death

When the perishable has been clothed with the imperishable,
and the mortal with immortality, then the saying that is written
will come true: "Death has been swallowed up in victory."

1 CORINTHIANS 15:54 NIV

Once, I heard a song that captured my heart. A bit enraptured
by the music, a powerful picture filled my mind. The song was
about a man named Joe, who now lives in glory. He is face-to-
face with Christ, his Savior. His battles are over, his victory won.
His joy is truly indescribable! But those left here on earth, who
loved Joe so deeply, will mourn, missing him with many tears.

Our God of all comfort will sustain, strengthen, and
bathe them in his peace. What a joy fills their spirit, though,
when they realize that one day, they will see their brother in
Christ again. All those who trust in Jesus will worship together
eternally before the throne. What a glorious future he has
prepared for those of us who believe in his name!

Lord, thank you for the many promises in your Word that testify
to these truths. Amen.

God Rejoices in You

The LORD your God is in your midst, a mighty one who will save; he will rejoice over you with gladness; he will quiet you by his love; he will exult over you with loud singing.

ZEPHANIAH 3:17 ESV

The Lord Most High, the all-powerful One, thinks about you and me. His thoughts toward us are always lovely, for he never condemns. He may chastise when we need it, but he still does this out of his great care and affection. He is always with us, right in our midst. He fights our battles and brings us to victory.

Do you hear that beautiful voice? That is your Creator, your Lord, your Abba, singing over you. Amazing, isn't it? He proclaims his pleasure in you and the beauty of who he made you to be. You can hear the joy in his song, for he is pleased with his creation. While he lifts his voice loudly, he extends his peace and care over you. The God of the universe has a love song just for you. May we never cease to marvel at the glorious thought that the Creator of all rejoices in song over his children.

Father, I am humbled by the knowledge that you sing over me. I don't deserve your grace, but I gratefully accept it. Amen.

Love and Peace

"You keep him in perfect peace whose mind is stayed on you,
because he trusts in you."

ISAIAH 26:3 ESV

Focusing on our sin, flaws, and imperfections is one great
robber of abiding in Christ's love and bathing in his peace.
Feeling despair over our transgressions is often a greater
obstacle than the sin itself. It causes us to run from God
when we should be running to him and giving him praise for
providing a way to be forgiven for your sins. Once you have
confessed, cast down any shame, for God never wants you to
live with guilt.

When God looks at our trespasses through the precious
sacrificial blood of Jesus, they vanish before the majesty of his
love. See your dirty rags made sparkling white. God loves us and
calls us his own. He remembers our frame and knows that we are
dust. Even when we falter and fail, he is our greatest supporter.
His arms are always open and waiting to hold us, enveloping us
in his magnificent love. Quietly lay your transgressions before
our loving God. We can experience peace of conscience when we
trust in him, our "everlasting rock" (v. 4).

Dear Lord, thank you for your perfect, amazing love and
wonderful, calming peace. May I be consumed by your love,
pouring it back to you and out to others. Amen.

We Are Free

For you have been called to live in freedom, my brothers and sisters. But don't use your freedom to satisfy your sinful nature. Instead, use your freedom to serve one another in love.

GALATIANS 5:13 NLT

What a gift God has given us in Christ Jesus, that we are no longer slaves to sin. There is no fear of condemnation, for Christ has already atoned for every trespass, former and future. Some people think this is too easy and continue in unbelief. If only they understood the enormity of what our salvation cost Jesus. He sweat blood in the garden just thinking about the type of death he would suffer to bring us life. His selfless act freed us from the requirements of sacrifice and the law.

Do not view this as a free pass to continue sinning. Some think if God is going to forgive them, they can indulge in sin. May it never be! Instead, we are to love and serve others as a testimony to our transformation in Christ. Show God gratitude for the freedom you have received by saying no to sin and putting the needs of others ahead of your own.

Jesus, I am grateful that your cross freed me from death. Help me use my freedom to honor you by being your hands and feet to others. Amen.

New Life

Praise be to the God and Father of our Lord Jesus Christ!
In his great mercy he has given us new birth into a living hope
through the resurrection of Jesus Christ from the dead.

1 PETER 1:3 NIV

Start this day by praising the Lord. Consider all the magnificent acts he has done on your behalf. Begin with the fact that you woke up this morning to his new mercies. Marvel at the first breath you took because he gave it to you. Look around and see his provisions for you and give him thanks. Rejoice with him over the loved ones he has placed in your life.

Remember that, at one time, we were without hope, unable to reach God, for our depth of sin stood in the way. We wandered through our darkness until the light of Jesus penetrated our soul. As our eyes were opened to view our sin, our hearts were torn over the trauma he endured to save us. By his broken body and spilled blood, God's mercy ushered us into salvation. Through his resurrection we have been raised to a new life. We will live with him for eternity. Let the meditation of our heart be one of worship continually to our magnificent Lord and King.

Lord, thank you for your amazing, pardoning, freeing, and
incomprehensible mercy. Amen.

Life-giving Properties

The law of the LORD is perfect, refreshing the soul. The
statutes of the LORD are trustworthy, making wise the simple.
The precepts of the LORD are right, giving joy to the heart. The
commands of the LORD are radiant, giving light to the eyes.

PSALM 19:7–8 NIV

There has never been nor will there ever be a book like the
Bible. It is alive, and its instructions have the power to help us
choose life or death. For those who ignore its wisdom, there is a
meaningless life ahead and an eternity spent without God. For
those of us who love the words of Scripture and accept them,
the life-giving properties will rescue our soul from hell.

The law rejuvenates our spirit. We have faith and
peace to face anything, for Scripture tells us that our Lord is
trustworthy. In its pages we find wisdom. We rejoice in his
precepts, for when we live righteously, our hearts are filled with
joy. We won't enter a wrong path if we follow his commands, for
our journey will be illumined to show us the way. Lift your eyes
and gaze on the face of your adoring Savior. He is gazing back
with the greatest affection.

Lord, help me live daily by your Word, committing it to memory.
May your Scripture always be on my tongue. Amen.

Speak Words of Life

Encourage one another and build each other up,
just as in fact you are doing.
1 THESSALONIANS 5:11 NIV

We all have days when we feel a bit blue. It can come in waves and varying degrees. Sometimes we have a justifiable reason for feeling down in the dumps. We may have lost a job or could be enduring a long illness. We may have experienced far too many changes in our lives all at once. Or maybe we simply didn't sleep well. We must consider the reason for our attitude and take it to God. Maybe we need to take our eyes off ourselves and focus on others. When we reach out to encourage one another, even though we may not feel like it, it brings us joy. Our day can turn around from gloomy to sunny because we blessed someone else.

Try it, because once you do, you will want to do it more and more. You will find your discouragement melting away as you lift up those around you, lend a helping hand, and speak words of life. So go check on your neighbor, call an old friend, or smile at a stranger and watch your own countenance start to glow.

Lord, thank you for being a friend who sticks closer than a brother. Amen.

His Image

God said, "Let us make man in our image, after our likeness. And let them have dominion over the fish of the sea and over the birds of the heavens and over the livestock and over all the earth and over every creeping thing that creeps on the earth."

GENESIS 1:26 ESV

We tend to make snap judgments about people. We might look down on them for the way they live, the way they dress, or the way they look. Maybe we decide they're a bit odd, so we reject them. We determine in the hidden places of our heart whether that person is worthy of our time or whether we should just avoid eye contact as we pass them. If we truly know Scripture, we know that we are not to favor anyone over another.

With a loving and accepting heart, we are to help all who need it. We must remember that each person who is now walking or has ever walked this earth was created in the image of God. His likeness and stamp of approval are on them. Think about that the next time you are faced with the opportunity to serve someone. Remember that Jesus said, "As you did it to one of the least of these my brothers, you did it to me" (Matthew 25:40 ESV).

Father, help me see your image on all mankind. Amen.

Your Refuge

From the ends of the earth I call to you, I call as my heart
grows faint; lead me to the rock that is higher than I. For you
have been my refuge, a strong tower against the foe.

PSALM 61:2–3 NIV

Often, when faced with trouble, we neglect to see the best
solution of calling out to God immediately. As our anxiety hits
a fever pitch, our first impulse is to fix our problems ourselves.
We panic over how this scenario will resolve. We pick up the
phone to complain to a friend when we should be getting on
our knees. We have made the Lord an afterthought. Only when
we face the truth that we are in a mess we can't clean up, we
finally turn to him.

Oh, we never forgot him, but we just haven't gotten to
the place in our faith where we value his help over our own
efforts. This is why we don't think first and foremost of running
to our strong tower. At the onset of difficulty, we should cry to
God, for he is the only one who can save us. Next time your
heart drops to your knees from the fiery trial, rush to your Rock
who will deliver you.

Lord, though the Enemy vigorously attempts to destroy me, may
I stand strong in you, my Rock. Amen.

Redeeming the Impossible

O Israel, keep hoping, keep trusting, and keep waiting on the Lord, for he is tenderhearted, kind, and forgiving. He has a thousand ways to set you free! He himself will redeem you; he will ransom you from the cruel slavery of your sins!

PSALM 130:7–8 TPT

Hope is about the future. Yesterday is done, but the dawning of today brings new promise. While trusting in God's goodness, we can find ourselves in a time of waiting. Maybe the thing you have been praying about for so long still seems out of reach. Possibly you are yearning to hear the voice of God and are feeling discouraged in the season he has you enduring. Ground your expectations firmly upon his unfailing love, mercy, and power to restore the situations that seem impossible.

Remember the widow's jars that were continually filled with precious oil? The redemption of vile King Manasseh? The resurrection of Jesus Christ? Often in history, things looked far too bleak to ever recover, but then God stepped in. Petition the Holy Spirit for great faith. Remember God's kindness and generosity. Trust in him to save you from the many temptations you face daily. Never give up. Believe him for the miracle.

Lord, thank you! Let me be a bearer of the hope that your life, love, mercy, and grace bring. Amen.

He Will Guide You

"I am the LORD your God,
who brought you out of Egypt,
out of the land of slavery."
ExODUS 20:2 NIV

Can you remember a time when you were a slave to sin? There are so many varying testimonies. As young children, some accept Jesus, so we don't have live with the memories of the times they chose self over Jesus. They never have to fight the Enemy when he attempts to shame them as he fills their mind with pictures of their rebellious past. Others live wild and dangerously before they come to the end of themselves and go to God. Some find him on their deathbed. Regardless of how or when, our Father desires to save everyone in his creation. He wants to deliver us from the bondage we have chosen and bring us to redemption, transforming us into the likeness of his Son.

Even after we have given our lives to Christ, we face temptation that tries to tear us away from a righteous path. Stop and recall all the times God has stepped in, giving you the strength to say no to temptation. If you turn to him for help, he will guide you away from the treacherous road to transgression.

Father, help me always turn to you when I am tempted. Help me choose the righteous way. Amen.

Ask and Receive

"Ask, and the gift is yours. Seek, and you'll discover.
Knock, and the door will be opened for you."
MATTHEW 7:7 TPT

Do you feel you fall short of God's command to love him with all your heart, soul, mind, and strength? Does it cause you to feel very inadequate in your affection for him? Don't linger on listening to the Enemy's whisper of discouragement. Realize that God never asks anything of us that he doesn't provide the power and wherewithal to fulfill. When we feel lacking in love, we should ask him to fill us to overflowing. If you need to, keep asking every day, for the truth is that we could always love him more.

We could always surrender more to his plan. We know we could be better students of the Word. We long to share the gospel more. There is no request too big for God. Don't settle, because Jesus said that all you need to do is ask. Remember the story of the man who woke his neighbor up to ask for bread for a late-night visitor? He persevered until he got what he wanted (Luke 11:5–13). That should inspire us! Be persistent in seeking God, and you'll see the mountain move on your behalf.

Lord, give me the faith to know I will receive what I ask of you.
Amen.

One Job

Jesus came close to them and said, "All authority of the universe has been given to me. Now wherever you go, make disciples of all nations, baptizing them in the name of the Father, the Son, and the Holy Spirit. And teach them to faithfully follow all that I have commanded you. And never forget that I am with you every day, even to the completion of this age."

MATTHEW 28:18–20 TPT

Possibly at one time, someone said these demoralizing words to you: "You had one job." Perhaps when you were a teenager, your parents left you at home and said, "Don't forget to do your chores," and when they returned, they found you watching TV and the tasks undone. Has a boss had to confront you about an assignment you forgot that resulted in dire consequences? Nothing will break our hearts as much as standing before Jesus knowing we neglected to fulfill the Great Commission.

When he left earth, he gave his followers one job, and that was to make disciples. Whether we feel called to go to a foreign land or stay at home, we're all to share the gospel and assist in the growth of those who receive Christ. We're to lead new believers to baptism. We must help them learn and follow God's commands.

Jesus, help me fulfill your Great Commission. Amen.

Wrong Motives

Even when you ask, you don't get it because your motives are
all wrong—you want only what will give you pleasure.
JAMES 4:3 NLT

Sometimes our prayer list can resemble a child's Christmas list.
It's a plethora of our wants, not our needs. If you feel like your
prayers are hitting the wall and remain unanswered, you may
want to review your requests. Ask why you are praying the way
that you are. Inquire of your own heart whom your desire will
benefit if granted. Will it bring glory to God, draw people to
Jesus, or just feed your own pleasure? We are to be heavenly
minded, storing up treasures in heaven by the good work we do
for the kingdom while on earth.

If all we are concerned with is asking God to give us the
same vacation that our neighbor had, we need to reboot. When
we desire to honor God, we will have a shift in what we ask of
him. We'll start to petition him for the things that are on his
heart. Refocus your purpose by agreeing with God, interceding
for others, and calling on him to fill you with his power to do
his will.

Jesus, help me pray the concerns that are on your heart. Keep my
requests heavenly minded. Amen.

Love without Limits

May [you] have power, together with all the Lord's holy people,
to grasp how wide and long and high and deep is the love
of Christ.

EPHESIANS 3:18 NIV

Do you ever feel that you are separated from God or from his
love? This happens when we have sinned or moved away from
our first love, replacing him with other things. Due to sin, we
retreat in shame. We find ourselves entertaining idols because
we take our eyes off Jesus and focus them on our pleasure. We
must confess and surrender to Christ. We need to then move
forward without any condemnation, for nothing can truly
remove us from his affection. Romans 8:35 asks, "Who shall
separate us from the love of Christ?" (NIV). The chapter goes
on to declare that nothing can. Even when we transgress again,
as we will while on this earth, God calls us to confess and be
forgiven.

Realize how great his love is for you. It surpasses any
human understanding. It is complete and without limits. May
we never distance ourselves from God but crave that every
minute brings us closer to him. May we all comprehend how
much he desires us and adores us. Let us return his love in the
way we obey and follow Jesus.

Father, I am grateful that your love for me is eternal. Amen.

Every Thought

You are so intimately aware of me, Lord. You read my heart like an open book and you know all the words I'm about to speak before I even start a sentence! You know every step I will take before my journey even begins.

PSALM 139:3–4 TPT

Consider that God knows every thought and every intent of your heart. He determined how your life will play out. Does that make you want to sit and have a long conversation with him, inquiring about what he has seen in you now and in your future? Or does it make you want to climb under the covers and stay there?

If you are afraid God will see the condition of your heart, confess it and start fresh with him. If you are frightened about his will for your future, ask for faith to trust him and wait in hopeful expectation. Find wonder in the fact that he knows the words you will speak or pray before you even say them. Rejoice that because he knows your yet-to-be-spoken requests, he is already at work preparing the answer. Praise him because wherever you place your foot, he has already gone ahead of you.

God, thank you for how intimately you know me and how you determine my path. Amen.

Unmovable

Neither death, nor life, nor angels, nor principalities, nor things
present, nor things to come, nor powers, nor height, nor depth,
nor any other creature, shall be able to separate us from the
love of God, which is in Christ Jesus our Lord.

ROMANS 8:38–39 ASV

Have you ever had the feeling that someone is following you?
Have you ever had a visitor come to your home and been unable
to influence them to leave? If you have ever had anyone with a
differing opinion continually try to wear you down until you
agree with them, then you know the meaning of what never-
ending feels like. These are situations you want to shake but
can't. It is a whole different story when we look at scenarios like
these in the light of today's verse.

We rejoice that God will always go with us and that our
relationship with him is unbreakable, lasting from now through
eternity. We are comforted that nothing, no person, and no
occurrence can remove us from his presence. Our standing with
God in Christ is unmovable, and we are sealed with his Holy
Spirit. Go boldly to do his will, believing that he will always be
right at your side, loving, guiding, and protecting you. Praise
him, for he is and always will be your Abba, best friend, Savior,
and constant companion.

Father, impart your love to me, not as a concept but as a lived
experience. Amen.

Eager to Share

Give reverent honor in your hearts to the Anointed One and treat him as the holy Master of your lives. And if anyone asks about the hope living within you, always be ready to explain your faith.

1 PETER 3:15 TPT

A non-believer once said, "If you Christians really believe what you say you do, you would really have to hate your neighbor not to share it." Convicting? Yes. True? Yes. If we do not care where others spend eternity, either we have a misunderstanding of how horrible hell is, or we just don't care. If it is the first, read what Jesus said about hell in Scripture. If it is the latter, then we probably need a heart check. Possibly even a look into our soul to see if we have truly made Jesus Lord of our life.

If you know him and are not open about your faith, do you really revere who he is and the gravity of the fact that he holds the keys to life and death? If persecution comes, are you ready to stand for Christ even if it means your demise? We must know in advance how we will tell the good news and what we'll say if someone asks us about our stance with God.

Jesus, help me to be eager to boldly share the gospel. Amen.

He Will Strengthen Us

Be strong and take heart,
all you who hope in the LORD.
PSALM 31:24 NIV

If we are in Christ, no matter what befalls us, he will strengthen and deliver us. Whether he delivers us on this earth or ushers us into his kingdom, we can trust that he always performs what is best for us. When we feel our heart failing, we should build it up by searching his Word, for his Word is truth. When our hope is dwindling, we must shore it up by submitting ourselves in prayer to his faithfulness. When we are confused, we should seek godly counsel and ask others to intercede for us to hear from God. If our faith is weak, we must ask the Lord to strengthen us. If we truly know and believe the Lord is who he says he is and we continually stay connected to our Vine, then we will have peace and confidence that cannot be shaken. If we believe our God for what he can do, we will never faint.

Our God is all-powerful, all knowing, sovereign, and the definition of love. He never fails us, cannot be thwarted, and will always have the victory.

Father, today, I will lift my voice to give you thanks. Your love never fails, and your presence never leaves me. Amen.

Point Them to Jesus

God has not destined us for wrath,
but to obtain salvation through our Lord Jesus Christ.
1 Thessalonians 5:9 ESV

Our world is in a current state where many people are thinking about the end times. Wars, rumors of wars, major earthquakes, and famines spring up in various places. The coming tribulation and antichrist are all reported in the Bible. Scripture tells us to be aware of the signs of the times. Toward the end of days, people will call evil good and good evil. Look around and you will notice that sin is in abundance.

How should a Christian regard these times? Look for every opportunity to share your faith and glorify God with your remaining days. As believers, we are not appointed unto wrath, for we have been redeemed by the blood of the Lamb. So many are still destined for God's punishment, and we should do all we can to point them to Jesus before it is too late. Today is the day of salvation. Don't hold off, for every day we get closer to the events of the tribulation and the return of Christ. Point people to Jesus before the day of wrath comes. How will they know unless we tell them?

Father, may I stay alert to your Word: your instructions, guidance, warnings, and promises. Amen.

August

Divine Defender

I lie down and sleep; I wake again,
because the LORD sustains me.

PSALM 3:5 NIV

The first thing we should do every morning is to thank God for blessing us with another day of life. From the sun coming up to the breath that we take, it is only because God ordains it. When David wrote this psalm, he was fleeing from someone who meant him harm. He recalled prior times when God rescued him from danger, granting David peaceful sleep and assurance that God's heavenly eye remained on him through the night watch. David knew beyond a shadow of a doubt that his salvation was from the Lord. He could praise him in the midst of trouble because God had a perfect track record for being his deliver and sustainer.

Would the Lord do any less for us? He will most definitely provide for and protect us just the same as he did David. God loves his children, and his promises extend to all who believe in and call on his name. If you are facing hardship or peril, trust your divine defender to fight for you, preserve you, and bring you through triumphantly.

Lord, thank you for always having your eyes on me. I gain great assurance from knowing you are in control of everything that affects me. Amen.

God's Provision

The LORD is a refuge for the oppressed, a stronghold in times
of trouble. Those who know your name trust in you, for you,
LORD, have never forsaken those who seek you.

PSALM 9:9–10 NIV

In the book *The Heavenly Man*, a pregnant woman's husband
was imprisoned for "preaching Jesus," leaving her and her
mother-in-law to run their farm despite having no experience
or knowledge about farming. When the time came to plant
potatoes, the women did their best. Their neighbors, who were
also farmers, refused to help them, for it was considered a
disgrace to have a husband in prison. They laughed and scorned
the women for planting the potatoes all wrong. But when
harvest time came, their neighbors' crops failed, and the women
had a bountiful harvest. Despite their neighbors' rudeness, the
women shared with them.[4]

God has unlimited ways of caring for those who seek and
serve him. The husband in the story was truly honored to suffer
for Jesus, and as he did, God provided spiritually, emotionally,
physically, and financially for the man's wife and mother.

Father, thank you for being my safe tower, my provider, and my
Lord. Amen.

---

4   Brother Yun and Paul Hattaway, *The Heavenly Man: The Remarkable
     True Story of Chinese Christian Brother Yun* (Grand Rapids, MI: Kregel
     Publications, 2002).

He Is Supreme

He is the Rock, his works are perfect, and all his ways are just.
A faithful God who does no wrong, upright and just is he.
DEUTERONOMY 32:4 NIV

God is perfection. He alone controls the sky, the sea, and all they contain. He determines the length of days for every life that exists or ever existed. Nothing happens in any capacity without God's foreknowledge or approval. He is never wrong, always righteous, and extends us his mercy and grace although we never deserve it. Have you ever known anyone else who fits this description? Oh, there may be many people who think themselves perfect, even godlike. But they are far from correct. All humanity is sinful, and only God is without transgression. We stand in stark contrast to the holiness of our heavenly Father.

Worship him and him only. Praise him because, in his supremacy, he determined you worthy of his Son's life. The Creator loved his creatures enough to take their wrongdoing on his own back, die for them, and give them life. Live in awe of your glorious God and King, for he gave everything that was precious to him in order to have you.

Jesus, I am grateful that, in your perfection, you reached down to save a sinner such as me. Amen.

Our Rescuer

Rejoice not over me, O my enemy; when I fall, I shall rise;
when I sit in darkness, the LORD will be a light to me.
MICAH 7:8 ESV

Have you ever heard a story where a bully was picking on
someone smaller and younger? The older one laughed at the
younger one. The littler one cowered, but upon remembering that
he had a defender, he puffed out his chest. He knew his protector
was more than able and would arrive on the scene just in time.
As the large aggressor raised a fist and aimed squarely at the
little boy's jaw, a sharp blow took the bully off his feet. A much
larger boy, the little one's older brother, stepped in to squelch the
attack. As the bully lay on the ground, the victor stood over him,
warning him never to come close to his brother again.

Do you know that we can place ourselves in that little
boy's shoes? We have a defender who will one day send our
enemy to his destruction. The next time Satan comes after you,
remind him of your Father and the damning future that awaits
the Evil One. God is our rescuer. We have a future and a hope;
our enemy does not.

Lord, thank you for lifting me out of darkness to stand in your
light. Amen.

Glimpse His Glory

Then one of the seraphim flew to me with a live coal in his hand, which he had taken with tongs from the altar. With it he touched my mouth and said, "See, this has touched your lips; your guilt is taken away and your sin atoned for."

Isaiah 6:6–7 NIV

Isaiah saw the Lord seated on his heavenly throne, surrounded by seraphim. These angelic beings repeated "Holy, holy, holy is the LORD of hosts; the whole earth is filled with his glory!" (Isaiah 6:3 ESV). Isaiah was immediately struck by his unworthiness and his unclean lips. God then sent one of the seraphim to touch Isaiah's lips with a burning coal taken from the altar. With this action, Isaiah's sins were atoned for. Then came the well-known question from God about whom he would send, who would go and deliver God's message. Can't you picture Isaiah jumping up and down, hand raised high, saying, "Here I am, choose me, send me!" And with that offer, the Lord revealed a message for Isaiah to take to the Israelites.

Isaiah had a glimpse of God's holiness that resulted in sanctification. May we recognize our great need and be eternally cleansed by the fire of the cross.

Father, I long for my life to be a sweet-smelling fragrance before you, my Lord—my Redeemer. Amen.

His Continued Presence

Because of you, I know the path of life, as I taste the fullness of joy in your presence. At your right side I experience divine pleasures forevermore!

PSALM 16:11 TPT

When someone first presents the gospel to us, we must make a choice. We face a fork in the road, and whichever way we decide to go will determine our life here on earth and where we spend eternity. For those who choose Christ, there is the promise of his continued presence with the believer. There is the expectation that God will flower our path in life with spiritual abundance. We will be filled with rejoicing as we experience a close walk with the Creator of the universe. There will be a change in our countenance, for we will shine with the light of life.

As we continue to trust in the Lord we will never be without and will never be shaken, for he will be our portion and our defender. We will maintain a different outlook than the world, for we will now store our treasures in heaven. The pleasure that was ours in this life will follow us into and throughout eternity, for we will always be with the lover of our soul.

Jesus, I am overwhelmed with joy that I belong to you. Amen.

Feeling Abandoned

About three in the afternoon Jesus cried out in a loud voice,
"Eli, Eli, lema sabachthani?" (which means "My God, my God,
why have you forsaken me?").

MATTHEW 27:46 NIV

There has been much concern in recent years regarding the
level of loneliness people in our modern times are experiencing.
The number of young men and women who report feelings of
frequent or chronic loneliness is staggering. More often than
not, adults are not relying on friends to share their burdens.
Even though all this may be true, we will never have to know
the depth of abandonment that Jesus felt while on the cross.
He felt, as we do at times, that his Father had left him. Can you
picture God turning away so that Jesus couldn't see him weep at
his Son's suffering?

The Lord never forsakes any of us. There is no place you
can go where your heavenly Father is not with you. You never
leave his sight or his tender care. Nothing can separate you from
the love of God.

Jesus, thank you for your promise to never leave me or forsake
me. I receive it, stand upon it, and rest and abide in it. Amen.

The Spirit's Intercession

Likewise the Spirit helps us in our weakness. For we do not
know what to pray for as we ought, but the Spirit himself
intercedes for us with groanings too deep for words.

ROMANS 8:26 ESV

If you have ever been at a loss for words, you probably identify
with today's verse. There are times when trials hit us so hard
that all we can do is cry. We wonder how God will respond to
our difficulty if we can't even tell him what we need. Be assured
that even if you can't verbalize it, God knows what you need
before you can even formulate a sentence. He even knows what
his answer will be prior to your inquiry. We also have the gift
of the intercession of the Holy Spirit. He anticipates when our
words won't come, and he prays for us.

Isn't that downright amazing? God's Spirit steps in
and goes to the throne on our behalf! The Spirit's groaning,
advocating, for us with a message beyond our comprehension
can give us hope. Our inability to pray should never discourage
us from approaching God, but in times of deep despair, we
know our Father hears our needs and will meet them.

Holy Spirit, I am grateful that when my hurt is so deep that the
words won't come, you are praying for me. Amen.

God Is in Control

> "Say to him, 'Be careful, keep calm and don't be afraid. Do not lose heart because of these two smoldering stubs of firewood—because of the fierce anger of Rezin and Aram and of the son of Remaliah.'"
>
> ISAIAH 7:4 NIV

You know that a situation is brewing that could rock your world and not in a good way. You panic and start to consider all the people who will be your allies. You strive to have everyone see your view of things and jump on your bandwagon. When it feels like you're in the middle of a battle, don't let panic overtake you, or you may find yourself in Ahaz's shoes, trusting the strength of man instead of the all-powerful God. Instead, intentionally come to the Lord and bring your battered emotions, concern, and doubts to him, asking him to help you trust in him alone. Don't exchange faith for fear. The Father will wrap you in his arms all while fighting your battle and bringing victory.

He admonishes us, helping us to remember that he is in control and we are not. God will establish and carry out the fight. We can be assured a win is in sight. His good will is going to be accomplished.

Lord, thank you for your abiding peace. I surrender to and trust in you. Amen.

Kindness, Justice, Righteousness

"Let the one who boasts boast about this: that they have the
understanding to know me, that I am the LORD, who exercises
kindness, justice and righteousness on earth, for in these I
delight," declares the LORD.

JEREMIAH 9:24 NIV

Consider the definitions of the words *kindness*, *justice*, and
righteousness, which describe our heavenly Father. *Kindness:*
"the quality or state of being kind; favor; affection."[5] *Justice:* "the
maintenance or administration of what is just especially by the
impartial adjustment of conflicting claims or the assignment
of merited rewards or punishments."[6] *Righteousness:* "acting in
accord with divine or moral law: free from guilt or sin."[7]

Would any of us treat with kindness, justice, and
righteousness someone who has sinned against us so heinously?
Unlikely. But our perfect I AM is loving, compassionate,
forgiving, merciful, righteous, wise, all-knowing, ever-present,
trustworthy, and so much more. So let's share who he is with the
world, proclaiming his faithfulness and love.

Jesus, I want the world to know how good you are. I want people
everywhere to praise you. Amen.

---

5   *Merriam-Webster.com Dictionary*, s.v. "kindness."
6   *Merriam-Webster.com Dictionary*, s.v. "justice."
7   *Merriam-Webster.com Dictionary*, s.v. "righteous."

The Good Shepherd

Come, let us bow down in worship, let us kneel before the LORD our Maker; for he is our God and we are the people of his pasture, the flock under his care.

PSALM 95:6–7 NIV

When you consider all that a shepherd does to care for and protect his flock, it should evoke a feeling of security and love to be one of the Savior's sheep. The shepherd is on duty round the clock. He leads his sheep, and they follow. He makes sure their needs are met. He keeps them safe as they sleep. If one strays, he gently leads it back with his staff. If that doesn't coerce it, he will use his rod. His flock responds to his voice.

We may not be actual sheep, but there are similarities. We must respond to the Savior's voice to be saved. We must follow him as he leads us. We can depend on him to supply our needs. We know that if we backslide, he will gently but firmly discipline us. We know that whether we're awake or asleep, his eye is on us, protecting us. He is the Good Shepherd, and we're his beloved sheep. Stay close to your Shepherd Savior, and he'll guide you safely to your eternal home.

Jesus, I rejoice that I'm your beloved sheep. Amen.

Be Obedient

"If you are willing and obedient,
you will eat the good things of the land."

ISAIAH 1:19 NIV

God is entirely gracious with us, forgiving us without limit, loving us when we do not return love, and remaining faithful even when we are unfaithful. This is an astounding affection that is hard to understand and one we are incapable of. We want to love him fully, but we fail, and in his grace, he accepts our confessions and assures us of his care. If we want to show how we delight in him, we will be obedient to his commands. We will choose good over evil passionately, keeping our feet firmly on the narrow road. When we reverence his ways, desiring to live as Jesus did, he will not withhold any good thing from us. We will experience abundance in our spirit and receive provisions that fulfill our needs.

What incredible mercy God shows us when we once again trample on his heart by giving in to temptation. We will not be void of sin this side of heaven, but instead of putting us in a corner of shame, he woos us with his invitation to come close, confess our sin, and encounter his extravagant love.

Jesus, help me to be willing to serve you no matter what. Give me a heart that longs to obey you. Amen.

He Trusts God

Reach down your hand from on high; deliver me and rescue me from the mighty waters, from the hands of foreigners.

PSALM 144:7 NIV

The Davidic king is appealing to God for deliverance for him, his people, and all their children. He begins with praise to his Lord, the one who steadfastly loves him, the One he runs to for refuge. This is clearly a man who knows and trusts God. He believes that when he boldly requests that the Lord stretch out his hand and save them from deceitful foreigners, God will do it. He knows that he and his people will be blessed, for the Lord is their God.

When he petitions God that their sheep will greatly multiply, their children will prosper, and their city will be free from suffering, he trusts that God will answer yes. He has undeniable faith that all he asks of his heavenly Father will come to pass, for he knows how trustworthy his God is. He does not wait to see the results before raising his voice in songs of praise. Worship him as you watch him reach down his hand from on high to protect and bring the victory to his own.

Lord, may I remember to sing my praises to you in worship and with a grateful heart. Amen.

His Goodness

"The LORD bless you and keep you; the LORD make his face
to shine upon you and be gracious to you; the LORD lift up his
countenance upon you and give you peace."

NUMBERS 6:24–26 ESV

If we could achieve a life that resembles a dream come true, the aspects of today's verse would describe it. What could be more fulfilling, more wonderful than having our eternal Father bless us, look at us with loving eyes, and gift us his amazing grace. Just to think that he even considers us, people whom the Bible refers to as "dust," is mind boggling. Yet he takes his divine eraser and blots out all our transgressions.

We are sinners, dirty to the depths of our soul, but he values us so much that he went to the most extreme lengths to cleanse us. He will not neglect to grant us forgiveness but has also gone to great lengths to give us the kingdom. He is the Lord Most High, whose face shines with pride as he looks at us. He desires to show us grace for all our days so that we may live a life of peace. Meditate on his goodness today and give him abundant praise.

God, I am overwhelmed by your great love. You are everything to
me. Amen.

Serving Our God

"See, I am doing a new thing! Now it springs up; do you not perceive it? I am making a way in the wilderness and streams in the wasteland."

Isaiah 43:19 NIV

At times, my soul feels as though I am in a dry wilderness—a wasteland of uselessness without purpose. Do you ever feel this way? The Holy Spirit can help you and me to go beyond our emotions and look to Jesus, the only one who can and will quench our thirst and fill our drained spirits with his boundless provision of hope and joy. That joy springs from the knowledge that God did not leave us in our deep hole of sin but created rebirth through the crucifixion of his Son.

There is no limit to what the Lord can do in and through us, anointing and equipping his new creations in Christ. When we commit to his will, what once seemed hopeless becomes full of possibilities. A person who once believed there was no future is now expectant with thoughts of completing the plan God created them for. The adventure of open doors thrills a heart privileged to join the Lord in the work he is doing. We are blessed to be serving our God.

Father, use me up, and may I fulfill your purpose for me. Amen.

Pray without Ceasing

After he had sent the multitudes away, he went up into the mountain apart to pray: and when even was come, he was there alone.

MATTHEW 14:23 ASV

If we need a perfect example to follow to get us into the mindset of consistent prayer, Jesus is it. It's a bit hard to understand the God-man praying to God, but if Jesus knew prayer was needed, how much more should we be engaging in consistent prayer. Jesus often went away by himself to pray, enabling him to focus solely on his heavenly Father. We, too, need that special place, a prayer closet to create that alone time with God.

We know from the Word that the fervent prayer of a righteous man carries much power with it. When we intercede with passion, it moves the heart of God. The Word says to pray without ceasing. We may have times during the day when we can't find a secluded spot, but we should still whisper our needs to the Lord regardless of where we are.

Father, help me place a priority on prayer. Amen.

Be Righteous Representatives

This is what the LORD Almighty says:
"Give careful thought to your ways."
HAGGAI 1:7 NIV

If we only had a dollar for every misspoken, flippant, or rude word we ever voiced, we would all be rich. Careful thought prior to opening one's mouth is a rare thing. When we act out on the hurtful or violent words we say, we can leave a wake of wreckage. Marriages, friendships, and work relationships can all be destroyed with that little tongue of ours that is capable of setting a fire.

Any type of relationship is hard to repair after being damaged by careless behavior. This is exactly why God tells us in his Word to give careful thought to our words and ways. What we do affects others, whether they are unbelievers, fellow Christ followers, or new Christians. People love to people watch, and what they see, they may choose to emulate. We want to be righteous representatives of Jesus. If you struggle with controlling your speech and the way you act toward others, confess and request help from the Lord. Once we do that, we can embrace the power of the Holy Spirit to help us change. He desires to help you become more like the Savior.

Dear Lord, may I give careful thought to the way I act, think, and speak. May I represent you well to others. Amen.

Brought Near

In Christ Jesus you who once were far off
have been brought near by the blood of Christ.
EPHESIANS 2:13 ESV

Oh, the glorious love of Jesus that he came to seek and save the
lost. We were so far from God that we might as well have been
in a deep dark hole. We think if we were the only living thing
lost in a secluded forest that no one could find us. We believe
that if we traveled secretly to a faraway land, we would stay out
of sight and mind. Not so when it comes to our heavenly Father.

He chose us before we were even a single cell. He
predestined the work we would do for his kingdom before we
existed in the womb. He understood that it would be impossible
for us to approach him without the sacrifice that spilled his
Son's blood. Yet he would go to the ends of the world to make us
his own. There's no greater act of love than the cross of Christ.
If it were possible for us to be in another galaxy, God would still
see us, come after us, and give his precious Son so that he could
know us and we could seek to know him.

Father, thank you for going to the greatest lengths, namely giving
up your Son, Jesus, to save me. Amen.

Holy Fear

"The LORD Almighty is the one you are to regard as holy,
he is the one you are to fear, he is the one you are to dread."

ISAIAH 8:13 NIV

The Hebrew word translated as "fear" in today's verse is closer to what we understand as "deep respect" or "worship." Love is the foundation of our relationship with God, but "fear of God" is the stabilizer that helps us make wise choices, demonstrating our love for him. This fear should make us want to obey and make us look up to God with the hope of pleasing him in all we do. It should move us to avoid his disapproving eye or his discipline. Scripture says the fear of the Lord is the beginning of wisdom. Once we attain understanding, we must stay on the straight and narrow to escape sin and temptation. We want to live our lives as his treasured, obedient possessions.

The Word says, "It is a fearful thing to fall into the hands of the living God" (Hebrews 10:31 ESV). At the judgment seat, those who rejected Jesus in life will be sentenced. This fear is one that should cause us to shudder, realizing that their separation from God will last for eternity. Revere the living God and always give him the esteem that is due to him.

Jesus, may I live in the fearful wonder of who you are, and may I
guard my heart at all times. Amen.

Presenting Ourselves

Let us draw near to God with a sincere heart and with the full assurance that faith brings, having our hearts sprinkled to cleanse us from a guilty conscience and having our bodies washed with pure water.

HEBREWS 10:22 NIV

If we became intimate friends with King Charles III, we would feel rather humbled. Yet that friendship would pale drastically in comparison to the intimate relationship the great Creator offers to us. There is no one more holy, righteous, or renowned than our God. Isn't it the most amazing thought that he longs for our fellowship, friendship, and intimacy?

God knows how often we run around in a state of high distraction, leaving him out in the waiting room of our lives. His love is constantly wooing us and longing for us. He desires to give us true meaning, relevance, peace, contentment, and joy, which can only be accomplished through him.

As we present ourselves before his throne, let us search our hearts and make them pure. Because of Jesus, we can go to him without guilt or condemnation. May we be bold in faith, knowing that our confessed sins have been forgiven, washed in the blood of Christ.

Lord, help me to listen as your Holy Spirit guides me then to be willing to follow where you lead. Thank you, God. Amen.

Share with All People

The apostles and the believers throughout Judea heard that the Gentiles also had received the word of God. So when Peter went up to Jerusalem, the circumcised believers criticized him.

ACTS 11:1–2 NIV

Have you ever found yourself judging another Christian for their differences? We are bonded in Christ while coming from various backgrounds and having individual personalities. We all have opinions, but some of those thoughts should never cross our lips. Peter was entrusted with the Great Commission by Christ and was with Jesus when he spoke to the Samaritan woman. He was filled with the Holy Spirit yet held on to the prejudice that the gospel's redeeming love was only for the Jews. How often we cling to concepts that impair our relationship with God and man!

Note that in Acts 11, Peter was in prayer when God sent the vision, saying, "Do not call anything impure that God has made clean" (v. 9 NIV). Let our hearts beat with the same love that led Christ to Calvary so that we share his gospel of saving grace with all people. Just as Jesus told Peter was told to share the good news with the world, so Jesus has also told us.

Dear Lord, please remove barriers that hold me from being about your business. Amen.

Losing Everything to Gain Christ

Jesus looked at him and loved him. "One thing you lack," he said. "Go, sell everything you have and give to the poor, and you will have treasure in heaven. Then come, follow me."

MARK 10:21 NIV

One thing that the Enemy has convinced this world of is that we need more, bigger, better, and that once we get it, we must hoard it. This was the case with the rich young ruler. He had accumulated wealth and couldn't part with it, not even for Jesus. This story is recorded in three gospels. He is perhaps the only person who encountered Jesus with hopes of finding that which his heart longed for and left the encounter feeling sad. He couldn't give up the lifestyle he so enjoyed, even though his soul yearned for eternal life.

We don't know if later this young man decided to follow Jesus, but we hope for his sake he did. God forgives us for the many times we choose our own paths and fail to surrender to him. May our lifestyles not deter us from daily committing to the path he chooses for us. Be willing to lose everything to gain Christ.

Jesus, I want to lose my life in order to gain it. Help me devalue material things and store up my treasures in heaven. Amen.

Receiving Correction

The ear that listens to life-giving reproof
will dwell among the wise.

PROVERBS 15:31 ESV

In our flesh, it is hard to receive correction. In the moment, we very seldom welcome correction as something we appreciate. We might feel offended or embarrassed or that our actions or words were misunderstood. After we determine that the giver has offered the advice with the right motives, we need to consider if the information is scripturally accurate. If it is biblically correct, we can take an honest look at ourselves and see where we need to make improvement. If what we have done requires forgiveness, we should rush to seek it. Then we are wise to pray, asking for God's help to make the necessary changes. We know that without Jesus, we can do nothing, so we should gain strength from acknowledging that he is doing the work in us. As we surrender to his correction and growth in us, we will gain wisdom, maturity, and knowledge about how to better walk with our Lord.

May we be willing to humble ourselves before God and those of wise council, accepting and pursuing his path. We will reap the reward, for God hears and answers the prayers of the righteous.

Dear Lord, help me be humble when you reprove me. Please guide the trajectory of my life. Amen.

Hold Others Up

Moses hands were heavy; and they took a stone, and put it under him, and he sat thereon; and Aaron and Hur stayed up his hands, the one on the one side, and the other on the other side; and his hands were steady until the going down of the sun.

EXODUS 17:12 KJV

While the Israelites were camped out at Rephidim, they experienced their first attack since leaving Egypt. Moses commissioned Joshua to take some men and go fight. The next day, Moses went with Aaron and Hur to the top of a hill and extended God's staff. Whenever Moses held the staff in his hand high, God worked to deliver the Israelites and they prevailed. When he succumbed to his weak human strength and dropped the staff, the Amalek's began to win. Aaron and Hur found a rock for Moses to sit on and lifted his arms, holding them up when he couldn't.

We should support others with service and prayer when they are in the midst of battle. Let's never let our busy schedule override the decision to run to aid another believer. May we lovingly come alongside them in agreement until their enemy is conquered as we look to Jesus, our Victor.

Jesus, help me do whatever it takes to assist others in Christ. Amen.

Humbly Submit

Hezekiah humbled himself for the pride of his heart, both
he and the inhabitants of Jerusalem, so that the wrath of the
LORD did not come upon them in the days of Hezekiah.

2 CHRONICLES 32:26 ESV

Sennacherib and Hezekiah were nothing alike. Hezekiah was
a great and righteous king with only one act of pride recorded
against him. Prior to the attack of Assyria, Hezekiah had prayed
for God to extend his life. When God granted his request,
Hezekiah became proud by parading his wealth before some
envoys from Babylonia. Hezekiah then incurred God's wrath,
which caused Hezekiah to humble himself and seek forgiveness,
and he and his people were spared.

Sennacherib, king of Assyria, was a violent and wicked
king. He bragged that God would never be able to deliver God's
people from their hand, but that is exactly what the almighty
Lord did. Sennacherib went home in defeat and was killed by
his own sons.

May we not allow our past to define our future, either
through thinking we are such vile sinners that God cannot
forgive us or through feeling we have lived so well that pride
flourishes.

Lord, may I daily submit to you in humility, remembering that
all good things come from you and faithfully sharing your love,
mercy, and grace. Amen.

At the Altar

"Will God indeed dwell with man on the earth?
Behold, heaven and the highest heaven cannot contain you,
how much less this house that I have built!"
2 CHRONICLES 6:18 ESV

Solomon knelt before all of Israel at the altar and asked God
to hear his prayers and the prayers of his people in that place.
Solomon had constructed a bronze platform and set it in the
court where all the assembly could have access. Solomon
requested that the Lord keep his eyes open day and night
toward this altar and on those who would frequent it to
intercede for themselves and others. He prayed that God would
hear from his heaven and forgive.

Although God does not sit on an earthly throne, he
always hears from his heavenly one. Not only does God walk
with us while we are on this earth, but his Spirit also lives within
us. With Christ as our Messiah, we experience an intimate
relationship with the triune God. Whether we are asleep or
awake, lighthearted, or burdened, God has promised to be with
us, never to leave us—and we can count on him. Even in our
sin, he is there, longing, in pure love, to set us free from that
which would destroy us.

Father, thank you for your continual presence and grace. Amen.

Pray for Wisdom

His delight shall be in the fear of Jehovah;
and he shall not judge after the sight of his eyes,
neither decide after the hearing of his ears.

ISAIAH 11:3 ASV

So many messages bombard us daily. Screens of all sizes beg
for our attention. We become anxious if we haven't checked
our cell phones in the last ten minutes. Worldly opinions,
advertisements, and the way people alter and conduct their lives
threaten to sway us to believe things that are contrary to God's
Word. At times, we would be better off if we wore blinders and
ear plugs.

The best thing we can do, truthfully, is to saturate
ourselves with God's Word. We need to attend church regularly
and be in fellowship with other believers. We must pray for
wisdom, discernment, and the knowledge we need to avoid
any of the pitfalls this culture or our enemy would place in our
path. May we surrender all that we are—thoughts, motives, and
actions—to God. May we be captivated with God's holiness as
we encounter his presence, not basing our faith on feelings or
our current circumstances. Ask the Spirit to protect us from the
words and actions of those who seek to quench our faith in God
and his Word.

Dear Lord, may my mind be stayed on God with a great desire to
please him. Amen.

Spiritual Wings

"As an eagle that protects its nest, that flutters over its young,
He spread out His wings and took them, He carried them on
His pinions."

DEUTERONOMY 32:11 AMP

The eagle knows when it is the right time to push her babies out
of the nest and let them try to fly solo. She keeps a watchful eye
on them, ready at any moment to swoop in if they experience
trouble. At the sign of a serious struggle, she saves the day by
scooping the one in danger up in the security of her wings.

This is a wonderful example of our loving, patient God.
He desires for us to mature in our faith, stretch our spiritual
wings, and grow in Christlikeness. He knows we will be tempted
and, at times, succumb to sin. It is then when he pricks our
conscience and draws our heart to confession so that we can
be restored to close relationship with him. He goes before us,
behind us, and all around, eyes always on us and ready at any
moment to fight our battles alongside us or for us. With God by
our side, we will spiritually mature and have security in victory.

*Dear Lord, thank you for nudging me over the edge toward new
adventure in you and for catching me while I learn to fly. Amen.*

Dark Deeds

It is shameful even to mention
what the disobedient do in secret.

EPHESIANS 5:12 NIV

This is a verse that Christians rarely talk about, yet it carries so much instruction. Think about how it must grieve God when he views the evil that his creation devises in their minds and perpetrates with their actions. There is nothing he does not know and nothing he does not see, and if we were privy to that view, we would most assuredly turn away. We must search our hearts to see if we indulge in discussing these dark deeds. Do we gossip about the wrongdoings we have heard through the grapevine? Do we work to walk as Jesus did then expose ourselves to media that opposes the Word of God? What excuse do we voice in our mind to make it acceptable to watch movies or television shows that lay bare and approve of what the disobedient do in secret?

There is great advice in today's verse, and we would do well to follow it. It is *shameful* to mention, let alone watch or dip our toe into, the things that those who live opposed to the Word of God do in the darkness. Don't enter into evil through what you view, read, or say.

Father, help me guard my heart and eyes from evil deeds. Amen.

Adopted in Christ

Because you are sons, God has sent the Spirit of his Son into our hearts, crying, "Abba! Father!" So you are no longer a slave, but a son, and if a son, then an heir through God.

GALATIANS 4:6–7 ESV

Do you remember the times as a child when you could jump up into your father's lap and call him daddy? If you had a dad who welcomed you, wrapping you in his arms at any moment, then you can envision how your heavenly Father responds to your approach. He tells us to call him *Abba*, the Aramaic word that Jesus used in reference to his intimate relationship with the Father.

If you can't imagine this type of parental treatment due to an unaffectionate or absent parent, then please know you have this relationship with your Abba. You are adopted in Christ and loved as God's own child with all the advantages of one born of the spirit. The days when we were estranged due to unbelief and sin are gone and forgotten. The knowledge that we are his and he is ours should cause our heart to rejoice. Today, go as a child to your heavenly Abba, expressing your love for him.

Abba, hold me close, keep me safe, and let me feel your loving arms around me. Amen.

Giving Our Best

Honor the LORD with your wealth and with the firstfruits
of all your produce; then your barns will be filled with plenty,
and your vats will be bursting with wine.

PROVERBS 3:9–10 ESV

There was a stark difference in the mindsets and the attitudes
with which Cain and Abel presented their sacrifices to God.
Abel brought the firstborn of his flock, indicating that he had
given his best and most valuable. This offering reveals a heart
that desired to give what is most costly to honor the Lord,
and this pleased God. Cain brought an offering of fruit. This
situation does not elevate one type of offering over the other,
meat versus fruit, but rather the intent with which the men
offered it. Cain revealed his attitude when he became angry over
God's response to his offering.

The Lord warned Cain that the condition of his spirit
put him in danger of falling prey to sin. Cain failed to master
his emotions, rising up in jealousy against his brother Abel and
killing him. One lesson we can take away from this event is
to pray for a heart that gives God the most valuable aspects of
our life, our tithe, and our devotion. Giving our best brings a
promise of God's provision for our lives.

Father, I offer you all that I have and all that I am. Amen.

September

Believe, Even in Battle

When they began to sing and to praise, the LORD set ambushes against the people of Ammon, Moab, and Mount Seir, who had come against Judah; and they were defeated.

2 CHRONICLES 20:22 NKJV

There was no human way that the king of Judah, Jehoshaphat, and his army could have defeated the multitude of nations coming to battle them. Other leaders might have sharpened their weapons or strategized battle plans, but Jehoshaphat called all of Judah to fast and pray. The king knew the collective prayer of the people would honor God and show their dependence on him. They had faith that the Lord would deliver them and marched into war singing songs of praise. Before the army of Judah reached the battleground, God caused their enemies to turn on each other, and all were dead. God fought their battle for them. After the great victory, they came together and blessed the Lord with praise and worship. As it turned out, their prayer was the most fearsome battle cry they could have uttered.

Take Jehoshaphat and his people as an example, and face your next difficulty with prayer, fasting, praise, and undeniable trust in the Lord.

Jesus, call me to fasting and prayer when I face trials. Help me to remember that it is you who fights my battle so that I may praise you in advance of the victory. Amen.

God's Path

Whether it be good, or whether it be evil, we will obey the voice of Jehovah our God, to whom we send thee; that it may be well with us, when we obey the voice of Jehovah our God.

JEREMIAH 42:6 ASV

Some of the Israelites approached the prophet Jeremiah and entreated him to pray and ask God the way they should go and what they should do. They said that whatever God instructed, whether it was good or bad, they would follow. After Jeremiah prayed and received instruction from the Lord, he shared the results with the Israelites. If the people would stay where they were and not go to Egypt, God would grant them mercy, saving them from the King of Babylonia. He would bless them by allowing them to remain in the land. However, if they went to Egypt, Jeremiah reported, God would pour out his wrath on them.

Unfortunately, after hearing this prophecy, the people accused Jeremiah of lying and declared they would go to Egypt, for they believed if they stayed, God would not protect them against the Babylonians. Choosing to disobey ended in their death by the sword, famine, and pestilence in Egypt, just as Jeremiah had warned. Stay in God's favor by trusting and resting assured in his perfect plan.

Lord, help me follow the path you have laid out, for your will be done, not mine. Amen.

Bad Company

Oh, the joys of those who do not follow the advice of the
wicked, or stand around with sinners, or join in with mockers.
PSALM 1:1 NLT

As believers, we have the Holy Spirit to help us determine good
from evil. Through his discernment, we can have a red flag pop
up in our conscience when we receive advice from a bad source.
We should always pray before allowing anyone to counsel us,
asking God to give us wisdom regarding whom to confide in.
We should always check with the Lord about any opinion or
direction we receive before jumping in with acceptance.

      We must always surround ourselves with other
Christians, not allowing our closest confidantes to be of the
world but engaging with them in order to share the gospel.
When we begin to allow a secular relationship to take priority,
we can get dragged into sin more easily than we can imagine.
People often judge who we are by the people we associate with.
Bad company can quickly sully our testimony for Jesus. You
will experience peace, joy, and righteous living by surrounding
yourself with like-minded brothers and sisters in Christ.

Jesus, help me guard my reputation as a Christ follower by
following godly advice and keeping company with others who
know and believe in you. Amen.

Daily Gratefulness

One of them, when he saw that he was healed, turned back,
with a loud voice glorifying God; and he fell upon his face at his
feet, giving him thanks: and he was a Samaritan.

Luke 17:15–16 ASV

While traveling between Samaria and Galilee, Jesus encountered
ten lepers. They remained at a distance but could still see with eyes
of faith that they were looking at the Savior of the world. They
cried out saying, "Jesus, Master, have mercy on us" (v. 13 ASV).
Seeing their belief, Jesus told them to go present themselves to the
priests, and while they were on their way, they were healed.

Wouldn't you think all ten would run back, fall at the feet
of Christ, and worship him for releasing them from the life of a
leprosy? Yet only one returned, praising God with all his heart
as he fell on his face to worship the Messiah. Jesus questioned
where the others were and why they also didn't return to offer
thanks and praise. He blessed the one who was thankful, telling
him his faith had made him well. How often do we forget to give
God thanks? Oh, that our heart would swell in gratitude to our
generous Father in heaven.

Lord, forgive my ungrateful heart, and may I be filled anew with
gratitude. Amen.

The Heart of Man

Jesus would not entrust himself to them, for he knew all people. He did not need any testimony about mankind, for he knew what was in each person.

JOHN 2:24–25 NIV

The heart of man is a deceitful and wicked thing if not transformed by the salvation and blood of Jesus. Today's is a bittersweet verse. Bitter in that we may identify with the fickle heart more than we care to acknowledge. Sweet in that our Redeemer knows our battles against the flesh, our pride, our unfulfilled good intentions, our thoughtless words, and all our other failures. God knows us inside and out. Jesus does, too, and that is exactly why he would not allow too many to be his part of inner circle. He chose twelve, and even those had flaws that he foreknew, yet he allowed them into his life of ministry anyway. Jesus as God-man could see with his omniscience the intent of all hearts. He continued to engage with and heal people, and he determined to leave the crowds at the right time.

As believers, we have access to Jesus all the time, in any circumstance, and anywhere. Keep your heart pure before him, entrusting yourself to Christ.

Jesus, I know that even when I am not faithful, you remain faithful. I am blessed that, through salvation in you, I have entered the veil. Amen.

Clinging to Christ

*Fasten your hearts to the love of God and receive the mercy
of our Lord Jesus Christ, who gives us eternal life.*

JUDE (JUDAH) 1:21 TPT

In the early 1990s, the contemporary Christian singer and songwriter Carman released an album and an accompanying song entitled *Addicted to Jesus*. That's how we should be, so enthralled, so surrendered to the Savior that we cling to him every single second. He deserves to be our everything, our purpose, and our first love. Show him your constant gratitude for his mercy, your salvation, and eternal life. From the introduction of Jude (Judah) in The Passion Translation:

1. Keep building up your inner life on the foundation of faith.
2. Pray in the Holy Spirit.
3. Fasten your life to the love of God.
4. Receive more mercy from our Lord Jesus Christ.
5. Have compassion for the wavering.
6. Save the lost.
7. Hate any compromise that will stain our lives.[8]

*Lord, may the deepest recesses of my heart be filled with the
wonder of your love for me. Amen.*

---

8   Brian Simmons, "Jude (Judah): Introduction: Purpose," *The Passion
Translation: New Testament with Psalms, Proverbs, and Song of Songs*
(Savage, MN: BroadStreet Publishing Group, 2020), 705.

The Greatest Sacrifice

"Take your son, your only son Isaac, whom you love, and go to the land of Moriah, and offer him there as a burnt offering on one of the mountains of which I shall tell you."

GENESIS 22:2 ESV

God gave Abraham a directive that made the promise of the Lord seem impossible. He told Abraham to take his only son, the one he had waited for until old age, and put him to death as a sacrifice. Can you imagine the thoughts that ran through the patriarch's mind as he heard his son comment that they had fire and wood but no lamb? Scripture doesn't tell us what Isaac said as his father bound him and laid him on the altar, but they were probably both bewildered. Just as Abraham raised his knife, God told him not to harm the boy. God provided a ram for the sacrifice in place of Isaac.

God understood what he asked of Abraham, for he would one day soon be asking the same thing of himself. Only this time, the sacrifice would be completed. God gave up his only Son to death for all of us. There is no greater sacrifice.

God, thank you for sacrificing your only Son so that I can live. I sacrifice my life to you in return. Amen.

Forever Forgotten

In that day you will say: "I will praise you, LORD. Although you were angry with me, your anger has turned away and you have comforted me."

ISAIAH 12:1 NIV

What a kind and compassionate God! Even though he is pure and holy and our sin is a heinous affront to him, he quells his anger and proceeds to provide our comfort. Honestly, when you think of all the reasons why he could be displeased with us, it is a pretty long list. We fail in so many ways, yet his forgiveness is unlimited. Once we confess, he welcomes us back with open arms and the promise to never bring up our sin again, for he has forgotten it forever. Our enemy may try to remind us, but we can shut him down by quoting the Word, proving that we are no longer a slave to any sin.

Sing joyous songs to the Lord Almighty, who, though he would be justified to turn his back and give up on us, never has and never, ever will. When we become his, we are sealed for eternity. This day I will praise God, my Savior, my gentle Counselor, and righteous King. He listens and restores me as I bring my praises into his presence.

Dear Father God, thank you for your abiding peace and indescribable joy. Amen.

Growing Up in God

Jesus increased in wisdom and in stature
and in favor with God and man.

Luke 2:52 esv

When we think of growing up, we naturally think of the progress of a young child as they mature. When it comes to spiritual growth, we can be any age in life when we begin the process of maturing and knowing Christ. This is due to that fact that people accept Christ at different stages of life.

No matter their age, they begin as a Christian newborn and are fed with spiritual milk. As time goes on and they are discipled, trained, and become students of the Word, they are ready for meat that will help them discern the depths of God's truth and promises. Whether you are a teen who has recently accepted Christ or a senior citizen who accepted Jesus years ago, pray that you will increase in wisdom, stature, and favor with God and man. May we continually grow in our walk with God emotionally, physically, and spiritually and in our relationships with others.

Dear Lord, as long as I am on this earth, help me be determined to do all it takes to become mature in Christ. Help me through the power of your Holy Spirit. Amen.

God Moves Our Hearts

Therefore, my dear friends, as you have always obeyed—not only in my presence, but now much more in my absence— continue to work out your salvation with fear and trembling, for it is God who works in you to will and to act in order to fulfill his good purpose.

PHILIPPIANS 2:12–13 NIV

Paul addressed the Philippians to encouraged them in their faith walk. They had obeyed God in the past, and he desired that they continued to live righteously. When he said they were to work out their salvation, he in no way meant that we are responsible for our own salvation. Nor did Paul want his readers to be concerned that they, on their own, would never be good enough to find favor with the Lord.

It's all the work of God and his grace that fulfills his purpose in us. We are to take seriously the responsibility for how we represent Christ and to have a reverent respect for the Lord. When it comes to the good we do, it is God who moves our hearts to make the right choices. We will never accomplish God's will without his influence and power to bring victory from our efforts in him.

Father, I praise you that everything good originates with and is done by you. Amen.

The Heart of God

"When he had removed him, he raised up David
to be their king, of whom he testified and said,
'I have found in David the son of Jesse a man after my heart,
who will do all my will.'"

ACTS 13:22 ESV

Doesn't your heart yearn to be called a person after God's own heart? Imagine the intimacy of a relationship that is given that description. Think about how important the Bible portrays David to be due to this precious closeness with his heavenly Father. Wouldn't you have loved to follow David in life to see what it was that made him the man that would do all God's will?

And yet, we know the story of David's downfall. It was massive, involving lust, adultery, and murder. When confronted about his sin, David did not deny it but immediately confessed. He fasted, prayed, and accepted God's decision regarding his punishment. He worshiped God even though God took his baby son in the wreckage of David's wrongdoing. Despite his many failures and flaws, David continued to seek, praise, and worship God, to ask forgiveness, be humble, and long to be near to the heart of God. Despite David's sin, the Lord continued to call David a man after God's own heart.

Father, I am glad that your second chances never run out. Amen.

Stand Out

Do not be conformed to this world, but be transformed by the renewal of your mind, that by testing you may discern what is the will of God, what is good and acceptable and perfect.

ROMANS 12:2 ESV

When Jim Caviezel, who played Jesus in *The Passion of the Christ*, speaks at churches, he wisely says, "You were not made to fit in. You were made to stand out." Lights stand out by shining bright, and Jesus said we are lights for him. As believers, we illuminate a testimony so we will be noticed. That attention may bring interest, and it may elicit persecution.

Either way, we should count it all joy to represent our Savior. We must stay separate from the world but engage when the spirit leads in order to share the gospel. Scripture tells us how to live a life in this way. Study the Word and then be bold in lighting the way to Jesus.

Lord, may I be your light to someone who is groping in darkness. Amen.

Generosity and Kindness

We will show mercy to the poor and not miss an opportunity to do acts of kindness for others, for these are the true sacrifices that delight God's heart.

HEBREWS 13:16 TPT

When we are experiencing trials, the best strategy is to take our eyes off ourselves and to serve others. If we truly believe who our God is and what he can do, we know that he will bring good from our situation, so there's no reason to fret. Tell the Lord you trust him and be busy showing the love of Jesus to others. Your faith and your works on his behalf will fill his heart with joy and cause his favor to fall on you.

Something that will lighten your load is worshiping amid difficulty. Gratitude is easy when all is going well. Praise that delights his heart is an attitude of trust that no matter the pain, fear, worry, or rejection, you will stand still in faith as he fights for you. Singing his goodness with a humble and contrite heart that surrenders to him will bring you joy. Then go forward and live with generosity and kindness, focusing on those in need.

Jesus, help me have faith big enough to take my eyes off my troubles and to help others with theirs. Amen.

Grow in Living Water

"At least there is hope for a tree: If it is cut down, it will sprout again, and its new shoots will not fail. Its roots may grow old in the ground and its stump die in the soil, yet at the scent of water it will bud and put forth shoots like a plant."

JOB 14:7–9 NIV

Very early this morning, I woke up with the words *tree stump* vividly in my mind. On a search, I couldn't find *stump* in my Bible concordances, but I came across the above passage in Job. How often, due to bad choices, illness, aging, or life circumstances, do we feel like useless stumps? Notice that at the scent of water, Jesus being our living water, we will bud again.

Samson lost his supernatural power due to yielding to temptation, yet in the end, through faith, he was more victorious than before. Peter felt like a failure after he cursed and denied his dying Lord, yet he later became a champion for Christ. Today, we have a multitude of warriors of faith who were once what some would have called "total losers."

Dear Lord, let me connect with you, the living water, so I will be as the tree in Psalm 1:3 (NIV) that "yields its fruit in season and whose leaf does not wither." Amen.

Stay the Course

Rejoice in our confident hope.
Be patient in trouble, and keep on praying.
ROMANS 12:12 NLT

If you have ever been the weaker participant in an arm-wrestling match, you know that it is hard to keep going. You feel like giving in so you can escape the embarrassment you perceive from those who are watching. We can rejoice in Jesus that when we are weak, he is strong. So in this sense, weakness is a good thing. It allows our Savior to step in and do what only he can: achieve the victory. While we are waiting on his deliverance, we can please him by staying the course with hope, patience, and faithful prayer. If prayer is difficult, remember that the Holy Spirit intercedes for you. Ask him to give you the power to believe.

Many times, Jesus said that someone's faith had made them well. That should encourage all of us to put our childlike trust to work. When we put absolute belief in our Messiah, he moves mountains for us. And even if your flesh is weak, his Spirit will bolster you by strengthening your belief in the only one for whom impossible is never possible.

Father, may your Holy Spirit represent me before your throne, praying on my behalf for greater faith and complete trust. Amen.

Righteous Anger

God did not send his Son into the world to condemn the world, but to save the world through him.

JOHN 3:17 NIV

Doesn't it make you "righteously" angry when you hear people blame God for the wrong that man does? We have all heard, "If God is good, then why is there so much evil in the world? Why doesn't he do anything to stop it?" If only they would pay heed to today's verse. The Lord did do something, and it was everything we needed in order to escape death and enter into his presence. He sent his Son. He allowed him to suffer and die for the sins of the world.

We must pray that the eyes of the world are opened to the truth of salvation and to God's goodness. We must ask the Holy Spirit to fill us with a burning fire to share the gospel. We should intercede for the lost that they will comprehend the love our heavenly Father has for them. Pray for revival and let unbelievers know that our Lord is not sitting on the throne planning how to punish but that there is no condemnation in Christ. Our God is love.

Father, I want the world to understand how good you are. Let my life represent that to all. Amen.

Praise God

"The wild animals honor me, the jackals and the owls, because
I provide water in the wilderness and streams in the wasteland,
to give drink to my people, my chosen, the people
I formed for myself that they may proclaim my praise."

ISAIAH 43:20–21 NIV

If Jesus cares about the birds of the air and the flowers in the
field, how much more does he care for us? There is no word in
the English language that can describe the greatness and extent
of his love for us. If wild creatures thank God for his provisions,
how much more should we? Instead, we doubt and question,
but God is not going to abandon you. He has told us that he
works all things for good on our behalf (Romans 8:28).

God promises to make the wilderness a place of flowing
water, refreshment, and satisfaction. It is a place of birthing for
glorious encounters of his love. Focus on the one who is with
you during your most difficult time. Remember the story of
the three Hebrew children in the fiery furnace (Daniel 3:8–25)?
God was right there with them. He will not abandon you in
your desert experience. Worship God in the midst of it.

Father, I praise you for your provisions and presence that are
constantly with me. Amen.

Heavenly Minded

"Lift up your eyes to the heavens, look at the earth beneath; the heavens will vanish like smoke, the earth will wear out like a garment and its inhabitants die like flies. But my salvation will last forever, my righteousness will never fail."

ISAIAH 51:6 NIV

There used to be a saying: "They are so heavenly minded they are of no earthly good." This could be true if our gaze is solely on our perception of heaven and not on our glorious King Jesus. If that is the case, then that saying might have merit. However, when life has us bogged down with anxiety, we are over-committed, we are under pressure, and we feel stuck, we often achieve a breakthrough by changing our perspective. God wants to be the filter between us and our problems. When we catch a glimpse of our glorious, loving heavenly Father, Savior, and Redeemer, earth and its often overwhelming problems and pressures lose their suffocating power.

Remind yourself today that this earth and all it contains will burn and pass away, but those who believe in the Lord Jesus Christ will live forever. Our salvation is secure in him. Oh, the joy of looking forward to living with Jesus with no end in sight.

Lord, I will keep my heart's gaze fixed on you. I will dwell in your peace and clarity. Amen.

Salvation for All

"Everyone who calls on the name of the Lord will be saved."
ROMANS 10:13 ESV

Do you recall the times in elementary school when captains who were your peers were picking teams? You wanted so badly to be chosen at the beginning and feared being the last one called. It was a popularity contest of sorts, and you did not want to be the odd person out.

Our Lord doesn't play favorites. His team has no limit on members, and he views us the same. His love is so great that he doesn't show partiality but invites all to be included. His call goes out to the world, and his desire is that everyone respond with a yes. Some think it's too easy to be true. They foolishly surmise that there must be some catch, some good acts or rituals they need to perform to earn salvation. There is nothing anyone can add, for it took the Son of God to make salvation possible. We're sinful creatures for whom God gifted complete absolution because Jesus died in our place. If you don't know the Savior, come to him. He is tender and will readily forgive when you confess, welcoming you with open arms as his very own.

Jesus, thank you for the greatest sacrifice, dying so that I could live. Amen.

Jesus Is Lord

"Everyone knows I am safe until I come to Jerusalem,
for that is where all the prophets have been killed."
LUKE 13:33 TPT

Herod Antipas was set on eliminating Jesus. Pharisees came to Jesus and told him to leave their city because of the imminent danger. Jesus responded by calling Herod a fox. He told the men to inform Herod that Jesus was casting out demons and healing people and that he would not cease tomorrow or until the third day (referring to his resurrection).

It was so ironic that Jerusalem, the center of Jewish worship, was a threatening city for any true prophet of God. The likes of the Romans, Herod, and the Sanhedrin plotted in many ways to try to silence Christianity. Yet even though there was such opposition, this was still a place where Jesus desired to gather its inhabitants as a hen gathers her chicks under her wings. Due to the resistance, Christ proclaimed that that they would not see him until they could proclaim, "Blessed is he who comes in the name of the Lord!" (Luke 13:35 ESV). One day, every knee will bow and every tongue confess that Jesus Christ is Lord.

Jesus, I long for the day when every knee will bow to you. Please save those yet to be saved and take us home. Amen.

Persecution

I received mercy for this reason, that in me, as the foremost, Jesus Christ might display his perfect patience as an example to those who were to believe in him for eternal life. To the King of the ages, immortal, invisible, the only God, be honor and glory forever and ever. Amen.

1 TIMOTHY 1:16–17 ESV

Many of our sisters and brothers in Christ across the world face persecution. Pastors are thrown in prison for speaking the Word of God. Marauding gangs kill students who won't deny Jesus at their command. Entire families who claim the cross of Christ are beheaded. We pray for these, that God will deliver them, comfort them, and make them to feel his presence.

Do we ever pray for those who are torturing and condemning Christians? Don't you wonder what would result if someone prayed for a man who made it his mission to kill as many Christ followers as possible? Possibly someone prayed for the transformation of Saul, who became Paul. God showed that he could transform a furiously dedicated Jew, who opposed all that Jesus stood for, and convert him to the Lord's servant. He then proceeded to allow Paul to share in Christ's sufferings, bringing many to salvation.

Dear Jesus, please transform me, as I am saved by grace and kissed by mercy. Amen.

The God Who Hears

I love the LORD, for he heard my voice; he heard my cry for mercy. Because he turned his ear to me, I will call on him as long as I live.

PSALM 116:1–2 NIV

We can call our Father *Jehovah Shema*, for in Hebrew, that means "the God who hears." His ears are always attentive to the voices of his own. Whether we are singing songs of joy or crying out in desperation, he draws near to rescue the children he loves. The psalmist was in danger from his enemies, feeling the snares of death surrounding him. He was brought low, but the Lord saved him. He had been lied to by those he trusted, and he learned that he could only find truth from the words proceeding from God's mouth. He had been afflicted but continued to give thanks to the one who had delivered him. He praised the Lord for dealing bountifully with his soul.

The reasons listed in this chapter are but a fraction of the reasons why our heart should burst with praise and thanksgiving to God. His love and tender compassions are ever before us. May his love cover and enfold us as we move through our days. He can fill us with hope as we listen for his answer.

Lord, thank you for always hearing me. Amen.

An Invitation to Conversation

"Call to Me, and I will answer you, and show you great
and mighty things, which you do not know."

JEREMIAH 33:3 NKJV

It feels so good when a friend asks to spend time with us.
Especially if that person is a confidante. It is a blessing to have
someone who is like-minded and trustworthy, one who gets us
and isn't shocked at our struggles. Someone who reciprocates,
sharing their hardships and difficulties in life as well as their
successes. The greatest invitation to any conversation is in the
verse above from Jeremiah. The Lord Almighty, God of the
universe, Creator of all wants to share his secrets with us. Could
anything be more amazing? All we need to do is follow his
instruction to call on his name.

Get away to a quiet place and position yourself to
hear from the Lord. Open your Bible and pray that the Holy
Spirit will lead you to truths you didn't previously understand.
You can trust that spiritual nuggets will appear that you have
read before but that now have so much more meaning. Ask
to hear God's voice in your soul then sit silently and wait on
him. He keeps his promises, and he will bow down to whisper
magnificent truths from his heart to yours.

Father, I'm ready. Speak, Lord, for your child is listening. Amen.

Small Things

"Who dares despise the day of small things, since the seven
eyes of the LORD that range throughout the earth will
rejoice when they see the chosen capstone in the hand of
Zerubbabel?"

ZECHARIAH 4:10 NIV

The young boy who traveled a distance to see Jesus willingly
gave away, without seeking attention or praise, all the food he
had. He had no idea of the miracle that was about to take place
nor that the small lunch he shared that day would be multiplied
many thousands of times over and memorialized in Scripture.

Whether the "small thing" was David the shepherd
boy, Gideon (who became a judge), Peter the fisherman, the
servant of Naaman's wife, or that young boy with five loaves
and two fishes—they each had a heart that served God ahead of
themselves.

The Lord can give us hearts that willingly and lovingly
sow seeds with eyes, ears, and hands that see, hear, and respond.
Be willing to share, for your offering may reap a miracle. Never
make your offering for praise or a good feeling but only out of a
passion for God and his kingdom.

Father, break my heart with what breaks yours. Give me a resolve
to be your heart and hands extended. Forgive my want and waste
as I breathe in your mercy and grace, always new every morning.
Amen.

Fully Trustworthy

Whoever dwells in the shelter of the Most High will rest in the shadow of the Almighty. I will say of the LORD, "He is my refuge and my fortress, my God, in whom I trust."

PSALM 91:1–2 NIV

There is nothing like feeling secure, protected, cared for, and at peace. When your life is surrounded and filled with the one who assures you that nothing happens without his approval, you can live in a perpetual state of comfort. There is no worry and no fear, for you have a champion who will always save you. He is the Lord Most High, Creator of all, and the lover of your soul, and he is fully trustworthy.

So why do we give in to feeling uneasy? Why would we ever be distraught? Even if death should come, the next second when we open our eyes, we will see Jesus. We will be in paradise. We will no longer be sick, sad, or striving to make an earthly life work. Whether we continue in this world for many years to come or the Lord calls us home tonight, our Savior will always be our shelter, our salvation, and our precious Bridegroom.

Dear Lord, thank you for preparing a place for me in heaven. Whether you leave me here or call me home, I will praise you. Amen.

Hopeful Expectation

May the God of hope fill you with all joy and peace as you trust in him, so that you may overflow with hope by the power of the Holy Spirit.

ROMANS 15:13 NIV

God never intended for us to be devoid of joy or security in him. When he placed Adam and Eve in the garden, God meant for it to be paradise. When the evil serpent did his dirty work and Adam and Eve succumbed to his temptation, all kinds of trouble appeared on the scene. Adam and Eve opened the door, allowing the Enemy to try to destroy God's children.

Satan continues today to find our weak spots so he can torment us relentlessly. He tampers with the believer's peace, but he can't separate us from our beloved. In Jesus, we have everything we need for victory. God wants us to live with peace, passion, and the power that the indwelling Holy Spirit gives us. We must vehemently resist the devil, and he will flee. We must draw near to God continually, meditating on his Word, his love, and all that we have inherited in Christ. If we keep our mind focused on the Savior, our joy and hope will be complete in him.

Jesus, please help me keep my eyes fixed on you so I can live in hopeful expectation and great joy. Amen.

Clothed in Mercy

I delight greatly in the LORD; my soul rejoices in my God. For he has clothed me with garments of salvation and arrayed me in a robe of his righteousness, as a bridegroom adorns his head like a priest, and as a bride adorns herself with her jewels.

ISAIAH 61:10 NIV

My precious granddaughter and I were reminiscing over a time when she was extremely unhappy with the clothing her mother had chosen for a family photo. At the time, she failed to understand that her mother was choosing what she felt was best, but the child still respected her mother's decision.

I'm sure we can all recall similar occasions when it comes to God's choices for us. How often we forget or ignore the magnificent armor that our Lord provides for a life of purpose, fulfillment, joy, rightness, hope, and peace. Instead, we choose our ineffective garments. We find ourselves trying to fight a spiritual war without protection, and we then wonder why we mess up. We must go to the Lord in humility. He faithfully forgives and gently reminds us of his desire for our victory and how he has supplied all we need to win the battle.

Today, let us choose to be dressed in the Lord's garment of salvation and righteousness.

Lord, guide me to don your armor every day. Amen.

God Conquers

God has not given us a spirit of fear and timidity,
but of power, love, and self-discipline.

2 TIMOTHY 1:7 NLT

No one needs to teach a child to be prideful; it comes with our human spirit. It originated when Lucifer's power and the desire for it sent him tumbling from heaven to the pit. The power that Christ gives is held in check by agape love and a sound mind. The prince of darkness tries to convince us we are better off with self-pride and control of our own destiny. Yet those who surrender to Jesus and are filled with his power see the Spirit of God in their reaction to trials and experience deliverance from evil.

Ask Betty Stan, who transcended death at the hands of Chinese communists, or Corrie ten Boom, who overcame the hate of a Nazi camp guard, or Elisabeth Elliot, who defeated tragedy by teaching the natives who killed her husband. These women would tell you that Christ's power is more than adequate for conquering any circumstance that confronts you.

Lord, be my strength. Thank you for the power found in Christ that enables me to be victorious. Amen.

Spiritual Wellness

Search me, God, and know my heart; test me and know my
anxious thoughts. See if there is any offensive way in me, and
lead me in the way everlasting.

PSALM 139:23–24 NIV

When we face temptation or trials, we employ strategies that
originate from sinful desires that we don't even recognize.
We are blinded by our need for justification or having our
perpetrator ask for forgiveness. We start to ruminate over the
offense and offend in return by responding without consulting
the wisdom of God, placing ourselves rebelliously out of his will.

We must continually search our hearts to see whether our
motives serve the Lord or ourselves. We must ask that he reveal in
us any hurtful way or unacknowledged sin. Only God can lovingly
expose our wounded, lonely, painful, deceitful, proud, resentful,
and unforgiving hearts and mend them back to wholeness
again. We may use man's counsel, clothed in God's wisdom, to
insightfully guide us on a path to spiritual wellness, but only God
can expose and flush away any impure root cause that exists in
our hearts to deceive us. Desire his blessings, keeping your way
honest and truthful and seeking spiritual wellness.

Lord, give me a willingness and a strong desire to allow you to
expose that in me which needs your freeing, healing touch and
obedience to your counsel. Amen.

Our Champion

Who then will condemn us? No one—for Christ Jesus died for us and was raised to life for us, and he is sitting in the place of honor at God's right hand, pleading for us.

ROMANS 8:34 NLT

What a relief to know that in Christ there is no condemnation. People may and will condemn us, whether it is displeasure from our boss or a close friend who strongly disagrees with us. Others may rightfully or wrongfully consider us to be the party at fault.

The one who matters most, though, will always forgive and erase any memory of our sin. He will never disown us over our wrongdoing because for those who are saved by the blood of Christ, condemnation does not exist in any form. Jesus is our forever champion and cheerleader. He has our back, and we can absolutely trust him. No human description can illustrate what our Savior gave up so that he could be our perfect rescuer. He continually prays and intercedes for us. What love! What mercy! What grace!

Lord, in this time of uncertainty and turmoil, may I fasten my spirit eyes, thoughts, and heart on you. As our Champion, Jesus paid it all. As I dwell on and surrender to this wondrous truth, I will be lifted up with joy unspeakable. Thank you, Savior. Amen.

October

Season of Trials

You have allowed me to suffer much hardship, but you will restore me to life again and lift me up from the depths of the earth. You will restore me to even greater honor and comfort me once again.

PSALM 71:20–21 NLT

God is in control. The psalmist knows the Lord has allowed and approved of the season of trials he is suffering. Scripture makes clear the fact that a believer's life is not all sunshine and roses but that troubles will visit them throughout. Consider what would happen if everything were perfect every single day of your life. Do you really think you would go to God? Would your dependance on him continue, or would you figure you've got it all covered?

There is a reason for the struggles God brings our way, for they draw us near to him. The strength and integrity of our character are defined and refined when times are most challenging and turbulent. The psalmist also has confidence that the faithfulness of God means he will provide us with his comfort and reward. God will raise us up with honor for the trust his children have exhibited. May God's love bring forth jewels, not hay and stubble.

Dear Lord, I praise you for your refining fire, knowing your love and faithfulness are ever with me. Amen.

On Our Knees

If my people who are called by my name will humble themselves and pray and seek my face and turn from their wicked ways, I will hear from heaven and will forgive their sins and restore their land.

2 CHRONICLES 7:14 NLT

If our world would ascribe to today's verse, things could look very different. Our world is a mess. Some explain it as part of the progression toward the end times. Morals are upside down, common respect for others is nonexistent, and expressing your own opinion or thoughts can get you into a lot of trouble. Or it might just be that we live on a planet plagued with evil and filled with sinful people.

Whether Jesus returns tomorrow or a thousand years from now, God has given us an invitation to bring healing to our land. If we, as his church, go to him in humility and turn from our transgressions, he will hear, he will forgive, and he will restore.

Merciful God, I humbly confess my sin against you and ask that you will forgive me and allow healing to repair our land. Amen.

Great and Precious Promises

Let your steadfast love comfort me
according to your promise to your servant.
PSALM 119:76 ESV

We have problems that include finances, health, and broken relationships. Yet probably few of us have ever had to escape from someone who was seeking to kill us. David was no stranger to this issue, however, for Saul and even David's own son sought to destroy him. It is extremely stressful to be looking over your shoulder, skulking away in dark, hidden places to try to stay alive. Even under great duress, each morning King David turned to God, recognizing his utter need and dependency upon the Lord for guidance, peace, forgiveness, wisdom, and hope.

Whether it is a dangerous or dire situation or a minor issue, we all need the Lord. If we don't know and believe the guarantees he has given us in his Word, we will stumble and fall when trials that come our way. He has given us his great and precious promises so that we can rest in faith, knowing that he is always working for good in our lives. Don't go your own way. Depend on him, allowing his love for you to fill you with comfort and hope.

Father, help me meditate on your Word, trust in your promises, and find comfort in the fact that you are in control. Amen.

Waiting and Still

Be still in the presence of the LORD, and wait patiently for him
to act. Don't worry about evil people who prosper or fret about
their wicked schemes.

PSALM 37:7 NLT

In the book of Ruth, we see that when the famine came to
Bethlehem, Elimelech fled to Moab with his wife and two sons.
The sons married, and after ten years, Elimelech and his sons
died. After such losses, Naomi, Elimelech's wife, returned to
Bethlehem and found her family and friends still there, living
well, unaffected by the famine Elimelech and Naomi had fled
out of fear. How often we rush ahead of God instead of being
still and waiting on him for guidance. We are wise to stay
surrendered to the Lord as he reveals his will.

After World War II, my dad was facing horrendous
difficulties, yet he waited on and stayed before the Lord, seeking
his direction and wisdom. God guided him through those
turbulent waters, and he came out victorious. It spoke volumes
to me, viewing my father's reliance on Jesus, learning the
valuable lesson to do the same in my life. I thank God for my
dad's example. He trained me spiritually by the way he trusted
his heavenly Father.

Lord, may I, in these times of testing, be still before you, seek
your plan, and be obedient to you and your guidance. Amen.

We Were There

He was despised and rejected—a man of sorrows, acquainted
with deepest grief. We turned our backs on him and looked the
other way. He was despised, and we did not care.

ISAIAH 53:3 NLT

When many people read the crucifixion account, they place all
the blame on the people in that day. When you imagine hearing
the shouts for Barabbas, it's easy to assume only those folks were
at fault. We forget that it was not only they but also all of us, the
entire span of humankind, who caused Jesus to go to the cross.
He was the most offended, dejected, lied about, hated, and
plotted against Man of all time. No wonder he was so intimate
with grief.

We may not have literally turned our backs on the cross,
but we were there. Every sin of every person who ever lived
hung on that cross. We didn't suffer the pain, the shame, or the
heartbreak he did, but we certainly reaped all the benefits. We
must never take for granted the extent of suffering Jesus went
through on our behalf. Look daily at the cross, remembering the
sacrifice and showing gratitude for the result. Christ gave all;
let's give our all for him.

Jesus, thank you for the cross and how you suffered to save me.
Amen.

Our Rock

"Anyone who listens to my teaching and follows it is wise, like a person who builds a house on solid rock."

MATTHEW 7:24 NLT

Some people never ask for advice but rely only on their own opinion. Others run wildly to as many sources as possible, asking for input so they can go with the concept that most pleases their fancy. There is one place to go for reasoning that is foolproof and completely trustworthy, and that is to the Lord. In his Word, he speaks great truth that will lead us to understanding and wisdom.

In addition, if we ask him, he will guide us to a pastor, brother, or sister in Christ who can prayerfully counsel us. We will find the ground we place our feet on is unstable if we employ our own strategies. Before long, we will see things collapsing around us as we fall prey to compromise, unwise decisions, and questionable actions. This life will succeed in righteousness if we position ourselves on our Rock, Jesus. Let's open our Bibles, fall to our knees, and seek the Lord, knowing we will find him.

Father, help me never rely on myself but rather meditate on your Word and surrender to you. Amen.

Daily Miracles

> Around midnight Paul and Silas were praying and singing
> hymns to God, and the other prisoners were listening.
> Suddenly, there was a massive earthquake, and the prison was
> shaken to its foundations. All the doors immediately flew open,
> and the chains of every prisoner fell off!
>
> ACTS 16:25–26 NLT

Our greatest test of faith, trust, love, and obedience to our Lord comes when times are difficult and uncertain. It is then when we discover whether we truly believe that he is who he says he is and can do what he claims in his Word. Scripture is filled with miraculous events in the lives of our biblical ancestors, accounts of occurrences that boggle the mind. The common denominator is faith in a perfect, loving, faithful Lord.

Those people in Scripture demonstrated that trust through obediently following him even when they didn't know where he would lead. They proved their undeniable faith in him by a denial of self and a desire to go wherever he led, whatever the cost. In gratitude, watch to see God's hand at work, whether it is the wonder of waking up to another day of life or the healing of a loved one from a terminal illness. Everything is possible with Jesus. He performs miracles for those he loves.

Lord, I praise you, waymaker, miracle worker, beloved Savior!
Amen.

The Deepest Peace

The peace of God, which passeth all understanding,
shall guard your hearts and your thoughts in Christ Jesus.
PHILIPPIANS 4:7 ASV

When you dwell in the shelter of the Almighty, treasures of relief from worry are at your disposal. If it were not true, God's Word would not proclaim it. Peace that is indescribable and inexplicable suddenly comes to rest on us. It is because we have a heavenly Father who is protective and compassionate and who desires to gather us under his wing where he can keep us close to his heart. He wants to shelter us from distraction that would divide our affection for him.

Our Father knows that he is what is best for us, not this world, not material things, not even another person, but him, first and foremost. When we realize that truth in all its beauty, we will desire him and his comfort more than anything else. We will thrill at the thought of him and marvel at being in his presence. We will discard other activities to spend time alone with Jesus. Once there, at his feet, we will find the greatest love, the sweetest unity, and the answer to all we could ever want or need.

Lord, as I bask in your unexplainable peace, I am filled with thanksgiving that I can dwell with God Almighty. Amen.

Can You Imagine?

"He will once again fill your mouth with laughter
and your lips with shouts of joy."

JOB 8:21 NLT

Job's friend/comforter spoke the words in today's verse during Job's great time of adversity, pain, utter frustration, and confusion. Job's friends delivered these comments to him after they had piously laid him low. At God's perfect time, this verse was abundantly fulfilled in chapter 41.

I had a best friend for over fifty years who survived polio in her youth. Sharon lived in an iron lung for six months, had numerous surgeries, and used a wheelchair. She survived cancer and endured many "comforters" who were quick with advice and counsel. Her trust in the Lord sustained her through it all. She found Jesus to be her truest friend and faithful Rock, and she glowed for him. Sharon was the first to share the song "I Can Only Imagine" with me. She went to be with Jesus shortly after that. Can you imagine what her life is like now? I can, and I envision her doing her happy dance in the presence of her Lord and Savior. Jesus has turned her mourning into joy and her pain into laughter.

Father, I am grateful that, no matter what I face on this earth, my confidence, joy, and delight are in you, and my heart is set on eternity. Amen.

The Originator of Your Blessings

"For I hold you by your right hand—I, the LORD your God. And I say to you, 'Don't be afraid. I am here to help you.'"

ISAIAH 41:13 NLT

Whether it is a dark night of the soul or a celebration of a long-awaited desire realized, God is there right by our side. His righteous right hand holds ours as we dive into the depths of his will for us when we still do not know where it will take us or how long it will last. Our concerns are allayed as we gaze at the one who never intended for us to have a spirit of fear. A calm washes over us as we realize we aren't and never will be alone in this life but have the assistance of the almighty God to bring beauty from ashes.

It is God's desire to help us. His presence is our joy, strength, and protection. When you find yourself in times of trial, turn quickly in faith to the one who will hold up your arms as you face the battle. If it's a time of rejoicing, make sure you are giving thanks to the originator of your blessings.

Lord, may I bask in the joyful confidence that even if I have nothing to fear, your loving presence encompasses me. Amen.

Open-Ended Invitation

Jesus said, "Come to me, all of you who are weary
and carry heavy burdens, and I will give you rest."
MATTHEW 11:28 NLT

As a society, we are addicted to working out, staying in shape, and being in the best physical shape we can possibly be. We go to extremes with diets, sports, personal coaches, and every cutting-edge exercise plan. We exhaust ourselves, starve ourselves, and restrict the foods we will eat to fit a specific plan, whether it be paleo, keto, carnivore, or something else. At the end of the day we collapse only to wake up and do it all over again. No pain, no gain, and we are the only ones who can convince our sore body to stick with the program.

When it comes to the heavy burdens of our hearts, we can't rely on ourselves but must turn to the only One strong enough to carry our load. Jesus left us an open-ended invitation to allow him to shoulder the weight of our troubles so we can take time to rest. He wants to help us heal. When he took our place on the cross, he intended to free us, transform us, and deliver our victory. Give praise to your great and mighty Savior.

Jesus, dispel the destructive fear that the Enemy would war against me. Help me stand still as you fight for me. Amen.

Agonizing over Possessions

"These things dominate the thoughts of unbelievers all over the world, but your Father already knows your needs. Seek the Kingdom of God above all else, and he will give you everything you need."

LUKE 12:30–31 NLT

Today's verse refers to worrying over what you will wear or what you will eat and drink. This type of concern leads to frantically seeking and agonizing over where your provisions will come from. It could lead to you becoming a workaholic in order to buy all you think you need. It could tempt you to steal if you felt you had no other choice.

This passage assures us that stressing over these things is a waste of time. We know that our Father owns the cattle on a thousand hills (Psalm 50:10), so surely he has more than enough resources to care for us. The question is, though, are we content or striving to pile up our possessions? Are we happy and thankful for what God has blessed us with, or do we feel cheated when we look at our neighbor? Draw near to the Lord, store up your treasures in heaven, and remember that only kingdom work will last.

Father, help me look toward heaven while living a content life on earth. I praise you and know that you will always provide for me. Amen.

Church Discipline

Your boasting is not good. Do you not know
that a little leaven leavens the whole lump?

1 CORINTHIANS 5:6 ESV

We never want others to find us agreeing with the world that
good is evil and evil is good. The world should not hear us
bragging about doing something that would displease our Lord.
Unbelievers engage with all sorts of sinful actions, whether
they are engaging in sin in their own lives, participating in the
lives of their friends, or watching it play out on the big screen.
Usually, people emulate this type of behavior because they want
to fit in.

   The Bible warns us about sin in the church and how
we should handle it. Church leaders rarely if ever speak about
discipline from the pulpit and even more rarely enforce it. In the
Corinthian church, a certain man slept with his stepmother. The
church turned a blind eye, essentially conveying their approval.
Paul had a come-to-Jesus meeting, reprimanding the church
and giving instructions on how to handle the situation (1
Corinthians 5:3–5). Are we, like the Corinthians, choosing what
we will adhere to in Scripture and what we won't? Correction
from our fellow Christians is a tough pill to swallow, but
allowing the sin to infect the whole congregation could cause a
sickness that leads to spiritual death.

Father, help me deliver a brother or sister from death. Amen.

His Kindhearted Forgiveness

O Israel, hope in the LORD; for with the LORD there is unfailing love. His redemption overflows. He himself will redeem Israel from every kind of sin.

PSALM 130:7–8 NLT

This is one of fifteen psalms that David wrote, which are referred to as the Songs of Ascent. In this psalm, David again remembers the wretchedness of his sins and the great wonder of God's redeeming love, mercy, and grace for him and all who embrace the wonder of God's unending forgiveness. He states that there is no sin, no matter how despicable, that our gracious Father will not forgive. He credits God's unfaltering love for the extravagance of his pardon.

May we never take lightly the great cost for our redemption or the passion of God's love that took our sins and buried them in the deep. Through Christ's heinous death and glorious resurrection, our merciful Father offers redemption's freedom to all who would accept his Son. If you have not come to salvation, don't hesitate. Come to Jesus, the only one who can save you from sin and eternal death. He offers life everlasting. Someday it will be too late. Today is the day of your salvation, so sinner, please come home.

Dear Lord, how I wonder at the grace of your limitless, kindhearted forgiveness. Thank you for your salvation that has redeemed me. Amen.

A Snake Slithered In

The serpent said to the woman, "You will not surely die.
For God knows that in the day you eat of it your eyes will be
opened, and you will be like God, knowing good and evil."

GENESIS 3:4–5 NKJV

If only Eve had obeyed God, our lives would be very different.
Maybe we would still be in the garden communing with God.
Adam and Eve might be walking alongside us today if death
had never entered, but a snake slithered in. The devil was so
overcome with greed for power that he was cast down from
heaven, and he wanted revenge. He went after God's children,
lying to them in order to destroy the beautiful relationship that
existed between the Creator and his own creation.

Satan caused Eve to question the Lord's goodness. He
told the truth, saying that if she ate the apple, she would know
the difference between good and evil. He left out the fact that
her disobedience would inject evil into the heart of all mankind,
giving birth to sin. Satan isn't clever, for he has perpetrated the
same scheme for ages. He whispers doubt in our minds about
God's best for us. Recognize your enemy and make him flee by
obeying, being faithful to, and praising the Savior.

Father, help me turn a deaf ear to Satan's lies. Amen.

No Fear Here

"Don't be afraid," he said, "for you are very precious to God. Peace! Be encouraged! Be strong!" As he spoke these words to me, I suddenly felt stronger and said to him, "Please speak to me, my lord, for you have strengthened me."

DANIEL 10:19 NLT

Daniel had much in his life to fear. As a youth, his country's enemies had dragged him from his homeland to a totally foreign culture and separated him from his family. He faced death unless he could interpret the king's dream. The king's high officials schemed against Daniel because of his faith and his prayer life. The king threw him into a den of hungry and ferocious lions.

When God tells us not to fear, he doesn't mean there is nothing to fear. In fact, we are foolish if we don't recognize that in this fallen world, there are threats, and recognizing this can lead us to lean and depend on God with faith. Place your fear in God, respecting his power. It is an absolute truth that as we focus our spiritual eyes on Jesus, trust and love envelops us as our gripping and destructive fears vanish. We can do nothing less than shout hallelujah!

Lord, I am grateful that I can come to you when I am afraid. Thank you for your presence in my lion's den. Amen.

Victorious over Sin and Death

To Him who loved us and washed us from our sins in His
own blood and has made us kings and priests to His God and
Father, to Him be glory and dominion forever and ever. Amen.
REVELATION 1:5–6 NKJV

Jesus was victorious over sin and death when he replaced the
human race on the cross. He provided freedom from eternal
damnation through the power of his blood and body that he gave
for us. As if that weren't enough, to get free redemption for our
trespasses, he also gave us royal positions. No one anywhere at
any time could ever grant us a greater kindness, love us more, or
display that love in the unthinkably extreme way that Jesus did.

Yet do we sometimes take it for granted? Do we get
so familiar with our salvation that it becomes commonplace?
Oh, let it never be, for the cost was much too high to not give
it the proper praise and greatest of gratitude. We are sons
and daughters of the Most High God, and the lungs of all his
children must shout his glory for eternity.

Jesus, fill my heart and revive my soul so that my faith may burn
brightly for you, all to your glory. Amen.

Brag about Him

I know that the LORD rescues his anointed king. He will answer
him from his holy heaven and rescue him by his great power.
Some nations boast of their chariots and horses, but we boast
in the name of the LORD our God.

PSALM 20:6–7 NLT

The Lord delivers his chosen king, but he is just as ready and
willing to be our Redeemer and Defender. God loves all his
children, not just those who hold high positions or have large
platforms. He may be closer to those who seek him, but he is
available for all who call.

Envision him in his righteousness, seated on the throne
looking in on your life, good times and bad. He will move
heaven and earth to help you when you need it. Worship him
and brag about him to all who will listen about how good your
God is. Make it a habit to recall all his faithfulness in your
times of trials. He has a perfect track record for coming to the
aid of his children. Oh, how our Savior loves to step into our
discouragement and anxieties and manifest his faithfulness!

Lord, may I remember the many times you have rescued me. Let
your love and hope spring up and overflow to those around me.
Amen.

Faith over Fear

The next day a great multitude that had come to the feast, when they heard that Jesus was coming to Jerusalem, took branches of palm trees and went out to meet Him, and cried out: "Hosanna! 'Blessed is He who comes in the name of the LORD!' The King of Israel!"

JOHN 12:12–13 NKJV

What caused the disciples and multitude of followers to magnify Jesus as he entered Jerusalem and a week later turn away, run, and hide in his hour of great need? I believe they were terrified. John 2:24 says, "Jesus did not commit Himself to them, because He knew all men" (NKJV). The Scriptures state 365 times that we are to not fear. It's oftentimes this pesky emotion that keeps us from sharing the love of Christ with those around us. Fear keeps us from venturing into new paths of service to which Christ is calling us, causing us to miss his blessings. It makes us worry about provisions, keeping us from tithing and giving generously to his kingdom. We are apprehensive about the unknown instead of walking in faith. Fear is a tool of your enemy.

The great news is that Christ has the power and desire to deliver us from evil. We can live in faith, not fear.

Lord, help me choose daily to have faith over fear. Amen.

His Beautiful Heart

Who has believed our message? To whom has the LORD revealed his powerful arm? My servant grew up in the LORD's presence like a tender green shoot, like a root in dry ground. There was nothing beautiful or majestic about his appearance, nothing to attract us to him.

ISAIAH 53:1–2 NLT

We see depictions of Jesus, and they come in all varieties. In some he looks pleasing to the eye—even striking. In others, he is not someone to whom we would give a second glance. It is our interpretation, but Scripture tells the honest story. He was not a person whom others would gaze upon for his good looks. He most likely would have just melded in with the crowd. He hung out with those whom society considered to be its dregs. He befriended the tax collectors, publicans, sinners, the poor, and the needy.

Jesus may not have been handsome on the outside, but the inside of his soul was magnificently beautiful. In the midst of unimaginable pain, consider the way Jesus asked his Father to forgive all who caused his crucifixion because we didn't know what we were doing…yes, all of us. Even though we weren't there physically, we were there, present in his beautiful heart that broke over our sin.

Jesus, rekindle and renew my love and commitment to you. Amen.

Run the Race

"Keep alert at all times. And pray that you might be strong enough to escape these coming horrors and stand before the Son of Man."

Luke 21:36 NLT

In the verse above, Jesus is talking to the disciples about the end times approaching his return. He warns them to stay spiritually alert. Boiling that down, remaining alert includes consistent prayer, meditating on his Word, being surrendered to his will, and fulfilling the Great Commission. Jesus compares his return to a thief in the night, breaking in when you least expect it and during the sleeping hours. If we are not walking closely with Christ, we will risk being caught off guard.

What will you be doing during that hour? Will you be contemplating compromise or weakening under the conditions of the day? Pray that you will not grow weary or lose heart in doing good. Determine to live your life for Jesus, sharing his testimony and bringing glory to his name. Prepare for his coming by growing ever closer to him and being like him through the power of his Holy Spirit. Pray to run the race with excellence as you look forward to hearing, "Well done, my good and faithful servant" (Matthew 25:23 NLT).

Holy Spirit, may I fulfill your will, running the race well, being faithful and diligent in my prayer life, and living victoriously. Amen.

The Cost of His Cross

He was pierced for our rebellion, crushed for our sins.
He was beaten so we could be whole.
He was whipped so we could be healed.

ISAIAH 53:5 NLT

Isaiah wrote his prophecy more than seven hundred years before the cross. The New Testament refers to Isaiah 53 eighty-five times as it was stunningly fulfilled. Not one word spoken about the cross was left undone, from the horror of Jesus' beatings to the nails in his hands to his resurrection on the third day.

May we be smitten anew with the horrendous cost of our total and complete forgiveness, through the suffering Christ bore and his blood poured out on the cross. Let us be filled with humble gratitude at his sacrifice, for without it, we would be lost. May we marvel daily at his rising again to become our glorified and living Lord.

Dear Father, may I count Christ's cost with thanksgiving, and may it cause my heart to burst with joy at the reality of the cross. Amen.

Our Treasure

He will be the sure foundation for your times, a rich store of
salvation and wisdom and knowledge; the fear of the LORD is
the key to this treasure.

ISAIAH 33:6 NIV

In wars recorded in the Old Testament, the victor would take
the spoils from their defeated enemy. They could go home
carrying gold and numerous treasures from their opponent.
Although this may have made God's people wealthy on earth,
nothing could compare to the reward of fearing the Lord.
Scripture calls this attitude our treasure. His discernment,
anointing, and saving grace are limitless resources for those
who are in awe of his name. This respect for the Lord is the
beginning of wisdom.

The book of Psalms shares that if we want to understand
what it means to have the proper reverence for the Lord, we
will keep our tongues from evil and our lips from speaking lies
(34:13). We will work toward living peaceably with all people.
In fact, we will pursue peace passionately (v. 14). In response
to giving God this type of fear, we will have a solid foundation
of faith as we continue to commit to staying under his loving
guidance and righteous commands for all our life.

Father, teach me the fear of the Lord and help me to remain in it
all my days. I want to please you more than anything else. Amen.

Narrow Road

Jesus told him, "Anyone who puts a hand to the plow and then looks back is not fit for the Kingdom of God."

LUKE 9:62 NLT

When you are driving your car, what would happen if you only looked to the left continually? You are destined to have a crash either in front of you, to your right, or from behind. If you make a commitment to a work project but then discard it halfway through, you might be out of a job. If you tell God you are going to serve him in a particular area then start to get doubts about whether it is your thing, you are looking back from the plow. We won't always be one hundred percent thrilled and satisfied with everywhere we serve, and that's okay. God can use our discomfort to grow us by making our ministry sacrifice or equipping us with excellence as we continue to be faithful.

Jesus made the statement in today's verse after explaining the cost of following him. How tragic it would be to make him your Lord and then lose interest and fall away. It's a frightening thought. Keep your eyes on him, be faithful in service, and follow the narrow road until it ends in heaven's eternity.

Lord, may I be willing and pliable as you continue to transform me. Amen.

Adoration

"I tell you, her sins—and they are many—have been forgiven, so she has shown me much love. But a person who is forgiven little shows only little love."

LUKE 7:47 NLT

In this chapter of Luke, the Lord is having a conversation with Simon. Jesus told a story about a moneylender who had two debtors. One owed a large sum and the other a small one. The Savior said the moneylender canceled the debt of his debtors, and then Jesus asked, "Who do you suppose loved him more after that?" (v. 42 NLT). Simon rightfully answered, "I suppose the one for whom he canceled the larger debt" (v. 43 NLT).

Jesus then pointed out that Simon did not even provide water to wash Jesus' feet when he entered his house. Jesus compared this to the sinful woman who wet his feet with tears of adoration and contrition. Jesus corrected Simon for not kissing Jesus or anointing him with oil as the woman continued to kiss his feet, pouring precious ointment on them. All this was to teach his listeners that those who are forgiven of much will love the Savior more. The warning that forgiveness for little leads to a lack of appreciation for our salvation should be a wake-up call for us to continually have the utmost gratitude for all Christ has done for us.

Lord, make me keenly aware and grateful for all that you have forgiven me. Amen.

Recipients of God's Provisions

Trust in the LORD and do good.
Then you will live safely in the land and prosper.
PSALM 37:3 NLT

Many of us have known families that have suffered trial after trial but remained great witnesses of God's goodness. We wonder how they can take so many hits and still be standing. We are encouraged and challenged by the faith they continue to exhibit even though facing heartbreaking times. They make it through because they trust the Lord. They know that no matter what happens, he stays close, and he gives comfort. They have seen miracles along the way, and every time they are given hope, they proclaim God's glory, speaking his praises to all they can.

Even though these suffering people are in need, they serve others. What they carry in their hearts is the confidence that God is for them, not against them. They realize they have been the recipients of God's provisions, and they have learned that he is always good. They have no doubt that the Lord will continue to walk with them when trials come. Their greatest prosperity is the life of Christ in them, and that is a magnificent testimony to all who hear their witness. In Jesus, they are rich.

Dear Lord, help me to put my trust in you, living with great faith, obeying, and loving you. Amen.

Lumps of Clay

When a potter makes jars out of clay, doesn't he have a right to use the same lump of clay to make one jar for decoration and another to throw garbage into?

ROMANS 9:21 NLT

Several passages in Scripture liken us to lumps of clay. The other material Scripture compares us to is gold. These substances are quite opposite in design and value, but one common denominator each requires to reach its final desired form is fire. With clay, the potter does a lot of touching, gently molding, splashing cool water when needed, and shaping. His eye is continually on forming something unique and beautiful. Then the fire! If not for the fire, the use of the newly formed clay item would be greatly diminished. When a clay pot is put through proper firing, a steel knife cannot even mar it.

The Lord allows us to face the heat of trials, and if we surrender, he will mold and form us so that he can use us for his glory. To be more like Jesus, jump into the fire, laying yourself on his altar for his good purpose.

Lord, when darkness and fire surround me, may I find comfort in the truth that you know the perfect time, tolerance, and temperature to bring me forth as a vessel of honor. Amen.

Keep Looking Up

As Moses lifted up the bronze snake on a pole in the wilderness, so the Son of Man must be lifted up, so that everyone who believes in him will have eternal life.

JOHN 3:14–15 NLT

Just as Jesus was lifted onto the cross and then was resurrected and ascended to heaven, so Moses lifted up a serpent in the wilderness. "Moses made a bronze serpent and set it on a pole. And if a serpent bit anyone, he would look at the bronze serpent and live" (Numbers 21:9 ESV).

When sin entered the world through Satan's lies and Eve's disobedience, the Enemy came in the guise of a serpent. Revelation refers to him as the "old serpent" in (12:9; 20:2 KJV). In Moses' day, if a serpent bit anyone, they would look up to the serpent on the pole and live. The attacking serpent was a picture of death as the bronze serpent was a picture of life. Jesus is the way, the truth, and the life. When we look up at him, accepting the cross's salvation, we find eternal life. If we follow the ways of the world, falling under the Enemy's domain, we will die in our sin. Keep looking up and following Christ.

Jesus, help me to always look up and live up to your perfect will for me. Amen.

A Contrite Heart

"Don't tear your clothing in your grief, but tear your hearts instead." Return to the LORD your God, for he is merciful and compassionate, slow to get angry and filled with unfailing love. He is eager to relent and not punish.

JOEL 2:13 NLT

Just as God looks at the heart of man, not his appearance, he also prefers a humble heart rather than the gesture of ripping your clothes. This was a practice in the Old Testament days. People would tear their garments over their regret for their sins or the people's sins. This was an outward demonstration of sorrow for sin, but what about the condition on the inside of the person? They could have been thinking about another event, a friend, or anything for that matter, while destroying their attire with false emotion regarding their transgressions.

God makes it very clear that he wants a contrite heart—a desire to turn from doing evil and a commitment to follow him. The Lord, in his abundant compassion, is eager to forgive the penitent person, one whose remorse about their trespasses is pure and true. Search your motives and make sure they are authentic as you go before the throne of grace to receive his generous mercy.

Father, thank you for your overflowing mercy and never-ending love. Amen.

Different Ways of Worshiping

David danced before the LORD with all his might.
And David was wearing a linen ephod.

2 SAMUEL 6:14 ESV

The elite troops of Israel were transporting the ark of the covenant with great care as it made its journey to Jerusalem. David was ecstatic because this meant that the blessing of God's presence would be with him in his kingdom. David proceeded to worship the Lord in passionate, enthusiastic dance while wearing just a simple linen robe. From her window, David's wife, the daughter of Saul, viewed David's exuberant display and despised him for it. Obviously, she did not feel as excited about the Lord's presence as David did and disapproved of his actions.

Many Christians have different ways of worshiping the Lord. Some churches still have choirs while others have bands. Some use colorful lighting and smoke machines while others exhibit more conservative measures. As long as Jesus is glorified from pure hearts, no one should disdain the way another chooses to honor God. It is our attitude in coming to him that the Lord views, and he receives pleasure from one who approaches with a sincere, undivided, and dedicated heart.

Father, may I worship you from a pure heart and never judge the differences in how others give you praise. Amen.

Eyes of Faith

The message of the cross is foolish to those who are headed for destruction! But we who are being saved know it is the very power of God.

1 CORINTHIANS 1:18 NLT

The Corinthians were having a bit of trouble with the content of Paul's teaching. In their society, they did not typically discuss anyone who was put to death by crucifixion. It was such a cruel, crude type of death reserved for the worst criminals that it was considered unfit conversation for proper company. This was undeniably an issue for some in Corinth who heard of the type of death Christ endured. It just didn't make sense that the Messiah would suffer this type of humiliation, and these opinions caused many to reject what the apostle shared about the gospel.

Some, though, could see with eyes of faith that Christ's death on the cross was the greatest exhibition of love there ever was, and they found in it the lover of their soul. Through the power of God, those who believed were snatched from the fiery furnace and given assurance that their sins were forgiven and eternal life was now theirs. God's ways are not our ways; his are always born of his love and provision for us.

Father, thank you for your methods. Even though I might not understand your ways, I know they are best. Amen.

November

What God Has in Store

As it is written: "Eye has not seen, nor ear heard, nor have entered into the heart of man the things which God has prepared for those who love Him."

1 CORINTHIANS 2:9 NKJV

Think back to the most beautiful sight you have ever seen. Try to recreate in your ears the sound of the most melodious music you have ever heard. Feel the emotions you experienced the last time you were surrounded by all your loved ones. These are wonderful things to imagine, but they can never compare to what God has in store for us.

Not only does he desire to give us an abundant, spirit-filled life on this earth, but he has prepared a place that is magnificently beyond our imagination in heaven. Gold streets with walls made of jasper and every jewel you can imagine. A city without a need for illumination for the glory of God gives this paradise light. There, we will sing great songs of praise before the throne as we view his glorious presence continuously. From his throne will flow the river of life, appearing like crystal and adorned by the Tree of Life on each side. Sounds too good to be true, but it's an absolute fact. He is coming back soon; be ready.

Jesus, I'm ready, Lord. Please come. Amen.

His Past Faithfulness

I pray that God, the source of hope, will fill you completely with joy and peace because you trust in him. Then you will overflow with confident hope through the power of the Holy Spirit.

ROMANS 15:13 NLT

When hard times come out of nowhere and hit you like a ton of bricks, it's easy to become hopeless. This is a time when our enemy comes at us with a vengeance because, coward that he is, he will always kick us when we are down. It is before these times arise that we must prepare by drawing close to God. We must have Scripture ready at hand to bolster our faith. We should understand through prayer and remembering his past faithfulness that he is in control and he will deliver us. We need to see with the eyes of our heart that he is close enough to collect our tears in his bottle.

Call on his Holy Spirit to give you wisdom to ascertain that this time is no different from any other troubled times, for your Lord is present and will defend you. Ask God to help you move forward with hopeful expectation of what you know for a fact your God will do: work all things together for good in your life.

Father, I trust you and will wait with faith and hope. Amen.

Caterpillars

Don't copy the behavior and customs of this world, but let
God transform you into a new person by changing the way you
think. Then you will learn to know God's will for you, which is
good and pleasing and perfect.

ROMANS 12:2 NLT

Just when the caterpillar thinks life is over, it becomes a
butterfly. For the caterpillar to become a butterfly, it first dies
to its old nature by literally digesting itself. An amazing process
ensues before the butterfly arrives. Every aspect of the journey
is important for it to become what God always intended it to be.
The Bible and life tell similar stories of struggle to victory.

Moses murdered a man and spent forty years in the
desert before becoming a great leader. Jonah rejected God's
mission and spent three days in the belly of a fish before
saving a city from destruction. John was exiled to an island,
where he wrote the book of Revelation. Mary Magdalene faced
tormenting demons before her glorious deliverance. Chuck
Colson endured prison for federal crimes before becoming
an evangelist and seeing multitudes of prisoners set free.
Amy Carmichael started life as a privileged girl before saving
thousands of children from ritualistic deaths and sex work.

That's the work of continuing grace in Jesus Christ:
eternal transformation!

Dear Lord, keep me from interfering in the transformation you
are desiring in my life. Give me your divine wisdom. Amen.

Remain in God

Jacob awoke from his sleep and said,
"Surely the LORD is in this place,
and I wasn't even aware of it!"
GENESIS 28:16 NLT

How often do we get so busy with our own lives that we fail to recognize when someone is trying to get our attention? When it comes to remaining in God's purpose for us, it is best to be constantly in relationship by confessing any sin. We must also be in the Word, recounting his goodness and provisions. We should be thankful in all circumstances, easy or difficult, for Scripture says this is his will for us. If we are not in close communion with the Lord, we can miss his direction and his plan for us.

Jacob was out under the stars sleeping and had a dream. Upon waking, he realized God's presence was there, and he had not previously recognized it. How often we miss the revelation glory of our holy, loving God because we are distracted. Jesus said he is truly, always with his children. He can come as a whisper, a dream, or through his Word to comfort, instruct, encourage, correct, and renew. May God make us aware of his presence and what he is saying to us.

Holy Spirit, may I be open anew to my encounters with the Lord.
Amen.

Nothing without Him

LORD, you poured out blessings on your land! You restored
the fortunes of Israel. You forgave the guilt of your people—
yes, you covered all their sins.

PSALM 85:1–2 NLT

We think that we make the decision to come to Christ, yet God
chose us before the foundation of the world. We believe we are
doing great spiritually, but we forget that it is through the power
of the Holy Spirit that we endure and mature. We pat ourselves
on the back for avoiding that particular sin only to realize that
pride moved in, taking the place of the victory.

We can do nothing of any value or any good unless we
do it through the Lord Most High. Recall that we are made from
the dust of the ground and the bone of a man, and it was the
breath of God that brought us to life. And when we had shown
nothing but disobedient disdain for his enduring love and
blessings, turning to other gods and going our own selfish way,
Jesus was the solution. So basically, we are nothing without him.
We should be praising him, humbly coming before him to sing
songs of worship every hour of the day and in the waking hours
of the night.

Lord, revive me, your child, to righteousness, holiness,
selflessness, and compassion. Amen.

The Joy Set before Him

You know that God paid a ransom to save you from the empty life you inherited from your ancestors. And it was not paid with mere gold or silver, which lose their value. It was the precious blood of Christ, the sinless, spotless Lamb of God.

1 PETER 1:18–19 NLT

Imagine getting a phone call from someone demanding a ransom for the return of a loved one. The panic and the attempt to decipher what is happening would send you reeling. And you would do everything possible to pay the ransom.

For the joy set before him, namely us, Jesus went to the cross to ransom us from sin. His Father had to watch his own creatures torment and destroy the body of his Son with vengeance and hatred. Still he offered the world redemption through the excruciating suffering of the Savior. This treasure, the One whose worth is more than any other, snatched us from the jaws of hell. God did all this for us although we were undeserving, sinful, rebellious, yet loved with an everlasting love. God desired us enough to pay our ransom with the blood drained from his Son's sinless body. Praise him for his redeeming love.

Jesus, mere words cannot express my gratitude for your sacrifice. I am yours. Work your will in me. Amen.

Spread the Gospel

No, despite all these things, overwhelming victory is ours
through Christ, who loved us.

ROMANS 8:37 NLT

The apostle Paul is the author of Romans. The particular chapter from which the above verse come ends with the beautiful assurance that nothing can separate us from Christ. We are guaranteed that even if we face tribulation, persecution, famine, or various other dangers, we will emerge as conquerors through Jesus. We have the confident assurance that "neither death nor life, nor angels nor rulers, nor things present nor things to come, nor powers, nor height nor depth, nor anything else in all creation, will be able to separate us from the love of God in Christ Jesus our Lord" (vv. 38–39 ESV).

So why do we get depressed, worried, or stressed out when this is our truth? How can anything bring us down when we know, as believers, that we are sealed as citizens of heaven forevermore? We should be joyously living to share the gospel so that others can experience his deliverance. We must get our eyes off this world and on Jesus so that we can represent him and help others find their way to salvation in him.

Jesus, forgive me for my lack of boldness in sharing the great
news of the gospel. Help me live every day with the purpose of
showing others the way to you. Amen.

Serve the Lord Only

"All right then," Joshua said, "destroy the idols among you, and turn your hearts to the LORD, the God of Israel." The people said to Joshua, "We will serve the LORD our God. We will obey him alone."

JOSHUA 24:23–24 NLT

There are laws set in place for our protection and that of others. There are red lights that warn us to stop before crashing into another car. There are consequences for stealing something that is the property of someone else. Joshua warned the people of his day what would happen if they served other gods. When the people swore that they would serve the Lord, Joshua struggled with their answer. He informed them that God is jealous and, if they forsook him, he would not forgive their trespasses. He instructed them to put away their foreign idols and serve the Lord only.

Don't we often look at these accounts and wonder how the Israelites could have been so foolish? Why in the world would they choose something else over the Lord? Then we notice the dust on our Bible and the remote in our hand. What do you gravitate to for knowledge or comfort? Is God truly first in your life? If not, turn your heart to him alone.

Lord, help me to put you first and serve you only. Amen.

God's Mercy and Forgiveness

"To the Lord our God belong mercy and forgiveness,
though we have rebelled against Him."

DANIEL 9:9 NKJV

Let's look at the definitions of three words.

Mercy: "forbearance shown especially to an offender or to one subject to one's power; a blessing that is an act of divine favor or compassion."[9]

Forgiveness: the act of "[granting] relief from payment."[10]

Rebellion: "opposition to one in authority or dominance."[11]

The first two words belong to God, for he is mercy and forgiveness. The third word belongs to us ashamedly, for we rebel against his goodness. And when we do, he eagerly waits for us to come to our senses, humble ourselves, and confess. He does not condemn; he does not guilt us or want us to feel shame, for those feelings were demolished on the cross.

We serve a Savior who offers limitless forgiveness. We did nothing to deserve his favor, yet his favor is ours in abundance.

God, you are generous, good, kind, compassionate, and forgiving. You are my everything, and I love you. Amen.

---

9   *Merriam-Webster.com Dictionary*, s.v. "mercy."
10 *Merriam-Webster.com Dictionary*, s.v. "forgive."
11 *Merriam-Webster.com Dictionary*, s.v. "rebellion."

God Is Victorious

"Don't be afraid!" Elisha told him. "For there are more on our side than on theirs!" Then Elisha prayed, "O LORD, open his eyes and let him see!" The LORD opened the young man's eyes, and when he looked up, he saw that the hillside around Elisha was filled with horses and chariots of fire.

2 KINGS 6:16–17 NLT

What do we put our trust in daily? Unfortunately, we often turn to ourselves instead of realizing how much we need the Lord. We walk around pretty clueless at times. If only we could see with our eyes all that surrounds us in the heavenly realm. Does that seem scary? Or does it give you confidence to know that, regardless of the raging war between angels and demons over your life, your God is victorious?

The Lord has kept some things a mystery from us for good reason. "Faith is…the evidence of things not seen" (Hebrews 11:1 KJV), and we must believe in God's plan and protection. How it glorifies and pleases our God when we trust, for while we are standing still, he will fight the battle. Elisha prayed for his servant, "O LORD, open his eyes and let him see!" When his eyes were opened, the man saw the hosts of God and nothing else.

Lord, open my eyes to your truth. Amen.

Made to Belong to Him

Create in me a clean heart, O God.
Renew a loyal spirit within me.
PSALM 51:10 NLT

So often we feel like we have made it, we are secure in our faith, and we are certain that we will avoid any temptation that pursues us. And then we fall. Just the pride of thinking we have it together spiritually can be a slippery slope to transgression. Scripture clearly states that all our righteousness is as filthy rags (Isaiah 64:6). Not just a stain, but absolutely, completely covered in dirt.

We have no means of cleaning ourselves up, but God provides the blood of Jesus to wash us white as snow. We are incapable of making a new heart within ourselves, but the God who loves us can give us a heart that is obedient and faithful. He can create a hunger for the bread of his Word that will fill and satisfy us like nothing else. He safely holds us close in the shelter of his wings, like a mother hen gathers her chicks. He delivers us from our enemy. We can do nothing, but nothing is impossible for God. We were made for his pleasure. We were made to belong to him and no one else.

Lord, stamp your image deep in my heart and on my life. Amen.

Run to the Father

The thief's purpose is to steal and kill and destroy.
My purpose is to give them a rich and satisfying life.

JOHN 10:10 NLT

Do you see the juxtaposition in today's verse between the two objectives? There are two plans at work here, two motives with completely opposite intents and results. One is a plot from the most despicable evil, and the other is provided by the greatest love that ever was or will be. We have the free will to choose which one we want to expose ourselves to.

We must wonder, *Why would anyone have any issue with making this decision immediately, for who would want to fall under the jurisdiction of Satan's deathly desires?* Look around, for a great number of people in the world have chosen the devil over God. Wouldn't you think the human mind would be smart enough and have a sense of survival that would make them run toward the Father and away from the murderer who is our enemy? Oh, that the world would come to know him, his goodness, his love, and his salvation. Today, may I be the one who sees the lost and endeavors to show them the love of Jesus.

Lord, thank you for my present abundant life in Christ and the eternal life in my future. Amen.

Choose

"If it is evil in your eyes to serve the LORD, choose this day whom you will serve, whether the gods your fathers served in the region beyond the River, or the gods of the Amorites in whose land you dwell. But as for me and my house, we will serve the LORD."

JOSHUA 24:15 ESV

Joshua had finished a long recitation of all the Lord had done for the people of Israel. He told how God had delivered them from a myriad of armies, including the Amorites, the Hittites, and the Canaanites, among others. He fought their battles, delivering their ancestors from Pharoah by parting the Red Sea. He gave them land they did not purchase and fruit to eat that they did not plant. Yet they still worshiped the foreign gods that their fathers had served in Egypt.

Joshua told them to choose their god, but regardless of their decision, Joshua and his house would worship only the Lord. The people cried out that they would also serve God. Joshua explained that God was jealous and would not forgive their sins if they turned away and returned to their false gods. Israel chose to serve the Lord for all the days of Joshua and the days of the elders who survived him. Whom will you and your house choose to serve?

Father, I choose you. Amen.

Filled with Pleasure

Praise the LORD! How good to sing praises to our God!
How delightful and how fitting!

PSALM 147:1 NLT

There is someone in my congregation who will never be asked to sing a solo, and for this, the rest of us are thankful. This person's worship is authentic and sincere, but he can't carry a tune in a bucket. He has no sense of rhythm but a heart that beats adoringly with love and devotion to God. It is beautiful to view the face of this child of God, for his eyes are alive, filled with joy as they look heavenward. Although the sound he makes will not inspire, his attitude and adoring heart speak volumes and encourage all who watch.

This brother in the church will not be remembered for his melodious rendition of a beloved hymn. However, other members of our congregation will think of him as an encouragement to love the Lord with all our heart, for he truly does. There will be no recordings of any tunes he sang in honor of the Lord, but many will speak of his testimony of a life lived well for Jesus. No matter the sound, if our heart swells up in praise and gratitude to our magnificent, beloved God, he is filled with pleasure.

God, help me focus solely on worshiping you and not on how I sound to others. May my feeble voice honor you. Amen.

Be Vigilant in Your Faith

These desires give birth to sinful actions.
And when sin is allowed to grow, it gives birth to death.
JAMES 1:15 NLT

We cannot stroll through life thinking that because we are
Christians, we will never give in to sin. As long as our enemy
is free to roam the earth, we will face temptation. If we cannot
master sin, it will master us, leading us down the path to death.
Hebrews 6:4–6 (ESV) says:

> It is impossible, in the case of those who have once
> been enlightened, who have tasted the heavenly gift,
> and have shared in the Holy Spirit, and have tasted the
> goodness of the word of God and the powers of the age
> to come, and then have fallen away, to restore them again
> to repentance, since they are crucifying once again the
> Son of God to their own harm and holding him up to
> contempt.

We must be vigilant in our faith, not backsliding but
growing up in the Lord and his Word. It is a slippery slope
the devil lays for us. Don't risk your relationship with God by
turning away after you have tasted his goodness.

Father, keep me close, guide my path, and discipline me if I need
it to keep me on your narrow path. Amen.

Amazing Grace

God saved you by his grace when you believed.
And you can't take credit for this; it is a gift from God.
EPHESIANS 2:8 NLT

Have you ever accepted accolades that you did not deserve instead of admitting the truth? Maybe you were part of a team effort, and you played up your participation a bit more than you should have to others. Possibly you said you'd pray for someone and, when they received their answer, they thanked you for your prayer and you accepted their gratitude. In your heart, though, you knew you had forgotten all about it, never uttering a word of intercession.

Sometimes we take the credit for our own salvation in the same way. We have no ability to obtain salvation on our own. It is only God who moves our heart to receive his free gift. Don't ever fool yourself into thinking you came to him of your own accord. He chose you in him before the foundation of the world. Any progress you make is the work of the Holy Spirit wooing you to the Savior to receive forgiveness and eternal life. What an amazing God we have, who would do anything and give everything to have us as his own.

Precious Lord, thank you for the beauty of your grace, your salvation, and the blessing of your love. Amen.

Bless Him

Accept my prayer as incense offered to you,
and my upraised hands as an evening offering.
PSALM 141:2 NLT

A dear friend and former neighbor shared a beautiful story with me recently: "As I was lying in bed listening to worship music, I lifted my hands in worship and praise to my Lord and felt, as it were, a bolt of energy flow through me. It was a most glorious and awesome experience! I had always been shy about lifting my hands unto the Lord." He went on to express that he can hardly wait to get back in church and join in the worship by lifting his hands. Praise the Lord for my brother's tender heart.

This friend experienced what Psalm 22:3 says: "You are holy, You who are enthroned upon the praises of Israel" (NASB). Some Bible translations say that God "inhabits" the praises of his people. If we ever wonder what attitude we should have in the presence of God, worship is definitely a way to do it. When we worship, God is right there with us. He takes pleasure in our praise, he loves us, and he gazes on us as his beloved children. It's a privilege to know that we can bless him with the words of our mouth, the movements of our bodies, and the intent of our hearts.

Lord, you alone are worthy of my praise. Amen.

It Will All Make Sense

Now we see things imperfectly, like puzzling reflections in a mirror, but then we will see everything with perfect clarity. All that I know now is partial and incomplete, but then I will know everything completely, just as God now knows me completely.

1 CORINTHIANS 13:12 NLT

When it comes to our attempt to try to fully understand or explain God, we need to remember this truth. "'My thoughts are nothing like your thoughts,' says the LORD. 'And my ways are far beyond anything you could imagine. For just as the heavens are higher than the earth, so my ways are higher than your ways and my thoughts higher than your thoughts'" (Isaiah 55:8–9 NLT). We are not meant to know everything now, for there is still mystery. God is God, and we are not. Study his Word to receive what he has freely shared with us presently and trust him for what is still unknown.

It is in his wisdom that the Lord withholds things we do not need to know now. Someday, when we're in heaven, we'll understand, and it will all make sense. We'll know beyond a shadow of a doubt that all he did on our behalf was righteous and perfect.

Father, I trust you and know someday you will help me see all things clearly. Amen.

Courage and Compassion

One day the girl said to her mistress,
"I wish my master would go to see the prophet in Samaria.
He would heal him of his leprosy."

2 KINGS 5:3 NLT

The girl was taken captive, torn from her family, brought to a foreign land with people who spoke a strange language, had strange customs, and ate strange food. She was forced to be a servant. Still, because of her faith in God, she risked her life to boldly proclaim, "I wish my master would go to see the prophet in Samaria. He would heal him of his leprosy." She wished the best for one who had enslaved her. She could have been fearful, bitter, angry, and resentful, yet she saw an opportunity to speak out about the one true God. She chose to step out in faith and trust her Lord for the result.

Such a story of faith, selflessness, courage, compassion, fervor to share God, and love for God is truly inspiring and convicting. God can give us boldness, wisdom, and clarity of speech to proclaim him and reflect him in the way we live. May we fearlessly share God with love, grace, wisdom, and fervor.

Dear Lord, forgive me for the many opportunities I've missed to share your great love and plan of redeeming grace. May I, who live in such freedom, be filled with your Holy Spirit, empowering me with compassion toward the lost. Amen.

Under His Gaze

You saw me before I was born. Every day of my life was recorded in your book. Every moment was laid out before a single day had passed. How precious are your thoughts about me, O God. They cannot be numbered!

PSALM 139:16–17 NLT

Contemplate the hand of God carefully weaving together every vein, creating every cell, forming every bone of your body while you were still in the womb. He had a supernatural view and an entrance to your developing frame that no one else could. He scheduled the day you would enter the world and the day you will depart from it. He determined your appearance, your personality, and the future work you would do for his kingdom. Then once you breathed his breath of life, he never took his eyes off you.

God desires to know us and for us to know him intimately. We have continually available to us a Counselor who knows and understands everything about us, our temperament, temptations, and traits. He knows what we have experienced and how those experiences have affected us. He longs for his children to come to him and his counseling Word. If we could understand even a trace of his amazing love toward us, we would seek him and follow his guidance.

Father, thank you for intimacy with you, for your love, and for your direction in my life. Amen.

Help the Lost

My brothers, if anyone among you wanders from the truth and someone brings him back, let him know that whoever brings back a sinner from his wandering will save his soul from death and will cover a multitude of sins.

JAMES 5:19–20 ESV

As believers, we know the saving grace of Jesus Christ. We know what we were before he redeemed us and our experience of the joy of his transformation, becoming new in him. We rejoice knowing we are no longer slaves to sin.

What about those around us who have not come to a knowledge of the Savior or know him and have turned away? It's our responsibility to live and speak the truth that guides them to Jesus. Those who know him but have allowed sin to reclaim a front seat in their lives need our counsel. We must go to those in both of these situations, through careful thought and prayer, to see if we can persuade them to make things right with God. We should go in humility and love, without condemnation. When we win a brother back or help the lost find their way, their sins are covered as they confess. The Lord will receive them, and we will have helped someone avoid spiritual death.

Jesus, give me boldness to share your truth. Amen.

We Are Loved

Dear friends, let us continue to love one another, for love
comes from God. Anyone who loves is a child of God and
knows God.

1 JOHN 4:7 NLT

We can all think of people we have known who exude love
for others. We can also recall those who are reserved and
tend to be shy around others. Either personality can show the
affection of Christ to others. You don't have to be the life of the
party to convey the heart of Jesus to another. It is the motive
of your approach and the desire you have to fulfill the Great
Commission or be the listening ear for one in distress that will
open hearts to the love of God.

We all need to know we are loved, and God has gone
above and beyond to let us know the depth of his love for us. In
community, we need to let other believers know we love them
as well. It brings joy and encouragement and warms a hurting
or needy spirit. It identifies us with the Lord when we love one
another, for he is love. It reveals to others that we know him,
for without him we would be incapable of showing his care.
Let everyone see who you are in Christ by carrying his love
everywhere you go.

Jesus, please put your love for others in my heart. Amen.

Faith

Elijah said to her, "Don't be afraid! Go ahead and do just what you've said, but make a little bread for me first. Then use what's left to prepare a meal for yourself and your son. For this is what the LORD, the God of Israel, says: There will always be flour and olive oil left in your containers until the time when the LORD sends rain and the crops grow again!"

1 KINGS 17:13–14 NLT

As we study the Bible, we see God's miraculous provision repeatedly, from the ravens feeding Elijah to our salvation through the cross of Christ. Doesn't it make you wonder why this has not been enough to give us unrelenting faith in the Lord's power? We think he will work wonders for someone else but not us. We should believe all things truly are possible. God is always working for good toward us. We must put our faith to work.

Today's passage focuses on a woman who had next to nothing, giving what she had to feed Elijah. Through faith, this woman gave him the first of the last she had. Her "works" accompanied her faith. God's miraculous supply kept pouring back into her life. What could change in your life today if you would only take God at his word and trust?

Father, give me great faith. Amen.

The Pride of Man

Isaiah said to Hezekiah, "Listen to this message from the LORD: The time is coming when everything in your palace—all the treasures stored up by your ancestors until now—will be carried off to Babylon. Nothing will be left, says the Lord."

2 KINGS 20:16–17 NLT

Pride is one of the most insidious sins. It slithers in and sneaks up unnoticed. Sad was the end of great King Hezekiah who had led and seen many great victories in battle. God had allowed him to build great cities and engineer great innovations for water supply. He was miraculously healed. God had blessed him, yet he became prideful when the son of the king of Babylon paid him a visit. He arrogantly showed off all his treasures as if he had attained them himself. The prophet Isaiah told him that great destruction was coming due to his boasting, but he was indifferent. He self-centeredly said, "At least there will be peace and security during my lifetime" (v. 19 NLT). He credited himself instead of praising God for the peace in his nation, and for that, his future was dim. All his goods soon belonged to Babylon, including his own sons.

Don't take credit for what only God can do. Give him the praise due to him.

Father, burn out my pride and rekindle my passion for you. Amen.

Cry Out

Shout with joy to the LORD, all the earth!
PSALM 100:1 NLT

How often do we sing the praises of our kids, our spouses, and even ourselves? We never hesitate to share what a great job little Johnny did in his presentation or at his chosen sport. We gladly share about the way our spouse treated us on our special day. We pretend to be humble when we casually tell others about our own achievement or latest promotion. So why do we reserve the best of our praise only on Sunday and in the relative privacy of a church building? We should be crying out his goodness from the rooftops!

We wouldn't be alive today if God's will and grace did not allow it. We have nothing without his power. We should be acknowledging that all we have is due to his mercy and lavish love. Our possessions and loved ones could be gone in a heartbeat, so it isn't wise to place all our trust in them. We must remember where our provisions for life, salvation, and security come from and be openly thankful consistently.

Seven reasons I will praise my Lord today: he is my firm foundation, patient, corrective, trustworthy, constant, faithful, and perfect. Your turn…shout to the Lord and let the earth hear your praise.

Father, forgive me for holding back gratitude. I want to worship and thank you continually. Your grace gives me life. Amen.

Divine GPS

"I can do nothing on my own. I judge as God tells me.
Therefore, my judgment is just, because I carry out the will of
the one who sent me, not my own will."

JOHN 5:30 NLT

What a great lesson we can learn from our glorious Savior.
Even though he was God as man, the Son never made a move
without direction from the Father. He didn't rush into anything
but always prayed, consulting the wisdom of the Lord. Once
he knew what his Father required of him, Jesus carried out
his will to the greatest detail. We have the Holy Spirit within
us to place a red flag in our way when we start to depend on
ourselves, making our own way. We must give ourselves over
to God daily so that we never venture into our own plan before
discerning what he wants from us. We must remember he is our
divine GPS when, in humility, we place ourselves in his hands.
Jesus gave himself over to the will of his Father. He could have
sought his own glory when his humanity was tempted, but he
submitted to God. We must follow his example and live fully
surrendered to him.

Jesus, may I, with passion and action, give my all to you. Please
forgive my waywardness. Once again, I surrender all. Amen.

Safe and Secure

"I am leaving you with a gift—peace of mind and heart.
And the peace I give is a gift the world cannot give.
So don't be troubled or afraid."

JOHN 14:27 NLT

These days, anxiety is at an all-time high. We can blame this on many things. Health crises, economic turmoil, mental illness, wars, school shootings, and crime bring worries about what tomorrow holds. This world offers no relief. Yet there has always been an answer.

The one and only solution is Jesus. He alone can provide the means to ease any concerns. He is the only one who can calm the sea, move a mountain, bring a dead person back to life, and save the souls of the world. His rest is like none other, for it is supernatural, bringing reconciliation to any disturbance life may present. We can't find rest without Jesus, for all that is good exists in him. Why spend another day living without the one who can replace your frenzied mind with his perfect peace. If you have not accepted his gift of peace, don't hesitate any longer. Come to him today.

Jesus, I confess my sin. Come into my heart and be my Savior. Be Lord of my life. Help me follow you. Thank you for redeeming me. Amen.

Unfailing Love

Your unfailing love is better than life itself;
how I praise you!

PSALM 63:3 NLT

Shortly after my parents were married, they were all packed to go to China as missionaries. They had an unfailing love for the country. Then the war broke out, and they were not allowed to go. Through the rest of their lives, they gave their prayers, money, and energy to China (as well as many other nations and peoples).

The Christians in China are now, and have been, under violent persecution beyond our imagination. Many pastors have been imprisoned for refusing to stop preaching the gospel. Yet the Christ followers in China continue to grow in number and to tell others of Christ's salvation to others. Many are going to other nations to share the love of Jesus. Let us pray for China and the nations of the world that they would know of Jesus' love and saving grace. May we be filled to overflowing with God's love and hear and respond to the cry of those in need—those longing to experience his unfailing love.

Lord, may I bask in your unfailing love today. Amen.

Safeguards

He also released a dove to see if the water had receded and it could find dry ground. But the dove could find no place to land because the water still covered the ground. So it returned to the boat, and Noah held out his hand and drew the dove back inside.

GENESIS 8:8–9 NLT

During the great flood, God provided a way to let Noah know when it was safe to leave the ark. Noah sent out a dove on a testing mission to find land. If she returned to the ark, Noah knew it was not safe for him and his family to leave the boat. God gives us many warnings and signs for our own safety. Unfortunately, we often ignore his blatant signs.

One night, a teen wanted to swim in a pool belonging to his neighbors, who were on vacation. They left a "no trespassing" sign on the gate to the pool, but the boy ignored the sign. In the dark, he dove into the pool. Unbeknownst to him, the neighbors had drained their pool to have it painted in their absence. His injuries from the dive left him paraplegic. Let us not advance in our own prideful strength. Follow God with an obedient heart. He desires to safeguard us.

Jesus, give me wisdom to see your warning signs and obey. Amen.

Strong Foundation

Let your roots grow down into him, and let your lives be built on him. Then your faith will grow strong in the truth you were taught, and you will overflow with thankfulness.

COLOSSIANS 2:7 NLT

Oak trees with deep roots can exist for a thousand years. The roots can extend to four feet or more below the surface. This support system also moves laterally and can extend three to seven times the width of the branches. The strongest root grows straight down, but the tree has many roots that thrive in the top eighteen inches of soil. It's abundantly clear that without the strength and provision of the roots, the tree would not survive.

So it is with our relationship with Jesus. If we don't drink daily at the well of his Word and in prayer, our Christian walk will suffer. We need to build our faith in him, what he has done, and what he has promised for the days ahead. Our strength must come from depending on him for all that we could ever need. Believe that he is the miraculous God of the Bible and trust him by building your faith on his strong foundation, and you will become more and more like Christ.

Jesus, help my roots grow deep in your Word, maturing me to be more like you. Amen.

December

Neighbors

"Now which of these three would you say was a neighbor to the man who was attacked by bandits?" Jesus asked. The man replied, "The one who showed him mercy." Then Jesus said, "Yes, now go and do the same."

LUKE 10:36–37 NLT

In Luke chapter 10, Jesus explains who our neighbors are. We do not choose them, but God chooses those whom he will put in our path. We are to show love, kindness, compassion, mercy, understanding, and, many times, forgiveness. Often this requires "inconvenience" of our time and an expenditure of our resources, including financial, emotional, and physical. We'll find ourselves befriending those we wouldn't necessarily choose but whom God has led us to.

Serving them with the right motive associates us with Jesus' heart. We become the only Jesus some people ever see. We are the hands and feet of Christ as we engage with those whom the Lord has allowed to cross our paths. Many of us have difficulty with this, and the solution is to pray and ask God to give you his love, his heart, and a passion to help others. We must humble ourselves to lead others to Jesus.

Jesus, so often, I am stiff-necked in the comfort of my daily life. May your Holy Spirit mold my heart and bend my neck to the desperate needs of others. Amen.

Valley of Bones

"'I will put my Spirit in you, and you will live again and return home to your own land. Then you will know that I, the LORD, have spoken, and I have done what I said. Yes, the LORD has spoken!'"

EZEKIEL 37:14 NLT

God took the prophet to a valley filled with dry bones. They discussed whether the bones could live, and Ezekiel answered that only God knew the answer. The Lord told him to prophecy over the bones, and God promised that he would revive them with sinew, flesh, and the breath of life.

As God fulfilled this prophecy, the bones stood up and numbered a great army. This was a sign to the despairing Israelites, for they had believed God had cut them off and that they were hopeless. The Lord said that the bones were the house of Israel, that he would place his Spirit in them so that they would live, and that he would place them in their land. God's people thrive when his Spirit is present in their lives. Many of us forget about the Spirit, focusing on only two persons of the Trinity. Make it your purpose to know the Holy Spirit intimately as he fills you and works in you.

Father, revive my dry bones with the breath of your Holy Spirit. Amen.

For Our Own Good

"They shall be My people, and I will be their God; and I will give them one heart and one way, so that they will fear Me always, for their own good and for the good of their children after them."

JEREMIAH 32:38–39 NASB

Everything that the Father has ever done for all of us who were made in his image has been for our own good. He desired so much to have us as his children and to be our Abba that nothing would stop him. It's astounding when you consider how much and in what great abundance God has taken on his own shoulders the responsibility for all that we need for life and salvation. The lengths he took to save us when we couldn't in any way save ourselves would never have even occurred to us.

In our state of sin, we would not have devised the plan of salvation, but he, in his perfect grace and eternal provision, did. Where would we be without his saving work in us? We would be lost forever, separated from him. He, however, creates in us an undivided heart with a reverent awe of his greatness. From his extravagant goodness, he does this for the benefit of us and our children. What an awesome God!

God, you are perfect love. Amen.

Obedience

Although he was a son,
he learned obedience through what he suffered.
HEBREWS 5:8 ESV

So often when we face trials in our life, we question God's goodness. We wonder if he really loves us as much as he loves those friends of ours who continually seem to skate through life. We doubt that anything positive could possibly result from going through this type of difficulty. When we look at today's verse, our perspective changes, especially if we desire to obey God.

If Jesus, who was both God and Man, had to suffer to learn obedience, how much more must we? Because it aligns us with him, we should rejoice in this shared suffering that our Savior understands better than anyone else. No one more than Christ will ever know the extent of what obedience costs. Through emotional agony, he was willing to do what the Father required of him, death on the cross in order to provide forgiveness for us. He learned what submitting to the Father's will wrought, for it brought our salvation.

Next time you are faced with the decision of whether to follow God's plan for you, remember what the obedience of Jesus bought for you. Choose to praise Jesus while suffering.

Jesus, thank you for being the perfect example of obedience to the Father. Help me also obey him in all things. Amen.

In Dark Times

"The mountains may move and the hills disappear, but even then my faithful love for you will remain. My covenant of blessing will never be broken," says the LORD, who has mercy on you.

ISAIAH 54:10 NLT

During those times when we feel our private world or the whole world is crumbling and everything is but a chaotic swirl, may we claim the promise of God's everlasting care and love. His love was with the three Hebrew men whom evil Nebuchadnezzar chained and threw into the fire. They came out without even their hair singed (Daniel 3:19–30). His presence was with Paul and Silas as they were beaten and imprisoned, later to bring the jailer and his entire family to Christ (Acts 16:16–40). It was also with Stephen as he was stoned to death (Acts 7).

In dark times, we must remember that he holds our future as we watch evil seemingly win in our world. A day is coming soon when all will acknowledge that he is God. Until then, the devil cannot chain us to fear, anxiety, anger, pain (physical or emotional), sorrow, or regret, for as believers, we are sealed in God's Spirit. No matter what assails us, God is there to deliver us.

Lord, as your child, I revel in and find comfort and courage in the knowledge that you, my Savior, will never leave nor forsake me. Amen.

The Way We Live

In view of all this, make every effort to respond to God's
promises. Supplement your faith with a generous provision
of moral excellence, and moral excellence with knowledge,
and knowledge with self-control, and self-control with
patient endurance, and patient endurance with godliness, and
godliness with brotherly affection, and brotherly affection with
love for everyone.

2 PETER 1:5–7 NLT

We need never add anything to our faith in an effort to
participate in the provision of our salvation. We're not saved by
works. However, if we are in Christ, a heart transformation will
take place that makes us want to show our salvation through
the way we live. We want to make wise decisions and avoid
temptation. A desire for God's Word will develop, not only to
read it but to insert Scripture into our soul so that we follow
it diligently. When faced with an angry assault, we will not
return anger but control our emotions, not seeking revenge but
offering love.

We will persevere, remembering the example of our Lord
and Savior as he endured the cross. If we struggle with loving
a sibling in Christ, we can pray for God to love that person
through us as he teaches us to sincerely carry his compassion in
our heart for all.

Lord, help me to live a life reflective of this verse. Amen.

The Center of Our Lives

Indeed I also count all things loss for the excellence of the knowledge of Christ Jesus my Lord, for whom I have suffered the loss of all things, and count them as rubbish, that I may gain Christ.

PHILIPPIANS 3:8 NKJV

The apostle Paul gave up an enormous amount of status to follow Jesus. In two verses preceding today's verse, he outlined his heritage. He explained that he was "circumcised on the eighth day, of the people of Israel, of the tribe of Benjamin, a Hebrew of Hebrews; as to the law, a Pharisee; as to zeal, a persecutor of the church; as to righteousness under the law, blameless" (Philippians 3:5–6 ESV).

After his trip down the road of Damascus, he came to the decision that all this was garbage compared to knowing Christ. He turned his world upside down, placing himself in the precarious position of now being misunderstood and abused by those he was once like, the Pharisees. Once he had been ruled by the law, but it no longer had any appeal. Christ as the center of his life was considered his greatest gain of all. Have you given up all, suffered loss for the cause of the cross? If not, will you?

Lord, may my eyes be centered and focused on you. Amen.

All for Good

> "You intended to harm me, but God intended it all for good. He brought me to this position so I could save the lives of many people."
>
> GENESIS 50:20 NLT

Can you imagine the terror in the heart of Joseph's brothers as they realized the brother they thought they had disposed of was now a man of great power? Do you think they remembered his dream in which they were all working in the field and their sheaves of wheat bowed down to his? Or what about the next dream in which the sun, moon, and eleven stars bent before him? Possibly now they believed what he had told them so long ago. They were most likely fearing that their death would come soon as payback for their evil deed. Instead, Joseph met them with compassion, provision, and his own testimony. He told them that, although they meant him harm, God worked something good to save lives. Even they would be saved as a result of their plan to harm their brother.

God can and will take whatever weapon that is forged against us and defeat it as we live according to his good will. Even though we may not understand it in the moment, trust God that his plan is right and his will is best.

Lord, I am grateful that your mercies are new every morning. Amen.

Go Forward with Strength

Be on guard. Stand firm in the faith.
Be courageous. Be strong.
And do everything with love.

1 CORINTHIANS 16:13–14 NLT

Even in the face of battle or an approaching army, God wants his people to maintain their trust in him. Moses explained to the Israelites that all they needed to do was stand still and watch as God fought for them. As the Red Sea parted, he promised that they would never again see the Egyptians who were chasing them (Exodus 14:13–14). When two mighty armies were coming after Jehoshaphat and Judah, the Lord assured them that they need not fear for the battle was his, not theirs (2 Chronicles 20:15).

When it comes down to any win, it will never be something we achieve on our own. The God of all creation brings victory for us. If we are Christ followers, everything we face in life comes under his scrutiny and the path of his plan. So go forward with strength, faith, and rejoicing that we serve the one true God who will deliver us from evil.

Father, I am blessed, knowing that I will never have to depend on my own strength but can stand still and see your deliverance on my behalf. Nothing will ever tear us apart. Thank you. Amen.

Called Us Out

Now, O Jacob, listen to the LORD who created you. O Israel, the one who formed you says, "Do not be afraid, for I have ransomed you. I have called you by name; you are mine."

ISAIAH 43:1 NLT

Paying a ransom releases the subject from captivity. When we dissect the above verse, we see once again that it is God who does all the work. He created us, forming us in his image out of dust. He wove us together in our mother's womb, carefully personalizing every part of us. He took our sin upon himself, paying the "ransom" for our souls. He chose us before the foundation of the world, called us out as his own.

Jacob was created, but Israel was formed by God. It took many years and many hardships before stubborn, spoiled Jacob was transformed from "deceiver" into Israel, "prince of God." Jacob came to the place in his life where he acknowledged and confessed his weakness and wrestled with an angel. It was a night of recognizing and surrendering his sinful self to God's powerful, perfect, transforming nature. It altered the trajectory of his life, changing him to one who belonged solely to the Lord.

Lord, may your continuing grace transform me into your image. Amen.

Endurance to Hold Up

We can rejoice, too, when we run into problems and trials, for we know that they help us develop endurance. And endurance develops strength of character, and character strengthens our confident hope of salvation.

ROMANS 5:3–4 NLT

A dear friend suffered an unjustified personal attack from a coworker. This attack continued over time with the coworker treating my friend in a passive aggressive way. Unable to leave the job, my friend had to endure what she didn't understand. So she went to Jesus and today's verse. She asked for endurance to hold up under pressure, and she found herself getting emotionally stronger. She saw changes in the way she handled things and developed gratitude that God was working in her heart.

She gained confidence, which gave her hope that the Lord would make things clear, redeem the relationship, and turn it into friendship. Then, realizing that her battle was not against flesh and blood, she started to pray for blessings on the one who was persecuting her. In the end, she found herself rejoicing that her faithful God took something that was meant to hurt her and used it to conform her to his Son's image.

Father, help me use today's verse as a strategy when trials and tribulations come. Help me humbly submit myself to you as you turn evil into good. Amen.

He Is Our Fortress

In that day he will be your sure foundation, providing a rich store of salvation, wisdom, and knowledge. The fear of the LORD will be your treasure.

ISAIAH 33:6 NLT

The world around us seems to be daily shaken to its core. Chaos and destruction spin with relentless force, and spewing fear and hate seems to be the norm. Senseless violence strikes down innocent lives. It is difficult to even try to comprehend how those who have rejected Christ manage living in this unstable environment. Where does their hope, if they have any, come from? One can only imagine that, if they experience any peace, it comes in the guise of a lie from Satan, for he would love to lull people into a false calm to keep them from seeking Christ.

As God's children, we have so many promises that we need never be afraid of the future, for he has it all planned out. He is our Rock and our redemption, and he fills us with his presence, power, peace, and perfect love as we abide in him. Be in awe of him as you submit to his requirements for you from Micah 6:8 to love mercy, seek justice, and walk humbly with your God.

Dear Lord, make me a healing oil, pouring forth your love, peace, mercy, grace, and compassion. Amen.

Dust and Ashes

"You said, 'Listen and I will speak! I have some questions for you, and you must answer them.' I had only heard about you before, but now I have seen you with my own eyes. I take back everything I said, and I sit in dust and ashes to show my repentance."

JOB 42:4–6 NLT

At the time Job made this statement, he was writhing in constant pain, greatly intensified by the discomforting words of his three friends. He had lost his children, and his wife rejected and deserted him. He had stated his case for what he thought was a life well lived. But after God spoke, Job began to see things as they really were, viewing God in all his power, wisdom, and sovereignty. These words are the result of what Job had to say after a Q & A between him and his Creator: "I had only heard about you before, but now I have seen you with my own eyes. I take back everything I said, and I sit in dust and ashes to show my repentance."

Take a truthful look at yourself; then see God in his purity, righteousness, justice, faithfulness, love, mercy, and grace. This should evoke awesome reverence and an urgency to bow in humility and surrender.

Lord, may I never question your goodness. Amen.

Songs of Praise

My mouth is filled with your praise,
declaring your splendor all day long.
PSALM 71:8 NIV

Remember how King Jehoshaphat and his people rejoiced in song and prayer when God defeated their enemies for them? The entire nation of Judah poured out their hearts to God that they had been powerless without him and that he alone was their defender and their portion, worthy of endless praise and worship.

Can you imagine how it pleased the Father's heart to know his people were looking only to him for their deliverance? Can you imagine how sweet the praise was to him? Each word must have been beautiful music to his ears, as it is even now in this day and age when we pray and sing to the glory of our heavenly Father. When we march into battle, we need only sing songs of praise. When we emerge victorious, we must put credit where it is due and sing songs of praise. And when we are walking through the valley, even in the midst of trial, we should still sing songs of praise. Trusting in the Lord, depending on him, and worshiping his name moves the heart and hand of God.

Lord, may faithful praises to you ever be on my lips. Amen.

Time Out

> The angel said, "Don't be afraid, Zechariah! God has heard
> your prayer. Your wife, Elizabeth, will give you a son, and you
> are to name him John. You will have great joy and gladness, and
> many will rejoice at his birth."
>
> LUKE 1:13–14 NLT

Zacharias walked righteously before the Lord. Scripture
actually uses the word *blameless* (v. 6 NKJV). Yet when faced
with what he thought was impossible because of his and his
wife Elizabeth's advanced age, he doubted and asked for a sign.
God in his kindness did not revoke his gift of a child but gave
Zacharias a time out to be quiet and contemplate the power of
God. Because of his unbelief, Zacharias became unable to speak.

When John (meaning, "God shows mercy and grace")
was born, neighbors came quickly to see the wonder. When they
asked the child's name, Elizabeth said John. But John was not
a family name, so the neighbors questioned this. They turned
to Zacharias, who wrote, "His name is John" on a tablet. Then
Zacharias' mouth was loosed, and he started to speak. The first
thing he did was bless the Lord his God (vv. 60–64). This should
caution us to trust the Lord and keep our doubt in check.

*Lord, when doubts arise, help me to humble myself before you,
asking for faith to arise instead. Amen.*

Faith during Testing

God blesses those who patiently endure testing and temptation. Afterward they will receive the crown of life that God has promised to those who love him.

JAMES 1:12 NLT

When we stay true to the Lord through difficult times, putting our faith to work so that we withstand the trial, it pleases him. He will never leave our side during these times. Today, Christ is with our brothers and sisters in China, Iran, and so many countries as they endure atrocities for his name's sake.

Christ was with Stephen, the first Christian martyr, who saw the glories of heaven in the moments before his death. Stephen saw the heavens opened, and maybe those being persecuted today also see this. Many of us will never experience martyrdom, but those who do will receive a reward. Revelation says these who died for their witness are under God's altar. They cry to him to avenge their death. When he says to wait a little longer for others who will be joining them, he gives them a white robe signifying victory and purity (6:9–11). What a privilege to bear his name and sacrifice for him!

My Lord, may your glory fill and surround those persecuted for your name's sake. Amen.

Joy, Gladness, or Tears?

"The Son of Man, on the other hand, feasts and drinks,
and you say, 'He's a glutton and a drunkard,
and a friend of tax collectors and other sinners!'"

LUKE 7:34 NLT

Did you know that there are more than five hundred references to joy, gladness, merriment, rejoicing, delighting, and laughing in the Bible? Only 158 referring to sadness, mourning, or tears? Jesus said that he has come that we might have life and have it more abundantly. The Pharisees of his day wanted to malign his reputation by judging whom he spent time with, hoping to turn people from him. As the Son of God, God clothed in human flesh, he was a Man of Sorrows, aware of his purpose: the giving of his life to redeem mankind. He came to redeem sinners, so why wouldn't he engage with those he came to save?

In Luke 7:31–35, Scripture says that "the Son of Man came, enjoying life" (PHILLIPS). As God-man, he wanted us to know true joy, bliss that invigorates and is our strength, undeniable delight. There is nothing more awesome and thrilling than experiencing praise to our Lord that lifts your spirit into his presence to a level of rapturous, inexplicable joy.

Jesus, thank you for coming to save a wretch such as me. Fill me with Holy Spirit joy. Amen.

Gifts or Glory?

Do not love the world or the things in the world. If anyone loves the world, the love of the Father is not in him. For all that is in the world—the desires of the flesh and the desires of the eyes and pride of life—is not from the Father but is from the world.

1 JOHN 2:15–16 ESV

The world we live in sees Christmas as a time of gaining a fortune in retail sales and over-spending on elaborate and unnecessary gifts. It's all about the jolly old man, parties, and everything in excess. Much of this results in high stress during the season and a feeling of relief once it has passed. This wasn't what God intended when he sent his Son as a babe to earth. The birth of Christ was about Bethlehem, a small manger, and a night of worship. There was no seasonal rush but a silent, calm, and meaningful evening in the presence of wise men, shepherds, and a newborn King.

How will you spend the birth of your Lord? Determine to slow down and look at Jesus. Don't conform to the world's way of celebrating but honor your Lord by making this season all about the Savior.

Jesus, forgive me for spending my time on buying gifts instead of giving you glory. Keep my attention focused on you. Amen.

A Leap of Faith

Joseph, to whom she was engaged, was a righteous man and did not want to disgrace her publicly, so he decided to break the engagement quietly.

MATTHEW 1:19 NLT

What utter trust and faith Joseph had. The angel didn't come to him as it had to Zacharias, Mary, or the shepherds, but rather he received his heavenly visitor during his sleep. With the dilemma Joseph was facing, discovering his new bride was pregnant, he could have thought the dream a coincidence. This scandal affected his character, reputation, and integrity. Mary's news for Joseph assuredly and initially caused him confusion and disbelief. Yet through faith, he put his own reputation aside and was obedient, taking Mary into his home, making her his wife, and raising Jesus as his own son.

Our idea of what faith is can sometimes be skewed. But "faith isn't the ability to believe long and far into the misty future," says Joni Eareckson Tada, Christian author and advocate for people with disabilities. Faith is "simply taking God at his Word and taking the next step." Joseph had no idea what the future would hold, but he obeyed. What God asks of us is always for our own good. May we, like Joseph, trust the Lord and remain willing to do whatever he asks of us.

Dear Lord, thank you for your forgiveness when I fear or dislike what you're asking of me and hesitate to say yes. Amen.

Do His Will

> "Not everyone who calls out to me, 'Lord! Lord!' will enter the Kingdom of Heaven. Only those who actually do the will of my Father in heaven will enter."
>
> MATTHEW 7:21 NLT

At first glance, the above verse can cause our hearts to drop if we are not secure in our faith. So often, we ask for prayer or seek God alone about his will for our lives. It is God's will that you receive the sacrifice of his Son on the cross. It is his will that you grow in his Word and in relationship with him. If you have come to Jesus with your sins, if you serve and obey him, if your heart motive is to put him first, you are saved. You have eternal life with him.

Don't let the Enemy make you doubt what God has promised. This verse was intended to help us avoid false prophets, people who claim to know Jesus but do not have a relationship with him. We adore and worship what we most highly value, what we put first in our lives, who we have made our Lord.

Jesus, I know that you have saved me, and I am forever yours. Thank you. Amen.

Our Precious Savior

"You will recognize him by this sign: You will find a baby
wrapped snugly in strips of cloth, lying in a manger."

LUKE 2:12 NLT

We have glamorized the stable and feeding trough, but in truth,
it was a lowly, ill-smelling, foul place to have a baby. It was a
place for animals, dirty, dusty, and not fit for a newborn. Yet
that is what the Father chose for his one and only Son as Jesus
entered the world in all humility.

He was born as Man, yet fully God. He was dependent
on the earthly parents God chose to feed him, change him, and
raise him. He looked like any other baby born to a woman, but
those who visited him that night knew he was the King. Many
would come to believe who he was, and others would do all
they could to silence him. Yet he would be victorious in the
completion of what his Father sent him to do. Today, let's pray
that God will enable us to celebrate our precious Savior with
continual gratitude in this and every season.

Jesus, I praise your mighty name. Thank you for coming as an
innocent babe, God as man to save the world. Amen.

A Son Is Given

To us a child is born, to us a son is given, and the
government will be on his shoulders. And he will be called
Wonderful Counselor, Mighty God, Everlasting Father,
Prince of Peace.

Isaiah 9:6 NIV

Most of us have held either our own newborn, a family
member's, or a friend's. There is nothing but pure joy at the sight
of a precious babe. We imagine what that child will become and
what they will do to make a difference in the world. We have
enthusiastic hope as we dream of the bright future ahead.

Don't you wonder what was going through the Father's
mind as he saw his Son as a human baby? He knew right then
and there what Jesus' future was, for he had planned it. Yes, one
day all the amazing attributes in today's verse would be ascribed
to him, but in that moment, the Father saw the cross. He saw
the rejection and the pain, but he also saw the redemption it
would bring to the ones he created. I believe the Lord was also
looking past this day to see the eternal future and the beloved
ones he would share it with because of his obedient Son, our
precious Prince of Peace.

Father, thank you for giving your Son so I could live. Amen.

The Wise Men

After this interview the wise men went their way. And the star
they had seen in the east guided them to Bethlehem. It went
ahead of them and stopped over the place where the child was.
When they saw the star, they were filled with joy!

MATTHEW 2:9–10 NLT

The wise men had just left an engaging conversation with King
Herod. He encouraged them to go to Bethlehem and search for
the child whose star they had seen. He wanted them to return
with the news of the child's location so he could go worship him
as well. Not knowing that the king actually wanted to kill the
newborn, the wise men went on their way.

The star rose in the night sky above them, and as they
followed with rejoicing in their hearts, they soon came upon the
manger where the baby King lay. They fell down and worshiped,
then gave him extravagant gifts of frankincense, gold, and
myrrh. As Mary looked on, she treasured in her heart all that
she saw. Later, God warned the wise men in a dream not to
return to Herod, for his intent was evil. They returned to their
own country praising God for the sight of their Messiah.

Dear Jesus, may I be wise to seek, come, worship, and give myself
to you. Amen.

The Shepherds

That night there were shepherds staying in the fields nearby,
guarding their flocks of sheep.

LUKE 2:8 NLT

The shepherds were intently doing their jobs. They made sure
the flocks were safe for the night and kept guard. It was dark,
and it was quiet. Can you imagine their reaction when suddenly,
a light that shone with the glory of the Lord broke through the
night? An angel appeared, and they rubbed their eyes, making
sure it wasn't a dream. The angel announced, "Do not be
afraid. I bring you good news that will cause great joy for all the
people. Today in the town of David a Savior has been born to
you; he is the Messiah, the Lord. This will be a sign to you: You
will find a baby wrapped in cloths and lying in a manger" (Luke
2:10–12 NIV). A choir of angelic beings sang "glory to God in
the highest heaven" (v. 14 NIV).

The shepherds rushed to Bethlehem, finding the baby
who would be their Savior. Filled with excitement, they told all
at the manger what they had heard from the heavenly hosts.
They returned to their fields praising their heavenly Father for
all they'd experienced that evening, for it happened just as the
angel had told them. Whether at Christmas or in July, we, too,
should praise our heavenly father for sending the Messiah to
us—praise him daily, in any way we can.

Jesus, I praise you, Savior of the world! Amen.

Birth of a Savior

She gave birth to her firstborn son. She wrapped him snugly in strips of cloth and laid him in a manger, because there was no lodging available for them.

LUKE 2:7 NLT

The animals in the stable were still as even they sensed the magnitude of who had arrived that night. As Mary labored to bring forth the newborn King, Joseph faithfully stayed at her side. Before long, guests started to arrive, and each bowed before the manger where the baby lay. Three men, with the brightest of intellect marveled at the sight of this babe who would be King. A few shepherds who boisterously led their flocks were silent as they gazed on the one whom the angel had said was the Savior, Christ the Lord.

There he was, the greatest of all, without a proper cradle, without a warm blanket, only strips of cloth to cover him. He entered the world humbly with accolades and praise, knowing he would exit it with scars and nail wounds. Both events were solely for our salvation. On the evening of his birth, he was recognized, but by very few. Jesus Christ will come again, as King of kings and Lord of lords, and all will recognize him.

Father, thank you for sending your Son to save a sinner such as me. Amen.

Longsuffering

We do this by keeping our eyes on Jesus, the champion who
initiates and perfects our faith. Because of the joy awaiting
him, he endured the cross, disregarding its shame. Now he is
seated in the place of honor beside God's throne.

HEBREWS 12:2 NLT

Joni Eareckson Tada and Nick Vujicic are two people who
have faced incredible physical difficulties yet still testify to
the goodness of Jesus. Enduring a lifetime of limitations, they
have turned the tide by using their restrictions to further
the kingdom of God and help others. Their testimonies have
brought many to Christ and encouraged other believers who
have disabilities. Those who suffer physically have found
courage to become all that God intended them to be by
watching the examples of Joni and Nick.

All of us face the possibility of long-term suffering,
disappointments, failures, loss, and heartaches. We never know
what tomorrow may bring. It's how we allow the Holy Spirit to
take us through these struggles, even if they last a lifetime, that
makes us better not bitter. How we respond and use whatever
may come to testify of Jesus has the potential to bring glory to
God and many lost ones to Christ.

Father, only you can see what my future holds. Whatever your
plan is, let me use it to testify of your goodness and salvation.
Amen.

Serve Joyfully

*You, brethren, have been called to liberty;
only do not use liberty as an opportunity for the flesh,
but through love serve one another.*

GALATIANS 5:13 NKJV

We often don't like the word *servant*. It denotes surrender and action that we're not always willing to offer. And then God adds *love* to it. In our human state, we often view people he calls us to serve as demanding, unkind, incompetent, or lazy. Yet he asks us to put them first. Jesus demonstrated this kind of service and love as he lived on earth. God, who created us and all that there is, became a servant of us all.

God desires us to do the same and sent the Holy Spirit to enable us to step into this position. His precious Holy Spirit melts our hearts anew before the Father, strengthening us for servanthood so that we can express his love in all we do. We live in a land where we often feel that others "owe" us something, and society tells us to make ourselves the priority. Our attitude must be as Christ's was. The world will know we are Christians if we offer our lives in loving service.

Lord, help me serve you and others. Forgive me for my selfishness and sins. Amen.

God's Choice

"How I wish today that you of all people would understand the way to peace. But now it is too late, and peace is hidden from your eyes."

LUKE 19:42 NLT

As Jesus looked down on the city of Jerusalem, he wept over their unbelief. The people had rejected the prophets of old who spoke of the coming Messiah, and many of those in Jesus' day disbelieved as well. "Now," Jesus said, "it is too late."

We know that whoever calls on the name of the Lord in faith will be saved. The Word says that God desires all to come to salvation. The hearts of those in Jerusalem were hardened by God. Yet God has also placed in our hearts the ability for us to receive Christ. The Scriptures say that God blinded their eyes so that they could not believe (John 12:40). Here we have a juxtaposition between God's will and man's choice. If God blinds their eyes, how can they be saved? Yet if they desire to be saved, they would have believed in the first place. It is an enigma about which we must trust God. He is good, he is loving, and he is faithful.

Lord, I know I won't understand everything this side of heaven. But I know you work for my best and love me with an everlasting love. Amen.

The Waymaker

"Run for your lives," says the LORD. "Hide yourselves in deep caves, you people of Hazor, for King Nebuchadnezzar of Babylon has plotted against you and is preparing to destroy you."
JEREMIAH 49:30 NLT

Gladys Aylward, a housemaid from England, saved her money to become a missionary to China. She found herself leading one hundred orphaned children fleeing Japan's invasion. It was a difficult and long journey over very dangerous terrain. When they came to the Yellow River, there was no way to cross as all boats had been hidden from the Japanese. One of the children reminded her of the Red Sea story, and they all knelt and began to pray. Just then, a Chinese military officer came by and sent boats to carry them to safety.[12]

Whatever the need, ask God! Whatever the journey, whether it be smooth or filled with danger, God will deliver us when we go to him humbly in prayer. He's the waymaker, the miracle worker, and he never leaves his children to fend for themselves. Listen for his direction and follow his voice, and he will get you to the destination he is sending you to.

Father, tune my ears to hear your voice and turn my spirit to obey and follow the path you set me on. Amen.

---

12 Jean Fischer, *Writing Courage on My Heart* (Uhrichsville, OH: Barbour Publishing, Inc., 2020).

Our Forever Home

All glory to God, who is able to keep you from falling away and will bring you with great joy into his glorious presence without a single fault. All glory to him who alone is God, our Savior through Jesus Christ our Lord. All glory, majesty, power, and authority are his before all time, and in the present, and beyond all time! Amen.

JUDE 1:24–25 NLT

As human beings, we have a very limited understanding of the greatness of God. Jesus and the power of the Holy Spirit enlighten us to understand Scripture and other supernatural things. Yet we will never see him as he truly is until the day we stand before his throne.

Once in heaven our eyes will be fully opened. "For now we see only a reflection as in a mirror; then we shall see face to face. Now I know in part; then I shall know fully, even as I am fully known" (1 Corinthians 13:12 NIV). One day, and that could be soon, we will witness the Lord in all his splendor. We'll stand before him faultless in Jesus. We'll sing praise to his magnificent name. We'll have our victory in Christ and a life of splendor with him in our forever home.

Father, may my time in eternity come soon. Amen.

Born as Sinners

I was born a sinner—yes, from the moment my mother
conceived me. But you desire honesty from the womb,
teaching me wisdom even there. Purify me from my sins, and I
will be clean; wash me, and I will be whiter than snow.

PSALM 51:5–7 NLT

Sin became a part of humankind in the garden. From the time
of our conception, we are destined to be born as sinners, yet
formed by the hand of God. His participation in our formation
tells us that his intent is to deliver us from our sinful state. The
fact that he instills wisdom and honesty in an unborn heart
reveals his desire for them to be cleansed of their sins and to
draw them to himself. Perhaps this provision is what causes the
psalmist to cry out for purification, to be washed whiter than
snow from his sins. What a relief when the soul is washed from
any wrongdoing, free to stand before the Holy One without
regret. We're born as sinners, but our Father's desire is to
redeem us as his own beloved children.

In this New Year, determine to stay pure before Christ
by confessing your sins immediately and being purified through
the power of his blood.

Lord, help me acknowledge my sin immediately and receive your
cleansing. Hallelujah!

Acknowledgments

I would like to thank my grandchildren, in particular Trenton, Corynne, and Morgan Anna. Without their vision, hard work, and love, the first *Mornings with Nana,* presented to me on my eightieth birthday, would never have been. To my beloved husband, Ted, whose love, faith, encouragement, and prodding made this book a reality.

About the Author

Marietta Terry is the founder of Plumfield Academy in Santa Ana, California, and is credited with opening several preschools within churches throughout Southern California. For decades, she has shared her love of Christ through her writing. Marietta and her husband, Ted, have been married for over sixty years and together share five children, seventeen grandchildren, and five great-grandchildren.